Asia and Policymaking
for the Global Economy

Asia and Policymaking for the Global Economy

KEMAL DERVIŞ
MASAHIRO KAWAI
DOMENICO LOMBARDI

editors

ASIAN DEVELOPMENT BANK INSTITUTE
Tokyo

BROOKINGS INSTITUTION PRESS
Washington, D.C.

Library of Congress Cataloging-in-Publication data

Asia and policymaking for the global economy / Kemal Derviş, Masahiro Kawai,
and Domenico Lombardi, editors.
  p. cm.
Includes bibliographical references and index.
Summary: "Examines the more dynamic role Asian nations are playing within
the G-20 and in multilateral organizations concerned with governance of global
economic and financial affairs, brought about by the rapid development of Asian
economies in recent decades"—Provided by publisher.
  ISBN 978-0-8157-0421-8 (pbk. : alk. paper)
  1. Asia—Foreign economic relations. 2. Asia—Economic policy. I. Derviş,
Kemal. II. Kawai, Masahiro, 1947– III. Lombardi, Domenico.
  HF1583.A83 2011
  337.5—dc22   2011003651

9 8 7 6 5 4 3 2 1

Printed on acid-free paper

Typeset in Sabon and Strayhorn

Composition by Circle Graphics, Columbia, Maryland

Printed by R. R. Donnelley
Harrisonburg, Virginia

Contents

Foreword

The sustained development in large parts of Asia has been one of the most significant signs of economic and social progress in the past half-century. Japan made the leap to industrialization first, followed soon after by the newly industrialized economies of Hong Kong, China; the Republic of Korea; Singapore; and Taipei,China. Then came the rapid development of countries now joined together in the Association of Southeast Asian Nations (ASEAN). More recently, we have seen the economic rise of the People's Republic of China and India, whose economies have exhibited extraordinary vitality throughout the past decade. Today, with a financial system exhibiting substantial resilience even at the apex of the global financial crisis, Asia is leading the world out of the worst recession in almost a century.

These recent decades of continuous and broad-based growth have transformed Asia from an economic hinterland into a crucial player in the global economy. Judging from current trends, the next ten years could see Asia's GDP, whether measured at market exchange rates or at PPP, far exceed those of the North American Free Trade Area and the European Union. Asia's per capita income should also rise rapidly.

Asia has become the new frontier of economic cooperation. At the regional level, the ASEAN+3 countries—the ten ASEAN member states plus the People's Republic of China, Japan, and the Republic of Korea—have consistently engaged in economic policy dialogue of unprecedented scope and depth. They implemented the multilateralization of the Chiang Mai Initiative in the spring of 2010 and have since decided to establish an independent regional surveillance unit, called the ASEAN+3 Macroeconomic Research Office, in the first half of 2011. Currently, efforts focus on building a truly regional bond market, creating an Asian financial stability dialogue, and consolidating overlapping free trade agreements (FTAs) into a single Asia-wide FTA.

Yet, against the backdrop of rising regional integration and its growing role as an engine of the global economy, Asia has not enjoyed a commensurate voice in the governance of global economic and financial affairs, which would enable it to fulfill its responsibility. With its elevation to a level of leadership, the G-20 now provides an unprecedented opportunity for a number of Asian countries to engage in global economic and financial discussions at the highest political level. As the scope of the G-20 summits is expected to broaden, so will the prospect for Asia to help shape the global agenda. Yet the effectiveness of this multilateral approach will also hinge on the extent to which Asian countries are prepared to fully articulate their vision of future global economic and financial governance. To do so, Asia must first further develop its own consensus regional position in the complicated arena of global economic relations, which is no small task.

This book, edited by Kemal Derviş of the Brookings Institution, Masahiro Kawai of ADBI, and Domenico Lombardi of the Brookings Institution and the University of Oxford, provides an insightful analysis of the emerging frontier of global economic cooperation and the role that Asia can play in it. By highlighting the contours of this unprecedented shift in the recent history of the world economy, the volume focuses squarely on Asia's accomplishments and opportunities, as well as the potential for Asia's new role in the global economy, without shying away from the challenges and the risks that the region will have to face. By gleaning insights from economics, economic history, and international political economy, Derviş, Kawai, and Lombardi provide a compelling account that explores the options for Asia to effectively engage in global economic cooperation. In so doing, this book significantly elevates the level of economic policy debate and represents a valuable reference for academics and policymakers in and outside Asia.

HARUHIKO KURODA
President, Asian Development Bank

Asia and Policymaking
for the Global Economy

ONE

Introduction and Overview

KEMAL DERVIŞ, MASAHIRO KAWAI, and DOMENICO LOMBARDI

Less than a decade ago, most economists and economic historians, looking at the nineteenth and twentieth centuries as a whole, or looking at the last decades of the twentieth century, still remarked that the process of global economic growth had been accompanied by a process of "divergence" of per capita incomes between a small group of rich countries and a large number of lower-income economies. The words of renowned growth theorist Elhanan Helpman are representative of most thought on the subject until quite recently: "Although the differences in income per capita among rich countries have declined in the post–World War II period, the disparity between rich and poor countries has widened. At the same time the number of middle income countries has dwindled. We now have two polarized economic clubs: one rich, the other poor" (Helpman 2004).

This "divergence" had been a puzzle for growth theorists, because essential aspects of growth theory, notably Robert Solow's neoclassical growth model, suggested that diminishing returns to capital deepening would lead to "convergence" of per capita incomes (Solow 1956; *Oxford Review of Economic Policy* 2007). These models suggested that for a while the developing countries with less capital per worker would grow more rapidly than the mature economies with their higher capital-labor ratios, as these richer countries were farther along in the process of diminishing returns to capital accumulation. The developing countries did not grow more rapidly, however, in the decades following World War II, when development economics became a subdiscipline within the economics

1

profession. Clearly the process of technological change that accompanied capital accumulation had been such that it more than compensated for the diminishing returns to capital in the advanced countries and allowed them to maintain their relative lead. Over the past two decades, and particularly since the turn of the twenty-first century, this has changed, with huge implications for the nature of the world economy, its growth dynamics, and the requirements for a system of global economic governance.

The global financial crisis of 2007–09 made the new convergence process due to more rapid growth in many emerging market economies very apparent. But the crisis merely underlined and accentuated a fundamental structural change in the world economy that had been taking place since the early 1990s. Convergence seems to have replaced the divergence referred to by Helpman. Emerging Asia is at the heart of the change, and the chapters in this book examine some of the key dimensions of this shift, which is continuing at full speed as we enter the second decade of the twenty-first century.

In the period following the Second World War, aggregate growth rates in the advanced industrial economies and growth rates in the rest of the world were not very far apart. Both groups saw much variation, with some countries and regions growing rapidly for certain subperiods and then far more slowly at other times. Parts of Latin America, for example, grew rapidly in the period from 1950 to 1980, and then stagnated during the 1980s and into the 1990s, before picking up new speed after the turn of the century. Many African countries experienced a few years of rapid growth after they gained independence, but soon most of them lost their growth momentum and many experienced negative per capita growth rates. Many developing countries also experienced high volatility, with good years followed by years of crisis and negative growth, often brought on by balance of payments difficulties.

Among the advanced countries, Japan grew spectacularly until 1990, and stagnated thereafter. From 1950 to 1970, Europe grew at a steady pace, even somewhat faster than the United States, but European growth slowed down significantly after the first oil crisis in the early 1970s. The United States also grew rapidly in the 1950s and 1960s, slowed down in the 1970s and 1980s, but picked up the pace in the 1990s. Overall, the period from 1950 to 1990 cannot be characterized as either a period of divergence or a period of convergence in per capita incomes, with the aggregate relative income gap between the advanced industrial economies and the emerging and developing countries neither widening nor narrowing significantly.

The picture started to change perceptibly in the 1990s, mainly because of the growth performance of the Asian countries. Growth in some Asian economies, such as Hong Kong, China; the Republic of Korea (henceforth, Korea); Taipei,China; and Singapore (the "Asian Tigers") had already reached relatively high levels in the mid-1960s.[1] Growth in the People's Republic of China (henceforth, PRC) picked up from the late 1970s onward, and in India it started in the 1980s. Nonetheless, since the four Asian Tiger economies had small populations and the PRC and India were still very low-income economies, the weight of Asia remained small in the world economy until the 1990s, and the rapid Asian growth did not compensate for the sluggish growth in many other developing countries in terms of impact on the aggregate relative per capita income gap between advanced and developing economies. By 1990, Asia had gained enough weight in relative GDP that its rapid growth started to lead to a narrowing of the aggregate income gap between advanced and developing economies, despite continuing slow growth in Latin America and Africa. This new "convergence trend" continued into the twenty-first century, after a brief interruption at the time of the Asian crisis in 1997 and 1998, reinforced after the turn of the century by substantially better performance, also in Latin America and Africa.

While the nineteenth and twentieth centuries were times of divergence, it appears that the twenty-first century will be a century of convergence in the world economy. Looking at the very long run, it now seems that the nineteenth and twentieth centuries, with their colonial empires and Western domination, may turn out to be a limited period, a kind of parenthesis in world history. As the twenty-first century unfolds, the world may become much less divided by income levels than it has been since the Industrial Revolution, returning to a structure—though at much higher levels of income and prosperity—that existed for centuries before the Industrial Revolution. Per capita income differences between the traditionally rich countries and the developing world will persist for decades, but they are likely to decline over time, while the overall size of the rich economies will soon be overtaken by the aggregate size of the developing country economies, even when measured at market prices. At purchasing

---

1. This book adopts the Asian Development Bank naming convention of referring to its member economies. The Brookings Institution takes no position on Taipei,China's legal status.

power parity prices, the emerging and developing countries have already caught up, in terms of aggregate size, with the advanced rich economies.

Climate and the environment may of course develop into new challenges, constraining growth for large parts of the world, advanced and developing; and there is unfortunately always the threat of devastating conflict that could create unforeseen upheaval. Some developing and emerging countries are particularly vulnerable to natural disasters. Moreover, some of the least-developed countries, where there is internal conflict and "state failure," are still "diverging," and extreme poverty remains a huge challenge, even in many middle-income countries. But looking at the world as a whole, a large percentage of the global population now lives in "emerging" countries that are closing the income gap that separates them from the mature advanced economies. Emerging Asia leads this process.

This volume analyzes the dynamics of growth in Asia comparatively and historically in a global context (chapter 2); appraises the scope for policy coordination among systemically important economies of the world (chapter 3); analyzes financial stability in Emerging Asia (chapter 4); and assesses the implications of the rise of Asia in the newly emerging global economic governance by focusing on the reform of the international monetary system (chapter 5). This introductory overview provides a brief summary of the topics analyzed in greater detail throughout the volume.

Structural Transformation in Asia and the World Economy

In chapter 2, Kemal Derviş and Karim Foda analyze the sources of the greatest structural transformation that the world economy has ever experienced in a three-decade period. Emerging Asia (EA), led by the PRC in terms of size and rate of growth, is very likely to reach close to one-quarter of world GDP at market prices by 2020, compared to 6.6 percent in 1990.[2] The weight of EA in the world economy approached 16 percent in 2010. These percentages are much higher when output is measured at purchasing power parity (PPP) prices. Barring any cataclysmic political events, it is likely that this group of countries will sustain its strong growth momentum through the next decade, at least from the supply side.

---

2. Emerging Asia includes Hong Kong, China; India; Indonesia; Korea; Malaysia; the PRC; Singapore; Taipei,China; Thailand; and Viet Nam.

To a degree, the rise of EA is in some ways similar to the rise of Japan during the postwar period. Over the three decades from 1960 to 1990, the share of Japanese GDP rose from 3.3 percent of world GDP to 13.3 percent. But the Japanese story involved about 120 million people, while the EA story involves close to 3 billion people—about 40 percent of the world's population. Japan's remarkable growth performance allowed it to join the club of the advanced economies. EA's growth performance is transforming in a very fundamental way the overall structure of the world economy and relocating its center of gravity.

In their analysis, Derviş and Foda point to two defining characteristics of the EA group: GDP growth rates and ratios of investment to GDP. In the aggregate, both investment rates and growth rates have been sufficiently high in EA countries to set them apart from most other countries. From 1999, the year after the Asian financial crisis, to 2008, EA growth was about three times as rapid as growth in the advanced economies and about twice the rate of growth in other emerging and developing economies. Over the same period, investment rates were high in EA countries, rising from about 29 percent of aggregate GDP in 1999 to about 38 percent in 2008, much higher than in any other part of the world.

Despite high investment rates, EA ran a significant current account surplus over the same period, indicating that the region has saved a higher proportion of income than the already high proportion it invests. This savings behavior has been providing the region with the ability to finance its own investments, and as EA's high growth rates indicate, the region has displayed the capacity and institutional effectiveness to translate investment into rapid economic growth.

EA has achieved this through the combination of rapid capital accumulation, driven by sustained high investment rates and fairly rapid technological progress as measured by the growth of total factor productivity. This is in contrast to what happened in the Soviet Union, which also had very high investment rates but was unable to generate much total factor productivity growth. Much of the growth in total factor productivity in EA can be attributed to the importation and adaptation of frontier technology (catch-up growth facilitated by openness to the world economy), large-scale rural-urban migration (moving labor from low- to higher-productivity activities), and improved factor allocation within the "modern sector" across industries and firms. In addition, many indicators of human capital formation, such as years of education, enrollment rates, and gender parity, have significantly improved in EA. In the PRC and Korea, tertiary school enrollment increased 16 and 18 percentage points, respectively, between 2000 and 2007.

The supply-side factors mentioned above will continue to be at work over the next decade at least, allowing growth at a pace similar to that of the recent past. The future sustainability of growth will also depend on the demand side. As a region with higher savings than investment, and thus a current account surplus, EA has shown that, in the aggregate, it does not need net foreign capital inflows to finance its high investment rates, but requires net foreign demand to ensure that potential growth is realized.

The debate over whether EA can sustain growth from the demand side centers on "global imbalances," where imbalances refer to current account surpluses or deficits. Most EA countries have run significant surpluses, with the PRC running the largest at $400 billion, or in the range of 10–12 percent of GDP, at its peak in 2007–08. On the other side of the Pacific, the United States runs very large current account deficits, which reached $800 billion, or 6 percent of GDP, at their peak in 2006.

In addition to EA running large current account surpluses, it has accumulated large volumes of foreign exchange reserves, a strategy that originated in the wake of the Asian financial crisis of 1997–98, partly, at least, as an attempt to self-insure against volatile international capital flows. Emerging countries more generally adopted this strategy, adding $4.7 trillion to their foreign exchange reserves between 1999 and 2008, with EA accounting for most of this accumulation. On the other hand, the United States experienced a current account deficit of $5.7 trillion over the same period. It is possible, to a certain extent, to view the EA surplus and the U.S. deficit as mirror images, although both the United States and Emerging Asia traded with a multitude of other countries in other regions as well.

Some argue that the existence of current account imbalances should not necessarily be considered a major problem, because globalization should be expected to reduce home bias in the allocation of savings. In a globalizing world, countries or regions should not be expected to balance their current accounts. However, in a world of sovereign nations, national currencies, herd behavior in markets, and volatile capital flows, not to mention national authorities that intervene in foreign exchange markets and accumulate foreign exchange reserves, the situation is much more complicated. A truly integrated world economy driven entirely by efficient markets does not exist.

Going forward, there is broad agreement that the United States cannot continue to run its pre-crisis current account deficits and that EA cannot continue its pre-crisis surpluses, because, among other reasons, the United States is unlikely to be able to sustain high domestic demand owing to the deleveraging process, large household debt, the need to rebuild household assets, high unemployment, and lack of investment demand. In other words, a rebalancing of supply and demand around the world is needed to help ensure sustainable growth in the long run. In particular, the high-surplus PRC should increase the share of its domestic demand in total growth, offsetting a desirable decline in domestic demand as a share of total U.S. demand. This "rebalancing" need not, and should not, however, involve only the United States and the PRC. Too rapid and too drastic a decline in the Chinese "structural" surplus might not be feasible in the short run without triggering a decline in the Chinese growth rate, which would hurt not only the PRC but world growth as a whole (on this, see also chapter 3 by Rajiv Kumar and Dony Alex).

There is also the special case of Germany, with a large surplus but a currency that could be dragged downward by weakness elsewhere in the euro zone, a paradoxical dilemma that poses a particular challenge to global (and intra-European) rebalancing. Moreover, many emerging and developing economies outside Asia have high returns to investment but relatively low savings rates. Given the huge need for infrastructure and other investments in these countries, and the much improved macro-economic frameworks in many of them, it would seem reasonable that they be net capital importers and run a moderate current account deficit in the aggregate. This would help counter the tendency for "ex ante" world savings to exceed "ex ante" world investment and help rebalance the world economy.

Derviş and Foda argue that it would be useful for policymakers to focus on the overall structure of savings and investment globally when trying to "rebalance" the world economy, as was tentatively agreed at the Seoul G-20 meeting in November of 2010. In this context it would be particularly desirable if more long-term capital could safely flow to capital-poor developing countries without creating the damaging "stop-and-go" cycles of the past. Besides private flows, official lending and guarantees from development banks can and should play an important role in reducing volatility and lengthening maturities. Official development finance remains relevant also in the context of resource transfers needed to fight climate change.

Looking to the next decade, Derviş and Foda argue that it is likely that the combination of high investment and savings rates, with continued technological diffusion and continued absorption of lower productivity labor by higher productivity sectors, as well as continued improvements in factor allocation within sectors, will allow emerging Asian countries to continue to grow at impressive rates, well above the world average. The ensuing structural transformation will be unprecedented and will need to be managed, including from a political economy perspective. If the transition is well managed, it will be compatible with growth in over-all prosperity. It will, however, imply a serious shift in the economic and financial weight of countries and thereby in their political influence and power over the next decade. What lies beyond 2020 is surely more difficult to predict.

The Rise of Asia and Implications for International Economic Coordination

In chapter 3, Rajiv Kumar and Dony Alex examine first the nature and magnitude of the global macroeconomic imbalances, and then some possible scenarios for redressing them. In doing so, they focus on the role that Asian economies can play in achieving a more balanced and sustainable global economic growth and greater coordination of macroeconomic policies.

Kumar and Alex explain that macroeconomic imbalances have almost always been a feature of the modern global economy. They were seen to facilitate faster growth by permitting a creditor country, with a current account surplus, to park its excess savings in safe assets (such as U.S. Treasury bills) for possible use in financing a future external current account deficit. However, very large macroeconomic imbalances can be seen as a symptom of deeper underlying distortions in the financial and monetary systems of the economies concerned. They can be attributed to a number of factors, such as a shift in saving behavior, productivity changes, the accumulation of foreign exchange reserves, movements in commodity prices, and also a shift in investors' attitude toward risk.

Kumar and Alex review the two contrasting explanations that have been given for the present state of global imbalances. The first view (notably put forward by Barry Eichengreen) attributes imbalances to a savings deficit in the United States, which translates into a current account deficit that is met by an inflow of capital from the rest of the world. The second view (supported by Ben Bernanke) argues that high savings rates in countries such as the PRC have made huge surpluses available; these surpluses, which lower the cost of borrowing, have contributed to huge current account deficits in countries such as the United States. In that view, the onus of correcting global imbalances falls also very much on surplus economies, which should be implementing policies to lower their domestic savings and raising their domestic consumption as a share of GDP.

Kumar and Alex argue that the global macroeconomic imbalances can be seen as the combined outcome of both explanations, with high U.S. current account deficits financed by rising savings in the PRC and the oil-exporting economies. To some degree, the imbalances are rooted in the Asian financial crisis of the late 1990s, which left the Asian economies bitter about not getting timely or adequate financial assistance from the IMF. In turn, this propelled them toward more contingent measures, such as achieving a degree of self-insurance against a future financial crisis through the raising of foreign exchange reserves (on this, see chapter 5 by Domenico Lombardi).

This process of accumulating reserves turned the current account of some countries from deficit to surplus. For countries such as the PRC, net exports also play an important role in sustaining high GDP growth rates. This has been achieved by keeping a fixed exchange rate with the U.S. dollar to maintain export competitiveness and, in turn, has led to a huge accumulation of reserves to prevent the currency from appreciating. However, the PRC is not the only country running a substantial current account surplus. Other countries, such as the oil-exporting economies, have perhaps been equally responsible. The case of Germany is more complicated, because it is part of the euro zone—but Germany too has had large surpluses in the current account.

The literature on the measures that can be taken to tackle global imbalances identifies two approaches. The first approach argues that the imbalances are just a manifestation of a short-term disequilibrium and that this will automatically adjust itself over time. The second approach, on the other hand, insists that these imbalances are the result of severe economic distortions that have to be rectified with coordinated and conscious policy actions. In this vein, measures to correct the macroeconomic imbalances in the Asia-Pacific region and the United States have to focus on serious restructuring of the U.S. and Chinese economies.

The thirteen largest Asian economies have a total GDP of US$13.9 trillion, which is similar in size to the U.S. economy of about US$14.1 trillion at 2009 prices. The economic crisis led to a decline in U.S. private sector demand. If the falloff in U.S. demand has to be compensated for by the thirteen largest Asian economies, Kumar and Alex argue that these would need to increase their aggregate demand by roughly a similar amount.

They say that there are three possible routes to raising aggregate demand in Asia. The first is to raise domestic private consumption, especially in the PRC and Japan, as well as in the ASEAN region. This would enable other countries, including the United States, to take greater advantage of external demand and to rebalance their own economies. While this would have some positive impact, especially in reducing the PRC's dependence on external demand to sustain its very rapid GDP growth, it is difficult for a country-by-country process of internal balancing alone to compensate for the weakness in demand-slowing growth in some of the advanced economies.

The second way forward would be for the oil-exporting economies to reduce their current account surpluses to push up aggregate world demand. The oil-exporting countries could be expected to spend more of their savings from sudden surges in oil prices, if they could be assured of more stable future income streams. This would be achieved through reforms in both the Asian and the oil producers' financial sectors to ensure that such savings could be suitably invested and would generate stable earning flows from Asia to the oil producers. A rise in domestic investment demand in these countries would help absorb skilled labor from labor-surplus Asian economies and also strengthen economic activity in general. However, the implementation of necessary reforms in the financial sectors will come about only in the medium to long term. As a result, the oil producers cannot be relied upon to substantially contribute to global rebalancing in the near future.

The third modality would be to boost regional economic activity in Asia even more, including in the lower-income Asian economies, by accelerating the process of pan-Asian economic integration and establishing institutional mechanisms for designing and financing regional infrastructure projects. One way to shore up regional demand would be to complete the process of trade and economic integration among the ASEAN+4—the ten ASEAN member states, the PRC, India, Japan, and Korea—so that it could contribute to greater dynamism in regional economic activity. Another option would be to establish an Asian Investment Bank (AIB), which would supplement the efforts of the Asian Development Bank (ADB) and other national development banks to finance infrastructure and connectivity in

Asia at levels comparable to those in Europe and the United States. The AIB could be managed independently of extra-regional interests and could focus on a more efficient utilization of savings generated within Asia. It could also help facilitate the development of Asian financial markets.

Kumar and Alex conclude that the strengthening of regional economic activity in Asia could contribute to the external demand stimulus for the U.S. economy and help both Asia and the United States achieve higher economic growth and employment. In their view and in the context of Asia-Pacific rebalancing, it is thus critical that intra-regional economic activity in Asia be bolstered through higher demand for regional public goods, supplemented by rising domestic demand in the economies with a current account surplus.

G-20 Financial Reforms and Emerging Asia's Challenges

In chapter 4, Masahiro Kawai underlines that the main lesson emerging from the crisis that began in 2007 is that a systemic financial crisis can be very costly in terms of fiscal resources as well as lost output and employment. In fact, the crisis severely affected the economies of the United States and Europe well beyond their respective financial systems. It then spilled over into Asia through the trade channel. The Asian financial system was largely spared, however, owing to the regulatory reforms that had been enacted in most Asian economies in the aftermath of the 1997–98 crisis, the ensuing reduction in short-term external debt and the accumulation of foreign reserves and, finally, a more conservative approach to risk-taking eschewing the widespread use of sophisticated structured products. Looking forward, the increasing globalization of financial activities, the sustained economic growth achieved by the region, and the new regulatory reforms on the agenda of the G-20 require Asian policymakers to upgrade their supervisory capabilities to continue to regulate and supervise financial firms and markets so as to promote financial innovation in a framework of systemic stability.

Against this backdrop, Kawai reviews recent progress on financial sector reforms in EA achieved as a result of the so-called G-20 process, focusing on the following issues: building stronger capital, liquidity, and leverage standards; addressing "too-big-to-fail" problems; designing macroprudential supervisory and regulatory frameworks; and strengthening international coordination of financial supervision and regulation. Such reforms are expected to strengthen the financial systems of the United

States and Europe, where the crisis originated in 2007. Yet, Kawai argues that Asian economies should not view them as relevant only to those advanced economies and that it is in their best interest to continue pursuing reform policies to further develop and deepen financial markets while preserving financial system stability.

A key aspect of the G-20 process has been the endorsement by the leaders of the Basel III capital and liquidity requirements. The aim is to introduce a fair amount of counter-cyclicality to the bank capital rules while increasing the provisioning against maturity mismatches that give rise to funding liquidity risks. EA banks will be less affected by the new supervisory framework thanks, to a large extent, to the reforms already enacted; they will benefit from the implementation of that framework in the United States and Europe. Similarly, because most EA banks are small internationally—although some are large in their domestic markets—they are unlikely to be affected by the emerging international regulation of systemically important financial institutions (SIFIs), although there is still merit in identifying and appropriately overseeing national SIFIs.

The 2007–09 crisis revealed that authorities in the United States and Europe had failed to accurately assess their financial system's ability to withstand systemic shocks owing to their traditional "bottom-up" approach of microprudential regulation and supervision of individual firms. Along similar lines, regulators tended to focus on specific areas of responsibility while no entity was in charge of assessing risk in the entire financial system or economy. In contrast, the aim of macroprudential regulation and supervision is exactly to remedy these shortcomings by providing a "top-down" framework for identifying risks in the financial system as a whole through a "systemic stability regulator." In Asia, many authorities have actively intervened in their respective financial systems in a macroprudential way without, however, a well-defined framework. At the international level, the prevention and detection of systemic crises will require concerted macroeconomic and financial surveillance as well as implementation of macroprudential policies through close cooperation between the IMF and the Financial Stability Board.

Following the 1997–98 crisis, Asian policymakers undertook significant reforms aimed at enhancing the quality of balance sheets and risk management practices of their banks. In this vein, financial firms have taken a conservative approach to risk, as reflected by their not relying on widespread use of structured products and by not expanding the securitization business. Partly as a result of national authority efforts, stock market capitalization and the total stock of bonds have increased rapidly in Asia, reflecting a more balanced financial system than in the past. Despite these favorable developments, there is an urgent need to continue to strengthen microprudential regulation and supervision and to establish a full-fledged macroprudential supervisory framework that focuses on economywide systemic risks. An important lesson from the global financial crisis is that monetary and macroprudential policies should play complementary roles in addressing systemic risks. Accordingly, a mechanism should be established that allows central bankers, financial regulators, and finance ministry officials to share information about systemic risk and to coordinate policies so as to prevent the buildup of excessive risk. Whether a single entity or a council, a systemic stability regulator should be established at the national level for that purpose.

Kawai argues that, given the traditional predominance of banks in providing formal financial services, a balanced financial system would require deep local-currency bond markets as a means to enhance the allocation of large Asian savings to sustainable long-term investments. In the context of the Asian financial crisis, local-currency corporate bond markets would have, in fact, provided corporations with a greater opportunity to obtain longer-term financing for local projects, thereby removing both maturity and currency mismatches. Against this backdrop, finance ministers of ASEAN+3 launched the Asian Bond Markets Initiative with the aim of enhancing the market infrastructure for local-currency bond markets and facilitating access to a diverse issuer and investor base. Relatedly, the Asian Bond Fund, also launched by the region's central banks in 2003, aimed at removing impediments to the listing of local-currency bond funds through their inclusion in central bank foreign exchange reserves. Yet regional financial integration remains low. The bulk of the region's massive savings are still largely invested in low-yielding foreign exchange reserves and intermediated through financial centers outside the region.

In 2010, foreign capital resumed flowing back into the region, fueled by the expansion of the liquidity that advanced economies have injected to stabilize their financial systems and prop up their domestic demand. These flows will test macroeconomic management capacities, exchange rate policies, and financial supervision frameworks in Asia. As for the first aspect, sterilized intervention has been the favorite instrument applied by many EA economies to prevent nominal appreciation of their exchange rates. Given that interventions in foreign exchange markets have been mostly unidirectional, sterilization is becoming an increasingly costly method of preventing the economy from overheating, while increasing the accumulation of net foreign reserves cannot be sustained indefinitely. Hence there is a need to allow greater flexibility in the exchange rates of EA countries.

Another way to deal with the current surge in capital flows would be to impose capital controls along the lines of the Chilean experience. But evidence on the effectiveness of capital inflow controls is mixed and, in any case, their impact tends to weaken over time as agents learn how to circumvent them while producing distortions and inefficient allocations.

In the absence of definitive measures at the national level to effectively manage capital flows, Kawai concludes that regional collective action can be an attractive alternative, as it expands the menu of options available to individual countries. By stepping up regional financial market surveillance, policymakers can mitigate the impact of investor herd behavior and financial contagion. A country's adoption of tighter prudential policies and capital inflow controls could push capital toward other countries. The establishment of a new high-level Asian Financial Stability Dialogue (AFSD) would bring together all responsible authorities—including finance ministry officials, central banks, and financial supervisors—to address regional financial market vulnerabilities and make efforts at regional financial integration through greater harmonization of standards and market practices. Regional collective action would also be needed in respect of exchange rate policies. In fact, if the fear of loss of international price competitiveness prevents a country from allowing its currency to appreciate, it could cooperate with its regional competitors to take action simultaneously. Collective currency appreciation would have the benefit of contributing to financial and macroeconomic stability in the region while minimizing the loss of price competitiveness, at least within the region.

Reforming the International Monetary System through the Lens of Emerging Asia

In chapter 5, Domenico Lombardi focuses on the asymmetry between the sustained globalization of economic and financial activities driven by the integration into the world economy of emerging economies, many of which are in Asia, and the capacity shown by the international monetary system (IMS) and the global economic governance institutions to adapt accordingly. Despite some changes that have occurred since the late 1960s, when, for instance, special drawing rights (SDRs) were introduced, the current IMS has maintained key asymmetric features. These features, in the face of their increasing integration into the global economy, have produced a pattern of reserve accumulation by several emerging and developing economies that cannot simply be traced to traditional mercantilistic motives.

According to Lombardi, the first structural asymmetry of the IMS relates to the well-known feature whereby pressure to adjust their external accounts is much stronger for deficit countries than it is for those in surplus. This feature was strongly noted by Lord Keynes in his preparatory work for the Bretton Woods Conference in 1944. He pointed out at that time that the fundamental asymmetry in the global monetary system would generate a global deflationary bias in the absence of any corrective measures. In the past, the lack of an authentic multilateral forum to discuss and formulate policy responses to these weaknesses and asymmetries in the global monetary system had left developing and emerging economies more vulnerable in an increasingly interdependent world. Policymakers from emerging economies have often complained that advanced countries do not adequately consider how their policy spillovers will affect the rest of the global economy.

The G-20, with its stronger representation of emerging economies, especially from Asia, and its recent elevation to the leaders' level, may finally be able to become a relevant forum where emerging economies can voice their concerns and constructively channel their criticisms. In September 2009, leaders at the G-20 summit in Pittsburgh agreed to the so-called "Framework for Strong, Sustainable, and Balanced Growth" proposed by the United States. Through this framework, they pledged to devise a method for setting objectives, developing policies to support such objectives, and mutually assessing outcomes. The IMF's involvement has been sought in providing analysis on various national or regional policy frameworks and how they fit together.

Lombardi underscores that this is the first relevant multilateral surveillance exercise on a global scale in recent history. There are, however, strong challenges for the G-20-led multilateral surveillance. First, the exercise appears, so far, mainly geared toward making national authorities aware of the international spillover effects of their policies and providing a context in which policymakers can exercise mutual pressure. The G-20 countries have committed to a peer-review process for their economic policies and to a broadly defined policy objective. This is not the same as committing to quantitative policy targets to which they can be held accountable in a multilateral forum. The effectiveness of this multilateral exercise will also hinge on the extent to which emerging Asian countries are willing to fully articulate their vision of how international economic coordination should work in practice.

Lombardi supports the view that a key structural source of instability in the IMS is the central position that the U.S. dollar enjoys as a global reserve asset. The reliance on the domestic currency of a single country as the principal international reserve asset makes it difficult for U.S. policymakers to reconcile, in the long run, their domestic macroeconomic goals with the (increasing) need for a net supply of dollar-denominated international assets, leaving the IMS vulnerable to unilateral adjustments in the economic policies of the reserve currency country. In this regard, the IMS has been remarkably resistant to change. In contrast to the obligation set forth in Article VIII of the IMF Charter about "making the special drawing right the principal reserve asset in the international monetary system," SDRs have played a marginal role as international reserves.

As the 2007–09 crisis unfolded and developing countries' economies increasingly needed to bolster their reserve asset position, the G-20 supported a general allocation of SDRs equivalent to $250 billion, and the IMF quickly implemented this in August 2009. Many experts, including a UN Commission, have called for expanding the role of the SDR through its regular or cyclically adjusted issuance, as a way of managing international economic risks posed for countries that do not issue hard currencies. Because SDRs are an artificial unit of account with limited scope for use within the existing parameters, the head of the Chinese central bank has proposed a significant overhaul to increase the role of the SDR. This proposal envisages a political bargain between structural reforms of the IMS and the restoration of the IMF's centrality in it. In the interim, the managing director of the IMF, the executive board, as well as the institution's governors have expressed interest in proposals for strengthening the role of the SDR, and the 2011 French presidency of the G-20 has made it an agenda item.

In Lombardi's analysis, a third asymmetric element of the IMS has been associated with the governance of the institution charged with the regulatory task of overseeing it. The distribution of voting power within the IMF has been heavily biased toward Western countries and has pointed to a serious legitimacy gap. Since many emerging Asian countries have carried inadequate weight in Fund decisionmaking, their positions, even on matters in which they may have the most relevant and immediate experience or knowledge, were less likely to be incorporated in the IMF's own policies and programs, as when, for instance, the Fund intervened in Asia in the late 1990s.

Another example of how the IMF's governance has affected the asymmetries of the IMS is the fact that, against the need for increased reserves, the issuance of "synthetic" assets such as SDRs requires approval of 85 percent of the voting power of the IMF membership. Besides the potential veto power that such a large supermajority affords to a few countries or groupings, the governance arrangements underpinning the creation of SDRs have reduced the IMF's ability to be responsive to the liquidity needs experienced by some segments of its membership. At the same time, it embeds a tension in the institutional mandate to pursue systemic stability, as it leaves decisions on regulating global liquidity in the hands of those countries issuing the hard currencies used as international reserve assets.

At the G-20 meeting in Gyeongju in October of 2010, the finance ministers agreed on a package of reforms that went beyond most expectations at the time by endorsing a shift of about 6 percent of voting power to dynamic and underrepresented economies. According to this agreement, approved by the IMF Executive Board on November 5, and endorsed by the leaders at the Seoul G-20 Summit, the PRC will become the IMF's third shareholder, while Brazil and India will be among the top ten members on the basis of their revised quotas. Moreover, the quota review, to take effect by the time of the IMF's Annual Meetings in 2012, will be linked to a recomposition of the board itself, with Western Europeans giving up two seats at any given time. The practical details of how this broad package will be implemented remain to be worked out but, in Seoul, G-20 leaders expressed a clear commitment in this respect, making it very likely that such reforms will be enacted within the envisaged time frame.

These latest developments would have not materialized without the political impetus provided by the G-20 with the presence of the large Asian economies. As long as countries with large stocks of reserves, like emerging Asian economies, perceived a gap between their relative international economic status and their position within the IMF's membership, they had an incentive to break away from the IMF and set up regional or plurilateral pooling facilities. Only by linking IMF reforms to structural changes in the IMS will the IMF gain strong support from emerging Asian countries for the Fund's role as the central institution in a reformed and truly global monetary system.

Looking forward, Lombardi concludes that, given Asia's increasing weight in the world economy, the region's support for the IMF, replacing the suspicion and disappointment rooted in the crisis of the 1990s will be key for the effectiveness of the institution in discharging its own mandate and for delivering better prospects for global economic policy cooperation.

References

De Brouwer, Gordon. 2007. "Institutions to Promote Financial Stability: Reflections on East Asia and an Asian Monetary Fund." In *The International Monetary System, the IMF and the G-20—A Great Transformation in the Making?* edited by Richard Samans, Marc Uzan, and Augusto Lopez-Claros. Basingstoke, UK: Palgrave Macmillan.

Guerrieri, Paolo, and Domenico Lombardi. 2010. *U.S. Politics after Seoul: The Reality of International Cooperation.* Washington: Brookings.

Helpman, Elhanan. 2004. *The Mystery of Economic Growth.* Harvard University Press.

Kawai, Masahiro. 2010. "East Asian Financial Cooperation: Perspectives on the CMIM, EPRD and AMRO." Tokyo: Asian Development Bank Institute.

———. 2007. "East Asian Economic Regionalism: Update." In *The International Monetary System, the IMF, and the G-20: A Great Transformation in the Making?* edited by Richard Samans, Marc Uzan, and Augusto Lopez-Claros. Basingstoke, UK: Palgrave Macmillan.

Lombardi, Domenico. 2010. *Financial Regionalism: A Review of the Issues.* Washington: Brookings.

Mo, Jongryn, and Chiwook Kim. 2009. "Power and Responsibility: Can East Asian Leadership Rise to the Challenge?" Working Paper no. 09-01. Seoul: Hills Governance Center at Yonsei.

Oxford Review of Economic Policy. 2007. "The 50th Anniversary of the Solow Growth Model." Vol. 23, no. 1.

Rueda-Sabater, Enrique, Vijaya Ramachandran, and Robin Kraft. 2009. *A Fresh Look at Global Governance: Exploring Objective Criteria for Representation.* Washington: Center for Global Development.

Solow, Robert. 1956. "A Contribution to the Theory of Economic Growth." *Quarterly Journal of Economics* 70, no. 1: 65–94.

Special Meeting of Finance Ministers and Central Bank Governors, Chairman's Statement turn. April 16, 1998 (www.ustreas.gov/press/releases/rr2375.htm).

United Nations. 2009. *Recommendations by the Commission of Experts of the President of the UN General Assembly on Reforms of the International Monetary and Financial System.* New York.

Woods, Ngaire, and Domenico Lombardi. 2006. "Uneven Patterns of Governance: How Developing Countries Are Represented in the IMF." *Review of International Political Economy* 13, no. 3: 480–515.

Zhou, Xiaochuan. 2009. "Reform the International Monetary System." Speech presented at the People's Bank of China (March) (www.pbc.gov.cn/english/detail.asp?col=6500&id=178).

TWO

Emerging Asia and Rebalancing the World Economy

KEMAL DERVİŞ and KARIM FODA

The thirty years from 1990 to 2020 will constitute the period of great-est structural shift that the world economy has ever experienced over a period as short as three decades. Broadly speaking, the ongoing shift is due to very rapid economic growth in Asia. The People's Republic of China (henceforth, PRC) dominates the figures and is the clear leader in terms of the speed of growth, but after decades of slow growth, India, with a population almost as large as the PRC's, has also gradually become a rapidly growing economy. Other smaller and medium-sized countries are contributing to the remarkable structural transformation and will con-tinue to do so.

It is possible to view Asian growth as happening in successive "waves" over the post–World War II period. First, there was the postwar recon-struction and very rapid growth of Japan, starting in the early 1950s and stretching to the end of the 1980s. The rapid growth of the early "Asian Tigers," particularly Hong Kong, China; the Republic of Korea (hence-forth, Korea); Singapore; and Taipei,China, started in the 1960s and is continuing, although at a somewhat slower pace. Somewhat later, other Asian countries, including Indonesia, Malaysia, and Thailand, started to grow very rapidly, particularly in the 1980–96 period, until the "Asian crisis" of 1997–98 interrupted their pace. Viet Nam started even later, but has become one of the star performers of the past two decades.

The PRC's growth started in earnest in the late 1970s, after the disaster of the Cultural Revolution, and has been gathering steam ever since, with growth peaks reached recently in 2007 and 2008. India, to the west of the "East Asian miracle" countries,[1] was a slowly growing economy until the early 1980s, when it picked up the pace somewhat. Indian growth slowly accelerated in the 1980s, but the trend was interrupted by a short crisis in 1990–91. Growth gathered momentum again after the reforms of the early 1990s and accelerated decisively in the early years of the twenty-first century.

If we define "Emerging Asia" (EA) as the group of countries comprising the PRC; Hong Kong, China; India; Indonesia; Korea; Malaysia; Singapore; Taipei,China; Thailand; and Viet Nam, their combined GDP at market prices is very likely to reach close to one quarter of world GDP in 2020, compared to 6.6 percent in 1990. And by 2020, the size of the PRC economy, at market prices, will come close to that of the U.S. economy. It is always risky to project a decade ahead, but the weight of EA has already reached 16 percent in 2010. Barring cataclysmic political events, EA will likely sustain strong growth momentum into the next decade. What will happen in the longer run is more difficult to predict,[2] but the projected movement toward a share of about one quarter of world GDP at market prices by 2020 is very likely.

If one measures Emerging Asia's weight in terms of GDP at purchasing power parity (PPP), it is of course much larger, reaching just over 25 percent of world GDP already in 2010. At PPP prices, the PRC alone is already larger in size than Japan and more than half the size of the United States.[3] There is some argument as to which measure of GDP to use. There is no doubt that if the objective is to compare living standards, PPP GDP is a much better measure than GDP at market prices. Moreover, one advantage that PPP comparisons have is that they are less affected by short-term variations in nominal exchange rates, which sometimes dominate comparisons using current market prices. If the objective is to discuss macroeconomic policies, trade, current accounts,

1. World Bank (1993).
2. See Dadush and Stancil (2010) for worldwide GDP projections to 2050, and Kharas (2010) for projections to 2040.
3. At PPP prices, the PRC accounts for 13 percent, Japan 6 percent, and the United States 20 percent of world GDP in 2010 (IMF, April 2010).

TABLE 2-1. **Structural Transformation of the World Economy:
The Rise of Emerging Asia, 1990–2020**

Percent of GDP at market prices

	(1) 1990	(2) 2000	(3) 2010	(4) 2020	(5) 2020[a]
Emerging Asia	6.6	9.9	16.0	24.4	26.5
People's Republic of China	1.7	3.7	9.0	15.7	17.7
India	1.2	1.4	2.2	3.4	3.3
Japan	13.3	14.5	8.6	7.1	6.9
United States	25.4	31.0	24.5	21.6	21.0
Euro area	24.1	19.5	21.1	17.1	16.6
Other advanced	12.2	11.4	11.3	10.1	9.8
Other EMDEV[b]	18.3	13.6	18.5	19.7	19.1
Advanced economies	75.0	76.5	65.5	55.9	54.4
EMDEV economies[b]	25.0	23.5	34.5	44.1	45.6

Source: IMF *World Economic Outlook*, April 2010; authors' calculations.

a. Column 5 incorporates a 2 percent annual appreciation of the renminbi and some other EA currencies with respect to the U.S. dollar from 2011 to 2020.

b. The newly industrialized Asian economies (Hong Kong, China; Korea; Singapore; Taipei,China) are here included in the EMDEV (emerging market and developing countries) aggregate, contrary to IMF practice.

and financial flows, however, then GDP at market prices is more appropriate as a basic measure of size. It does not make sense, for example, to express a current account surplus or deficit, measured in market prices, as a share of GDP at PPP prices. This chapter uses market prices to measure size, except when indicated otherwise. It should not be forgotten, however, that GDP comparisons are often made using PPP prices and that these measures would be more appropriate if the objective were to compare living standards.

Table 2-1 provides an overview of this unprecedented structural transformation in the world economy. The projections to 2020 given in column 4 take the IMF *World Economic Outlook* (*WEO*) real growth projections available for 2010 to 2015, and extrapolate them to 2020, except for the PRC, for which we project a growth rate of 9 percent for 2016–20, compared to the 9.8 percent growth rate projected by the IMF for the 2010–15 period. In column 5 of table 2-1, these projections are adjusted by assuming a 2 percent yearly appreciation of the renminbi between 2011 and 2020, resulting in an approximately 22 percent real appreciation of that currency over the decade. The same appreciation is assumed for EA currencies traditionally linked closely to the renminbi.[4] These translate into changes in GDP shares measured in current prices that are higher than what real growth differentials alone would lead to. Table 2-1 also shows that the emerging market and developing economies (EMDEV) as a whole are likely to come close to one half of world GDP at market prices by the beginning of the 2020s, compared to only one quarter in 1990.

The projections reflect a conservative measure of the renminbi and other currencies' potential to appreciate. On the other hand, the real GDP growth projected for the PRC by the IMF in its Spring 2010 *World Economic Outlook* may be a little on the high side. The combined real growth + exchange rate appreciation projection should be robust, however, as we argue below.[5] We return to a discussion of exchange rates in the section on rebalancing the world economy.

There has never been a transformation of the world economy as dramatic as the one we are likely to see over the thirty-year period from 1990 to 2020. To a degree, the rise of Emerging Asia has something of a precedent in the rise of Japan during the postwar period. To consider a similar period of three decades, Japanese GDP rose from 3.3 percent of world GDP in 1960 to 13.3 percent in 1990. The share of Japanese GDP in the world continued to rise until the mid-1990s, although that rise, reaching 17.8 percent in 1995, was due entirely to a steep appreciation of the Japanese currency in relation to the U.S. dollar and not to Japanese real growth, which stalled in the early 1990s and never recovered.

---

4. Hong Kong, China dollar; Taipei,China dollar; and Singapore dollar. Note that the 22 percent real appreciation projected in the last column is, if anything, conservative. Fred Bergsten of the Peterson Institute, for example, has argued that the renminbi is undervalued with respect to the U.S. dollar by about 40 percent. If correct, it would be likely that the renminbi would appreciate by more than just 22 percent over the next decade. See Bergsten (2010). In the long run, real exchange rate changes are expected to reflect productivity growth differentials: the Balassa-Samuelson effect. See Balassa (1964) and Samuelson (1964). More on productivity follows later in this chapter. On the other hand, some argue that with greater liberalization of capital flows, there would eventually be substantial outflows of capital from the PRC, and that this might put a brake on real appreciation. When trying to make a reasonable projection of the renminbi's exchange rate with respect to the dollar, a lot depends of course also on the value of the dollar in relation to other currencies. The IMF *WEO* Spring 2010 figures were based on exchange rates before the European debt crisis and the ensuing loss of value of the euro that took place in the late spring of 2010.

5. At the time this chapter was finalized in late June 2010, and just before the G-8 and G-20 meetings in Canada, the PRC announced that it would increase the flexibility of the exchange rate of the renminbi with respect to the U.S. dollar.

The rise of Japan in the period 1960–90 was truly spectacular, and there is no doubt that many Asian countries, particularly the PRC and Korea, were influenced, and in many ways encouraged, by the Japanese performance, just as, later, the PRC's performance has had an impact on India. But the Japanese story involved about 120 million people. The Emerging Asia story involves close to 3 billion people—about 40 percent of the world's population. Japan's remarkable growth performance allowed it to *join* the club of advanced economies. Emerging Asia's growth performance is *transforming* in a very fundamental way the overall structure of the world economy and *relocating its center of gravity.*

The Emerging Asia aggregate used above is, like any grouping, to some degree arbitrary. In particular, the group referred to here is not a strictly geographic one. It does not, for example, include the Pacific Island states; nor does it include several other Asian countries, such as the Philippines. Including or excluding a few of the smaller countries would not significantly alter the structural change story. The EA group is of course dominated by the sheer weight of the PRC and increasingly India. The countries in the EA group share some characteristics. Two key characteristics defining the group are the GDP growth rates and the ratios of investment to GDP. It is these indicators that define the EA group discussed in this chapter, in addition to their geographic location in Asia. These two characteristics have not always been similar in all EA countries at all times during the period considered, but on the whole, both investment rates and growth rates have been high in EA countries, sufficient to set them apart from most other countries. Table 2-2 describes the growth rates achieved by EA countries. In the ten years from 1999, the year after the Asian crisis, to 2008, EA growth averaged 5.9 percent if we take a simple average of country growth rates, and 7.7 percent if we weigh by GDP or take the group's GDP as a single aggregate. Aggregate EA growth has been about three times as rapid as growth in the advanced economies and about twice as rapid as growth in other emerging and developing economies (EMDEV).[6]

As we discuss in the second section of this chapter, over the same period the simple average investment rate in EA was about 27.6 percent and

6. Including the year 2008, the second half of which was marked by the beginning of the worldwide "post–Lehman Brothers" crisis, lowers the growth average significantly for some very export-dependent EA economies such as Hong Kong, China; Singapore; Taipei,China; and Thailand. Their average over the decade remains quite high, however.

TABLE 2-2. Post–Asian Crisis Growth in Real GDP, 1999–2008

Percent

	1999	2000	2001	2002	2003	2004	2005	2006	2007	2008	1999–2008 avg.
Emerging Asia	6.8	7.3	5.2	6.9	7.4	8.2	8.4	9.4	10.1	7.2	7.7
People's Republic of China	7.6	8.4	8.3	9.1	10.0	10.1	10.4	11.6	13.0	9.6	9.8
Hong Kong, China	2.6	8.0	0.5	1.8	3.0	8.5	7.1	7.0	6.4	2.1	4.7
India	6.9	5.7	3.9	4.6	6.9	7.9	9.2	9.8	9.4	7.3	7.1
Indonesia	0.8	5.4	3.6	4.5	4.8	5.0	5.7	5.5	6.3	6.0	4.8
Korea	10.7	8.8	4.0	7.2	2.8	4.6	4.0	5.2	5.1	2.3	5.4
Malaysia	6.1	8.7	0.5	5.4	5.8	6.8	5.3	5.8	6.2	4.6	5.5
Singapore	7.2	10.1	−2.4	4.2	3.8	9.2	7.6	8.7	8.2	1.4	5.7
Taipei,China	6.0	5.8	−1.7	5.3	3.7	6.2	4.7	5.4	6.0	0.7	4.2
Thailand	4.4	4.8	2.2	5.3	7.1	6.3	4.6	5.1	4.9	2.5	4.7
Viet Nam	4.8	6.8	6.9	7.1	7.3	7.8	8.4	8.2	8.5	6.2	7.2
GCC[a]	0.1	6.3	1.4	1.3	9.0	7.3	6.9	5.4	4.2	6.3	4.8
Japan	−0.1	2.9	0.2	0.3	1.4	2.7	1.9	2.0	2.4	−1.2	1.2
United States	4.8	4.1	1.1	1.8	2.5	3.6	3.1	2.7	2.1	0.4	2.6
Euro area	2.9	3.9	1.9	0.9	0.8	2.2	1.7	3.0	2.8	0.6	2.1
Other advanced	3.8	4.2	2.0	2.3	2.3	3.3	2.9	3.1	3.1	1.0	2.8
Other EMDEV[b]	2.0	5.2	2.4	3.4	4.6	6.6	5.6	6.4	6.5	4.4	4.7
Advanced	3.5	4.0	1.4	1.4	1.8	3.0	2.5	2.8	2.6	0.4	2.3
EMDEV[b]	4.0	6.1	3.6	4.9	6.0	7.4	6.9	7.7	8.1	5.8	6.0

Source: IMF, *World Economic Outlook*, April 2010.

a. GCC (Gulf Cooperation Council) includes Bahrain; Kuwait; Oman; Qatar; Saudi Arabia; and the United Arab Emirates (UAE).

b. Newly industrialized Asian economies (Hong Kong, China; Korea; Singapore; Taipei,China) are classified under EMDEV (emerging market and developing economies).

about 33 percent in the aggregate, with a strong rising trend, the latter moving from about 29 percent in 1999 to about 38 percent in 2008. Given these high investment rates it is all the more remarkable that EA also ran a significant current account surplus over the 1999–2008 period, averaging 5.8 percent across countries and 4.3 percent of GDP in the aggregate. EA as a "region" has thus saved even a higher proportion of income than the high proportion it invests, allowing it to run this aggregate current account surplus. Because this group of countries also attracts a substantial amount of capital from abroad, reserve accumulation has been due not only to the current account surplus, but also to a surplus on the capital account.[7]

This chapter discusses EA in the context of the world economy, focusing on some of the key issues related to the huge structural transformation in the world economy. The next section takes a qualitative look at the drivers of growth; it underlines what has been special in the Asian growth experience and why "supply-side" considerations indicate that, at least in the near future, growth is likely to continue at a rapid pace. Second, the discussion focuses on the lively "rebalancing" debate, due to the larger-than-historically-observed current account imbalances that have characterized the world economy in the first decade of the twenty-first century. The main problem is perceived to be the large PRC current account surplus, augmented by some significant surpluses in other Asian countries, and the large current account deficit that the United States has experienced for most of the recent period. To what extent could these "global imbalances" turn into a "demand-side" constraint on Asian growth? Finally, we integrate the points made in the first three sections and offer concluding thoughts on the policy debate surrounding Asian growth and its impact on the world economy. The objective is not a detailed quantitative analysis, but a strategic and qualitative discussion of some of the most important policy issues that are coming to the forefront, and that are likely to become even more central in the years ahead. These issues are at the heart of the G-20 mutual assessment process in the context of the "strong, sustainable, and balanced growth" objective adopted for the world economy by the G-20.[8] They are likely to remain central to the G-20 process, to discussions at the IMF and the World Bank, and to the political debate in Asia, the United States, and the world as a whole.

The Drivers of Growth

Why has emerging Asia grown so fast, and why is it likely that this growth momentum will last well into the coming decade? Before turning to global imbalances, and the debate about the need to "rebalance" the structure of

---

7. While there has been a current account surplus in the aggregate, some countries have been running modest current account deficits, most notably India. For the EA aggregate, the capital account has been in surplus over the years 2001–2007, with a cumulative surplus of $397.5 billion (IMF Balance of Payments Statistics, June 2010).

8. G-20 Finance Ministers and Central Bank Governors (2009a and 2009b).

world demand, this section discusses the nature of EA's growth from the supply side.

The key supply-side drivers that explain the impressive growth of EA and the ensuing worldwide shift in income shares are: capital accumulation; technological progress, in particular the speed of diffusion of knowledge and technology; factors relating to the labor supply and human capital; and finally, the quality of institutions as well as political variables. The "convergence" story here is one concerning a few decades. In terms of theoretical growth models, we are not discussing long-term steady states, but medium-term transitions.[9]

Emerging Asia invests a much larger fraction of its GDP than the rest of the world—indeed this is one of the selection criteria used by this chapter to define the EA group. Table 2-3 gives the figures for the broad groups of countries already distinguished in table 2-2.

In the pre-crisis decade, Emerging Asia invested about 33 percent of its aggregate GDP, compared to less than 20 percent by the United States and about 21 percent by the euro zone. Note that Japan's investment rate went down to 24 percent from levels above 30 percent during its high-growth period, a modest percentage compared to Emerging Asia, but still "Asian" when compared to the United States or Europe. It is also instructive to contrast the investment rate in "Other Emerging and Developing (EMDEV)" countries, which averaged only 22.1 percent, to that of Emerging Asia's 33.1 percent.[10] The story is more complicated, therefore, than one of simple income level–driven convergence, where all poorer countries would have higher investment rates encouraged by higher rates of return on capital, in turn due to lower capital-labor ratios. There are many developing countries poorer than or at income levels close to EA countries that invest a much *smaller* fraction of their incomes. As illustrated by figure 2-1 below, there is no systematic relationship between per capita income and investment rates.

---

9. For a discussion of "how long is the long run" in the context of theoretical steady-state growth models, see, for example, Atkinson (1969). The time span relevant to long-run growth theory is measured in centuries. The world we observe and the policy discussions that accompany it, is one of transitional dynamics where decades are a more useful unit of time.

10. Note that Indonesia had a more difficult time recovering from the shock of the Asian crisis, with both growth and investment rates very low in 1999. The investment rate recovered strongly, however, reaching 27.8 percent in 2008.

TABLE 2-3. Investment as a Share of Country or Group GDP
Percent

	1999	2000	2001	2002	2003	2004	2005	2006	2007	2008	1999–2008 avg.
Emerging Asia	29.3	29.6	29.3	30.5	32.9	35.2	36.0	36.5	36.1	36.7	33.1
People's Republic of China	36.7	35.1	36.3	37.9	41.2	43.3	43.6	43.6	41.7	42.5	40.1
Hong Kong, China	24.8	27.5	25.3	22.8	21.9	21.8	20.6	21.7	20.9	20.5	22.7
India	25.9	24.3	22.8	25.2	27.6	32.1	34.3	36.0	37.6	35.6	29.7
Indonesia	11.4	22.2	22.0	21.4	25.6	24.1	25.1	25.4	24.9	27.8	22.4
Korea	29.1	30.6	29.2	29.2	29.9	29.9	29.7	29.9	29.4	31.2	29.8
Malaysia	22.4	26.9	24.4	24.8	22.8	23.0	20.0	20.5	21.7	19.1	22.4
Singapore	32.2	33.3	26.5	23.7	16.0	21.8	19.9	20.3	20.7	30.1	23.8
Taipei,China	23.6	23.3	18.4	18.0	18.4	22.7	22.7	22.7	22.1	22.7	21.3
Thailand	20.5	22.8	24.1	23.8	25.0	26.8	31.4	28.3	26.4	28.9	25.6
Viet Nam	27.6	29.6	31.2	33.2	35.4	35.5	35.6	36.8	43.1	41.1	34.6
GCC[a]	19.3	17.2	19.7	20.9	21.2	21.2	19.8	20.7	22.9	22.4	20.5
Japan	24.8	25.4	24.8	23.1	22.8	23.0	23.6	23.8	24.1	22.5	23.8
United States	20.6	20.9	19.3	18.7	18.7	19.7	20.3	20.5	19.5	18.2	19.6
Euro area	21.4	22.0	21.1	20.1	20.1	20.4	20.8	21.6	22.2	22.2	21.2
Other advanced	20.2	19.9	19.2	19.1	19.2	19.6	20.3	20.9	21.6	21.0	20.1
Other EMDEV[b]	21.3	21.6	21.6	21.0	20.7	21.8	21.7	22.8	24.5	25.0	22.1
World	22.8	22.6	22.8	22.3	22.2	22.6	21.6	21.0	21.2	22.1	22.1
Advanced	21.6	21.9	20.7	19.8	19.9	20.4	20.9	21.4	21.3	20.7	20.9
EMDEV[b]	24.4	24.7	24.5	25.0	25.8	27.2	27.1	27.9	28.9	29.6	26.4

Source: ADB (2010) and ADB (2009); IMF, International Financial Statistics, June 2010; IMF, *World Economic Outlook*, April 2010.

a. GCC (Gulf Cooperation Council) includes Bahrain; Kuwait; Oman; Qatar; Saudi Arabia; and United Arab Emirates (UAE).

b. Newly industrialized Asian economies (Hong Kong, China; Korea; Singapore; Taipei,China) are classified under the total EMDEV (emerging market and developing economies).

In a simple regression of investment rates on per capita GDP and a dummy variable for countries in Emerging Asia, the coefficients on the EA dummy variable indicate that those countries had investment rates approximately 6 percentage points higher, on average, during the period from 1999 to 2008 (see table 2-4). Higher per capita income, however, does not systematically lead to higher investment rates. Of course, this simply reflects part of the selection criterion for the group and is not some

FIGURE 2-1. Investment and GDP per Capita, 1999–2008

Percent of GDP

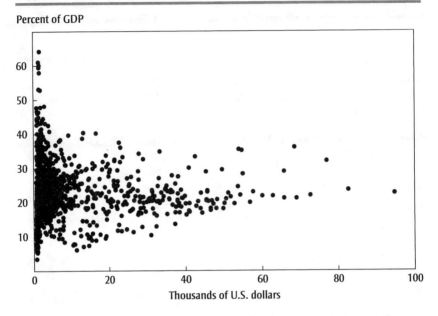

Thousands of U.S. dollars

Source: ADB (2010) and ADB (2009); IMF, International Financial Statistics, June 2010; IMF, *World Economic Outlook,* April 2010.

kind of test for causality, but it shows that the group is "different" in terms of its investment rates.

While all of Emerging Asia has high investment rates, there is significant variation in the group, with the PRC at the top reaching above 40 percent, and the Southeast Asian countries at the lower end in the 25 percent neighborhood. Both the PRC and India, the two biggest countries, show a clear

TABLE 2-4. Investment Rates, Income, and Emerging Asia, 1999–2008

Dependent variable: investment rate	
GDP per capita	−0.01
	(0.014)
EA dummy	6.07***
	(0.778)
Observations	1,161
R^2	0.044

Notes: Robust standard errors in parentheses.
***$p < 0.01$.

increasing trend in the investment ratio, which translates into an increasing trend for the aggregate EA investment rate.

Calculations performed using the basic growth accounting framework suggest, not surprisingly, that a significant part of Emerging Asia's much higher than average GDP growth rate is due to these higher investment rates, which lead to more rapid capital accumulation. It is worth remembering, though, that economic history has examples of countries with very high investment rates not growing particularly rapidly over a period of decades. One such country was the Soviet Union, which had long periods of investment rates comparable to the PRC's current investment rates, accompanied by mediocre growth rates.[11] Other examples can be found in the experience of oil exporters, such as Algeria.

A key factor that has made the rapid growth and "convergence" of Emerging Asia possible is the *combination* of rapid capital accumulation with fairly rapid technological progress, conventionally measured by the growth of total factor productivity, something that was absent during the later periods of Soviet history, and is also absent from the histories of many oil exporters. *What is special and unprecedented in EA, and particularly in the PRC, is that very high investment rates have been accompanied by decent total factor productivity growth.* There is some wasteful investment in EA, but the story is not at all similar to what had happened in the Soviet Union, where the huge sacrifices represented by large investment efforts in the end led to very little progress because of inefficiency, waste, and slow absorption of advances in knowledge outside the defense sector. A very big part of the Asian story is in fact the rapid diffusion of technology and know-how coming from the advanced economies through trade, foreign investment, licensing, and adaptation.

Barry Bosworth and Susan Collins, for example, in their comparative study of India and the PRC over the 1978 to 2004 period, estimate that in both countries total factor productivity (TFP) growth accounted for almost half of the growth of GDP per worker.[12] Other studies, including

11. Note that eminent Western economists such as Robert Solow and Paul Samuelson, in the late 1950s and early 1960s, were of the opinion that Soviet GDP per capita would converge with that of the United States because of those high investment rates. On Soviet growth, see Ofer (1987).

12. In the PRC, output per worker grew at an average annual rate of 7.3 percent, of which 3.2 percent was due to physical capital accumulation and 3.6 percent to TFP growth. In India, the rates are 6.4 percent for output per worker, 2.4 percent for physical capital growth, and 3.5 percent for TFP growth. Bosworth and Collins (2008).

studies of other Asian countries, document a significant positive contribution of TFP, often accounting for close to one third of growth in output per worker.[13] TFP performance may not always appear spectacular in itself, but it is significant, and it is this decent total factor productivity performance complementing rapid capital accumulation that explains why, despite very high investment rates, one does not observe significant declines in the return on investment. In a recent study on the PRC, for example, Chong-En Bai and co-authors conclude that the aggregate rate of return to capital "fell from roughly 25 percent between 1979 and 1992, to about 20 percent" and remained steady close to that value thereafter. A rate of 20 percent is high in comparison with that in both advanced economies and most developing economies.[14]

Part of what shows up as aggregate total factor productivity growth reflects a more productive allocation of inputs between sectors, most importantly workers relocating from low-productivity rural activities, mostly in agriculture, to more productive activities in urban industry and services or modern agriculture. This "relocation effect," well recognized since Arthur Lewis's seminal contribution on "economic development with unlimited supplies of labor,"[15] has been important in EA, accounting for 26 percent of growth in India and 14 percent of growth in PRC in the 1993–2004 period, according to Bosworth and Collins. Looking toward the next decade, both the PRC and India, as well as the other lower-income EA countries, retain growth potential from this labor reallocation effect, because there are still large amounts of underutilized rural labor. What has been called the "Lewis moment," when surplus labor runs out in a developing economy, is not yet imminent for the PRC and India, although for the PRC it is a medium-term prospect.[16] This is no longer true in the higher-income "newly industrialized" emerging Asian

13. See Hsieh (2002).

14. See Bai, Hsieh, and Yingyi-Qian (2006). Both Olivier Blanchard and Richard Cooper in their comments on these estimates express doubts about the quality of the data, but the possible data-induced biases are not all in the same direction, and overall, it is clear that the return to capital in the PRC remains high by international standards, despite the very high level of investment.

15. See Lewis (1954).

16. See Minami (1968) and, also, Yiping and Tingsong (2010) who perform interesting comparative static simulations of the consequences of the "Lewis moment" for the PRC. The "Lewis moment" can be more than a moment, of course, and stretch over a number of years. The PRC still has reserves of rural labor. But given the pace of growth, they may not last beyond this decade.

economies such as Korea; Taipei, China; or Singapore, where there is no more surplus labor to be drawn into the modern sectors.

Apart from the traditionally recognized Lewis-type productivity growth due to rural-urban migration, there is also total factor productivity growth due to improved factor allocation *within* the "modern sector" across industries and firms. A study by Chang-Tai Hsieh and Peter Klenow, for example, using microeconomic data on manufacturing, finds much wider dispersion in the marginal products of labor and capital in the PRC and India than in the United States.[17] In the period analyzed by the authors, this led to strong aggregate TFP growth in the PRC, because the dispersion in marginal productivities decreased; the authors did not, until 1994, observe the same phenomenon of dispersion reduction in India.

Empirical growth economics has traditionally distinguished the outward shift of the technological frontier, due to advances in basic knowledge, from the movement toward the technological frontier by firms and economic actors that absorb existing knowledge and adapt it to their specific conditions. The dispersion reduction observed by Hsieh and Klenow reflects this "learning and diffusion" mechanism inside an economy, including the reallocation of productive inputs from lower-productivity to higher-productivity firms. Learning and diffusion also occurs, of course, across international borders. A lot of total factor productivity growth in Emerging Asia is of that "catch-up" type, as Asian firms import technology and adapt it to suit their specific circumstances. Some firms are sector leaders in importing technology, but then diffusion occurs inside the domestic economy as other firms learn and adapt. The fact that they invest a lot has allowed this technological diffusion to take place on a grand scale, as much of the imported and adapted technology has been embodied in capital equipment, including information technology.

All this stands in stark contrast to the high-investment-rate Soviet experience. The difference is surely due to the very different institutional framework characterizing the Soviet and the EA experiences. In EA, markets function reasonably well, and resources are channeled to enterprises and sectors in a more efficient way than was the case in the hyper-centralized Soviet system. One does not have to be an unconditional supporter of unfettered markets to believe that a mixed economy, where markets play a considerable role, allocates resources better than a centralized

17. See Hsieh and Klenow (2009).

TABLE 2-5a. Education Participation

	Net enrollment in primary education (percent)[a]		Gender parity[b]	Gross enrollment in tertiary education (percent)[c]	
	2000	2007	2007	2000	2007
Emerging Asia					
People's Republic of China	n.a.	100	n.a.	8	22
Hong Kong, China[d]	93	94	0.99	n.a.	32
India	79	90	0.96	10	13
Indonesia	94	95	n.a.	n.a.	18
Korea	99	99	0.98	78	96
Malaysia[d]	97	97	1.00	26	30
Taipei,China	n.a.	n.a.	n.a.	n.a.	n.a.
Thailand	n.a.	n.a.	n.a.	n.a.	n.a.
Viet Nam	95	n.a.	n.a.	n.a.	10
World					
Advanced[e]	98	97	1.00	53	65
Other EMDEV[f]	80	86	0.98	18	30

Source: *Education for All Global Monitoring Report 2010* (UNESCO Institute for Statistics).

a. Net primary enrollment is the number of pupils of official primary school age who are enrolled in primary education as a percentage of the total children of the official school age population.

b. Gender parity is the ratio of net primary enrollment for females to net primary enrollment for males.

c. Gross enrollment is the number of pupils of any age who are enrolled as a percentage of the total children of the official school age population.

d. Data for Hong Kong, China, are for years 2001 and 2005; data for Malaysia are for years 2000 and 2006.

e. Advanced is a simple average of advanced economies.

f. Other EMDEV is a simple average of emerging and developing economies that are not in EA.

n.a.: not available.

bureaucratic system. The high investment rates of EA are not only accompanied by the rapid absorption of technical know-how, but are also taking place in an institutional setting that is much more conducive to an efficient allocation of resources than was the case in the Soviet system.[18]

Another factor that can help explain the remarkable growth performance of EA is the considerable progress EA has made with human capital formation. Tables 2-5a to 2-5c show data on several measures of

18. There is of course a debate relating to the perceived inefficiencies of the state enterprise and state banking sectors not only in the PRC but also in India, and the efficiency of resource allocation can surely be improved. But these inefficiencies are minor in comparison with what characterized the later decades of the Soviet system. The share of state enterprises in total output is of course also much smaller than it was in the Soviet Union, and it is declining. Increases in the overall level of efficiency will show up as TFP growth.

TABLE 2-5b. Schooling and Literacy Changes

	Average years of schooling, age 15 and over[a]		Adult literacy rate (%)[a]	
	2000	2010	2000	2008
Emerging Asia	5.9	7.0	91	93
People's Republic of China	7.1	8.2	91	94
Hong Kong, China	8.8	10.4		
India[b]	4.2	5.1	61	63
Indonesia[b]	4.3	6.1	—	92
Korea	11.1	11.8	—	—
Malaysia	9.0	10.1	89	92
Singapore	8.1	9.1	93	95
Taipei,China	9.9	11.3	—	—
Thailand	6.3	7.5	93	94
Viet Nam	5.1	6.4	90	93
World				
Advanced[c]	10.6	11.0	93	97
Other EMDEV[c]	6.4	7.3	76	82

Source: Average years of schooling from Barro and Lee (2010); literacy rates from *Education for All, Global Monitoring Report 2010* (UNESCO Institute for Statistics).

a. Population-weighted average of EA countries for schooling data; simple average for literacy data.

b. Literacy rates for India are for 2001 and 2006; literacy rate for Indonesia is for 2006.

c. For schooling, Advanced and Other EMDEV are population-weighted averages of advanced economies and emerging and developing economies that are not in EA. For literacy, Advanced and Other EMDEV are simple averages.

human capital: school enrollment rates, average years of schooling, literacy rates, and international test scores. Primary school enrollment rates in the countries of EA were already fairly high in the year 2000, but further increases have occurred in the enrollment rate and gender parity in some countries, most notably in India.[19] Increasing percentages of people are also seeking higher education throughout the world, and some EA countries have made large gains. Korea's tertiary school enrollment increased 18 percentage points, to a large 96 percent, between 2000 and 2007, and the PRC's enrollment increased by 16 percentage points in the same period.

Average years of schooling in a population has been estimated by R. J. Barro and J. W. Lee as a measure of the stock of human capital available

19. The net enrollment rate in primary education increased from 79 percent to 90 percent, as seen in table 2-6, and gender parity in primary education increased from 0.83 in 2000 to 0.96 in 2007.

TABLE 2-5c. International Test Scores: Achievement in
Math and Science

	Cognitive[a]	Basic[b]	Top[c]
Emerging Asia	4.87	0.87	0.10
People's Republic of China	4.94	0.93	0.08
Hong Kong, China	5.19	0.94	0.12
India	4.28	0.92	0.01
Indonesia	3.88	0.47	0.01
Korea	5.34	0.96	0.18
Malaysia	4.84	0.86	0.06
Singapore	5.33	0.95	0.18
Taipei,China	5.45	0.96	0.22
Thailand	4.56	0.85	0.02
Viet Nam	—	—	—
World			
Advanced[d]	4.75	0.88	0.09
Other EMDEV[e]	4.25	0.65	0.03

Source: Hanushek and Woessman (2009), based on the standardized average of scores on twelve international student achievement tests in math and science, conducted between 1964 and 2003. Not all countries were represented for all tests.
a. Cognitive is the average test score in math and science, from primary through end of secondary school.
b. Basic is the share of students reaching basic literacy in math and science.
c. Top is the share of high-performing students in math and science.
d. Advanced is a simple average of advanced economies.
e. Other EMDEV is a simple average of emerging and developing economies that are not in EA.

contemporaneously as an input to production.[20] India, Indonesia, and Viet Nam have lower average years of schooling than other EA countries, but their recent gains are quite large, ranging from a 22 percent increase for India to a 46 percent increase for Indonesia. The EA countries as a whole have a lower average years of schooling than other emerging and developing countries, 7 years compared to 7.3 years, but they have gained more in the decade 2000–10, increasing 17 percent compared to 13 percent in emerging and developing countries. EA countries have also seen increases in literacy rates over the same period, with only India remaining below a 90 percent adult literacy rate, of the EA countries with data available.

In a recent study of the relationship between education, cognitive skills, and growth, Eric Hanushek and Ludger Woessman develop a new metric to track student achievement across countries and over time, by standard-

20. See Barro and Lee (2010).

izing results from several international achievement tests in reading, math, and science.[21] This measure has the benefit of capturing skill differences between countries, which come from differences in education quality or from outside the formal education environment. On average, the shares of students achieving basic literacy in math and science in EA countries are comparable to those in advanced economies and are higher than those in other emerging and developing countries. EA countries compare with advanced economies for the shares of high-performing students as well. The various measures of human capital show Emerging Asia acquiring more highly skilled populations at a rapid rate.

Looking forward, for all the reasons touched on above, supply-side considerations suggest that the growth momentum of EA is likely to continue for at least another decade, certainly in the lower-income EA economies, as well as the PRC and India. High investment rates can continue to be accompanied by significant total productivity growth, which in turn means that rates of return to capital can remain high, encouraging further investment.

In the Soviet experience, there was rapid capital accumulation, comparable to the pace observed in EA, but very little total factor productivity growth. On the other hand, in many other emerging and developing countries today, there is the same process of diffusion and absorption of technology observed in EA, but investment rates are much lower, restricting the scale of the process of catch-up growth.

It is the *combination* of rapid capital accumulation, including human capital accumulation, with institutions supportive of technology absorption and reasonably efficient markets, that has been at the heart of Emerging Asia's success. It is this *combination* that distinguishes the Asian experience from other experiences with very high investment rates, such as the Soviet experience, as well as from the current experience of other emerging market countries constrained by lower investment rates.

Rebalancing the World Economy?

Looking at EA countries from the supply side, it would appear most likely that rapid growth can continue for the next decade, based on continued high investment rates, availability of both unskilled and skilled

21. See Hanushek and Woessman (2009).

labor in most economies, particularly in the PRC and India, and decent total factor productivity performance based on continued rapid diffusion of technology, increases in intrasector efficiency of resource allocation and continued reallocation of resources, notably labor, from low- to higher-productivity activities. Supply-side factors determine the growth of "potential output." For potential output growth to be matched by actual output growth, there has to be sufficient effective demand, something the macroeconomic events of 2008–09 have again reminded us of. What about the demand-side factors affecting growth in the EA economies?

What is perhaps even more remarkable than the high investment rates characterizing EA is the fact that this investment is financed, in the aggregate, by even higher savings rates. Table 2-6 describes EA savings rates in the global context. The aggregate savings rate of the EA countries is a whopping 37.4 percent of their GDP. The leader and outlier is the PRC, with a savings rate averaging 44.8 percent in the pre-crisis decade. All the EA countries are high savers, even the relatively richer ones and those whose investment rates declined markedly after the Asian crisis. In 2008, 25 percent of total world savings took place in EA, compared to the 14 percent share of world GDP that EA had in that year. Across the world, the only group of countries that have savings rates comparable to what prevails in EA is the Gulf oil exporters group, particularly in recent years, reflecting higher oil prices.

The savings rates reported in table 2-6 have two major implications. First, on the positive side, they suggest that the high EA investment rates discussed in the preceding section are easily financed. In the aggregate, EA does not need net foreign capital inflows to finance its high investment rates. Domestic savings more than cover the financing requirements. In some countries, notably India, domestic savings have fallen short of investment, but not by much. In the aggregate, the "savings surplus" has been substantial and durable. This in turn suggests that high investment rates can continue into the future without running into a *financing constraint.*[22]

The second implication of the savings and investment numbers and of the ensuing current account surplus is that Emerging Asia's domestic

---

22. Note that this does *not* imply that EA countries don't benefit from foreign direct investment (FDI). FDI is one key factor allowing "catch-up growth," and EA does attract large amounts of FDI. This inflow that comes on top of current account surpluses is more than compensated for by reserve accumulation.

TABLE 2-6. Savings as a Share of Country Group GDP, 1999–2008
Percent

	1999	2000	2001	2002	2003	2004	2005	2006	2007	2008	1999–2008 avg.
Emerging Asia	32.8	32.2	32.0	33.9	36.9	38.9	40.7	42.7	43.3	42.7	37.4
People's Republic of China	38.1	36.8	37.6	40.3	44.0	46.9	50.8	53.1	52.7	51.9	44.8
Hong Kong, China	31.1	31.6	31.2	30.4	32.3	31.3	32.0	33.8	33.2	34.1	32.1
India	25.2	23.3	23.1	26.6	29.1	32.2	33.0	34.9	36.6	33.4	29.4
Indonesia	15.1	27.0	26.3	25.4	29.1	24.7	25.2	28.4	27.3	27.8	25.3
Korea	34.4	32.9	30.8	30.1	31.8	33.8	31.5	30.5	30.0	30.6	31.6
Malaysia	38.1	35.9	32.3	32.8	34.8	35.1	35.0	36.9	37.4	36.6	35.4
Singapore	49.6	44.9	39.5	36.9	39.4	39.3	41.9	45.2	48.3	49.3	43.2
Taipei,China	26.3	26.0	24.8	26.8	28.2	28.5	27.5	29.7	30.5	28.9	27.7
Thailand	30.7	30.4	28.5	27.5	28.4	28.5	27.1	29.4	32.7	29.5	29.2
Viet Nam	31.7	33.1	33.3	31.5	30.5	32.0	34.5	36.5	33.3	29.2	32.5
GCC[a]	21.9	31.6	29.1	28.1	33.9	39.5	47.0	49.3	45.6	46.5	36.1
Japan	27.4	28.0	26.9	26.0	26.0	26.7	27.2	27.7	28.9	26.7	27.2
United States	17.4	16.7	15.4	14.4	14.0	14.4	14.4	14.5	14.4	13.3	14.9
Euro area	21.9	21.4	21.2	20.8	20.6	21.6	21.2	22.1	22.6	21.4	21.5
Other advanced	21.4	20.0	20.0	20.3	21.0	21.0	21.3	21.9	22.4	21.9	21.1
Other EMDEV[b]	18.5	20.0	18.8	19.0	19.8	20.7	22.3	23.3	22.5	21.5	20.6
World	22.0	22.4	21.4	20.7	21.1	22.1	22.9	24.2	24.3	23.9	22.5
Advanced	21.2	21.2	20.1	18.9	18.8	19.5	19.7	20.5	20.1	19.0	19.9
EMDEV[b]	24.8	26.4	25.7	26.7	28.4	30.1	31.5	33.3	33.4	33.5	29.2

Source: ADB (2010) and ADB (2009); IMF, International Financial Statistics, June 2010; IMF, *World Economic Outlook,* April 2010.

a. GCC (Gulf Cooperation Council) includes Bahrain; Kuwait; Oman; Qatar; Saudi Arabia; and UAE.

b. Newly industrialized Asian economies (Hong Kong, China; Korea; Singapore; Taipei,China) are classified under the EMDEV (emerging markets and developing economies) group.

demand had to be supplemented by net foreign demand for aggregate demand to match aggregate supply. It is this observation that is leading to questions relating to the sustainability of EA growth coming not from the supply side, but from the demand side.

The great crisis of 2008 again reminded us that economic performance is not determined entirely from the supply side. Effective demand still matters, even in the medium term. Demand has to expand at a rate close to the trend growth of potential output for potential output to become "actual" output. It is when looking at the drivers of growth from the demand side, therefore, that many observers have voiced the need for EA to be less reliant on exports as a source of demand expansion. The debate is one centering on the "global imbalances" that emerged in the first decade of the twenty-first century, where "imbalance" refers to current account deficits or surpluses. In the aggregate, EA savings have exceeded even the very high investment rates realized in the region. This implies current account surpluses. By far the largest of these current account surpluses appeared in the PRC, in the range of 10–12 percent of GDP, close to $400 billion in absolute terms, at its peak in 2007–08. Other EA countries such as Hong Kong, China; Singapore; and Taipei,China, also contributed to the aggregate surplus. On the other side of the Pacific, the United States ran a very large current account deficit, at its peak reaching 6 percent of GDP, or close to $800 billion in absolute terms, in 2006.

Global current account imbalances have taken center stage in the international debate on the causes of the great crisis of 2008, and in the discussion on prospects for lasting recovery. The PRC surplus, because of its absolute size and its size relative to PRC GDP, is naturally at the center of the debate and has led to strong arguments relating to the need for the PRC to revalue its currency. Global imbalances are no longer just an economic issue. They have become a highly charged political issue, and they are one of the sources of serious tension among the major economic powers, between the United States and the PRC in particular.[23] A letter to Secretary of the Treasury Timothy Geithner and Secretary of Commerce Gary Locke, drafted by U.S. Representatives Michael Michaud and Timothy Ryan and signed by 130 members of Congress in early spring 2010, is a good reflection of these political tensions:

> China's currency manipulation essentially subsidizes Chinese exports and imposes tariffs on foreign imports. This presents an insurmountable trade barrier to U.S. manufacturers. . . . If the administration fails to act on this issue it will hold back our economic recovery and hurt the ability of American small businesses and manufacturers to increase their production, keep their doors open, and create jobs.[24]

23. For an interesting perspective, see also Wyplosz (2010).
24. "130 Members of Congress Push for Action on China Currency Manipulation," Office of U.S. Representative Mike Michaud, March 15, 2010.

Arvind Subramanian of the Peterson Institute and the Centre for Global Development proposes that the World Trade Organization (WTO) be given the role of enforcing exchange rate policies·

> The key is to recognize that the renminbi is a problem not just for the U.S. but the world and, as such, requires a multilateral rules-based solution rather than a bilateral confrontation between Washington and Beijing.
>
> The World Trade Organization is a natural forum for developing new multilateral rules. First, undervalued exchange rates are de facto protectionist trade policies because they are a combination of export subsidies and import tariffs. Second, the WTO has a better record on enforcement of rules. Its dispute settlement system, although not perfect, has been reasonably effective in allowing members to initiate and settle disputes. The WTO has greater legitimacy than the IMF—developing countries, even smaller ones, have been active in bringing disputes to the WTO. Tiny Antigua (population 69,000) managed to successfully challenge U.S. gambling laws.
>
> What is needed is a new rule in the WTO proscribing undervalued exchange rates. The irony is that export subsidies and import tariffs are individually disciplined in the WTO but their lethal combination in "an undervalued exchange rate" is not.[25]

In late June 2010, the PRC announced that it will allow greater flexibility in the renminbi-U.S. dollar exchange rate, that decision coming after a sharp appreciation of the renminbi with respect to the euro due to the latter's loss of value triggered by the Greek, and later "southern European," debt crisis.

In academic writings as well as in policy circles, there are strong disagreements on how global imbalances should be viewed and what role they play in the world economy. A particularly interesting and sharp exchange took place between Ronald McKinnon and Günther Schnabel on one side of the argument, and Michael Mussa, former chief economist of the IMF, at the Seventh BIS Annual Conference in Lucerne, Switzerland, in June 2008. McKinnon has generally put forward the viewpoint that exchange rates do not matter much in determining current account

25. Subramanian (2010).

positions, which reflect gaps between saving and investment. He supports a strict fixed exchange rate policy for the PRC. Michael Mussa calls this "economic nonsense."[26]

Disagreements are also strong in policy circles. Mervyn King, governor of the Bank of England, in a speech delivered on January 19, 2010, had the following to say about the role of global imbalances in causing the great crisis:

> The massive flows of capital from the new entrants into western financial markets pushed down interest rates and encouraged risk taking on an extraordinary scale. Banks expanded their balance sheets and new instruments were created to satisfy the search for yield. In the five years up to 2007 the balance sheet of the largest UK banks nearly trebled. The build up of risk came to threaten the stability of the entire financial system. Capital flows provided the fuel which the developed world's inadequately designed and regulated financial system then ignited to produce a firestorm that engulfed us all.

And looking forward, he sees the global imbalances that are again increasing as a major threat to recovery and stability:

> The reason why continuing large deficits are not sustainable indefinitely is that for every current account deficit there is an equal capital flow in the opposite direction. Even if those flows remain constant in size, they imply an ever increasing stock of international asset and liability positions. . . . Adding inexorably to the stock of international assets and liabilities is like adding one brick on top of another to form a tower. With skill it can be done for a surprisingly long time. But

---

26. What explains such sharp differences between renowned economists? See Mussa (2008). While there is no space here to analyze them fully, an important part of the disagreement is due to different underlying models of the economy in the minds of the authors. Exchange rates do not matter much in models of open economies with homogeneous products that are essentially all tradable. They matter much more in models where there is a distinction between tradable and nontradable products and where, in addition, there is strong product differentiation between products produced in different countries. When there is no product differentiation, devaluation does not lead to terms-of-trade effects; when there is differentiation, a country that devalues can reduce the relative price of its traded products compared to products produced elsewhere, while increasing the price of its tradables with respect to its nontradables.

eventually the moment comes when adding one more causes the tower to fall down."[27]

On March 30, 2010, the five leaders of G 20 countries Canada, France, Korea, the United Kingdom, and the United States wrote a letter to all G-20 leaders with the following language:

> Ongoing trade, fiscal and structural imbalances cannot lead to strong and sustainable growth. Without cooperative action to make the necessary adjustments to achieve that outcome, the risk of future crises and low growth will remain. All G-20 countries must move quickly to implement the first steps of the new Framework agreed to in Pittsburgh—to report robustly on what each of us can do to contribute to strong, sustainable and balanced global growth.[28]

It is very interesting to contrast the views expressed by the governor of the Bank of England and the five leaders with the views expressed by Alan Greenspan, in 2007, not too long after he stepped down from his position as chairman of the Federal Reserve System:

> Cross-border current account imbalances impart a degree of stress that is likely to be greater than that stemming from domestic imbalances only. But in a flexible economy, are any of these as significant as we tend to make them? I do not deny that nation-defined current account imbalances do have important implications for exchange-rates and terms of trade. But I suspect the measure is too often used to signify some more generic malaise, especially in the context of the so-called twin American deficits, with reference to our politically determined federal budget deficit, which has quite different roots and policy requirements than those of the market determined current account balance.[29]

Greenspan, as well as others with strong faith in unfettered markets, tends to see current account imbalances as a consequence of the reduction in "home bias" in the allocation of a nation's savings and, in fact,

---

27. King (2010).
28. G-20 Leaders Statement (2009b).
29. See Greenspan (2007).

as accompanying a more efficient, market-driven, worldwide allocation of capital:

> A decline in home bias is reflected in savers increasingly reaching across national borders to invest in foreign assets. This engenders a marked rise in current account surpluses among some countries and an offsetting rise in deficits of others.[30]

The vision underlying Greenspan's remarks, and shared by many, is that of a truly integrated and globalized world, with fully flexible prices, including exchange rates, efficient markets and strong property rights, where savings and investments would be allocated by the global market according to relative returns and risk. In such a world it would be surprising indeed if current accounts, the result of a myriad of investment and savings decisions made by private firms and households, would happen to be close to balance. In such a world there would not be much more reason for national current accounts to be in balance than there is reason to expect the current accounts of individual firms or households to be in balance. To push this reasoning to the extreme, if all economic activity were to be carried out by purely profit-maximizing private actors, with no political motives, in a world of perfect and unrestricted markets, with flexible exchange rates, the very notion of national current accounts loses relevance. In such a world, one should expect a dramatic reduction in home bias in the allocation of savings translating into large national current account differences reflecting differences in productivity growth and other factors affecting the rate of return to capital invested. Note that in such a world there would not seem to be a need for countries to hold significant foreign exchange reserves.

It is useful to keep these different perspectives in mind when discussing the challenges facing EA and the "rebalancing" of the world economy. An efficient allocation of capital worldwide indeed requires that there is a flow of capital from high savings areas to areas where savings are scarce, provided the rate of return is higher in the latter. But in a world of sovereign nation-states, national currencies, herd behavior in markets, and volatile capital flows, as well as national authorities that intervene in foreign exchange markets and accumulate foreign exchange reserves, the

---

30. Greenspan (2007).

TABLE 2-7. Current Account Balances, 1990–2009
Billions of U.S. dollars

	1990	2000	2005	2008	2009
Emerging Asia	9.4	81.7	242.8	511.2	456.0
People's Republic of China	12.0	20.5	160.8	426.1	283.8
Hong Kong, China	4.8	7.0	20.2	29.3	23.4
India	−7.9	−4.6	−10.3	−26.6	−25.9
Indonesia	−3.2	8.0	0.3	0.1	10.6
Korea	−2.0	12.3	15.0	−5.8	42.7
Malaysia	−0.9	8.5	20.7	38.9	32.0
Singapore	3.1	10.7	26.7	36.2	33.8
Taipei,China	10.9	8.9	17.6	25.1	42.6
Thailand	−7.1	9.3	−7.6	1.6	20.3
Viet Nam	−0.3	1.1	−0.6	−10.7	−7.2
GCC[a]	8.0	49.2	167.8	260.0	57.0
Japan	43.9	119.6	165.7	157.1	141.7
United States	−79.0	−417.4	−748.7	−706.1	−418.0
Euro area	—	−35.9	45.3	−106.0	−43.8
Other advanced	—	−0.9	47.2	36.6	61.1
Other EMDEV[b]	−32.8	0.9	118.6	19.8	−48.8
World (error)	−123.2	−177.0	40.0	180.4	174.4
Memo:					
Germany	45.3	−32.6	142.8	245.7	160.6
Russia	—	46.8	84.4	102.4	47.5
Spain	−18.1	−23.1	−83.3	−153.7	−74.1
United Kingdom	−38.5	−39.1	−59.8	−40.7	−28.8

Source: IMF, *World Economic Outlook,* April 2010.
a. GCC (Gulf Cooperation Council) includes Bahrain; Kuwait; Oman; Qatar; Saudi Arabia; and UAE.
b. Newly industrialized Asian economies (Hong Kong, China; Korea; Singapore; Taipei,China) are classified under the EMDEV (emerging markets and developing economies) group.

situation is much more complicated than in the simple and idealized vision of a truly integrated world economy driven entirely by efficient markets.

Tables 2-7 and 2-8 describe the recent evolution of the current account balances of the EA countries in a global context. The tables show that the EA current account surplus grew steadily until the 2009 crisis year, mirrored by an increasing U.S. current account deficit. The U.S. current account deficit was about twice as large, however, as the EA surplus in the pre-crisis years, with others, such as Japan, the Gulf oil exporters, and also Russia contributing surpluses. Germany has also been a significant contributor of surplus, although the euro zone as a whole has not, with Spain notably running large deficits on current account.

TABLE 2-8. Current Account Balances, 1990–2009
Percent of GDP

	1990	2000	2005	2008	2009
Emerging Asia	0.6	2.6	4.7	6.0	5.2
People's Republic of China	3.1	1.7	7.2	9.4	5.8
Hong Kong, China	6.2	4.1	11.4	13.6	11.1
India	−2.5	−1.0	−1.3	−2.2	−2.1
Indonesia	−2.5	4.8	0.1	0.0	2.0
Korea	−0.7	2.3	1.8	−0.6	5.1
Malaysia	−2.1	9.0	15.0	17.5	16.7
Singapore	8.5	11.6	22.0	19.2	19.1
Taipei,China	6.6	2.7	4.8	6.2	11.2
Thailand	−8.3	7.6	−4.3	0.6	7.7
Viet Nam	−4.0	3.5	−1.1	−11.9	−7.8
GCCᵃ	4.1	14.4	27.2	24.1	6.6
Japan	1.5	2.6	3.6	3.2	2.8
United States	−1.4	−4.2	−5.9	−4.9	−2.9
Euro area	—	−0.6	0.4	−0.8	−0.4
Other advanced	—	0.0	0.8	0.5	0.9
Other EMDEVᵇ	−0.8	0.0	1.8	0.2	−0.5
World (error)	−0.5	−0.6	0.1	0.3	0.3
Memo:					
Germany	2.9	−1.7	5.1	6.7	4.8
Russia	—	18.0	11.0	6.2	3.9
Spain	−3.5	−4.0	−7.4	−9.6	−5.1
United Kingdom	−3.8	−2.6	−2.6	−1.5	−1.3

Source: IMF, *World Economic Outlook*, April 2010.

a. GCC (Gulf Cooperation Council) includes Bahrain; Kuwait; Oman; Qatar; Saudi Arabia; and UAE.

b. Newly industrialized Asian economies (Hong Kong, China; Korea; Singapore; Taipei,China) are classified under the EMDEV (emerging markets and developing economies) group.

Looking ahead, what is the evolution of these current account imbalances likely to be? Will the reduction of the imbalances that occurred during the crisis year of 2009 be permanent? Or will the previous trend toward widening of the imbalances reassert itself after the crisis?

The IMF *WEO* published very interesting projections in October of 2009. Table 2-9 summarizes these projections. One amazing and telling part of these figures was that the world was "projected" to have a current account surplus of over $800 billion with "outer space" by 2014! Part of the problem relates to the genuine "errors and omissions" that exist in the trade data. Since the world does not of course trade with outer space, the surge, in what is described as an error term, was also due to the fact that

TABLE 2-9. **Current Account Projections, Fall 2009, for the Period 2010–2014**

Billions of U.S. dollars

	2010	2011	2012	2013	2014
Emerging Asia	538.3	598.2	690.2	744.0	800.2
People's Republic of China	451.2	507.6	594.9	642.1	694.8
Hong Kong, China	23.9	23.1	22.8	21.7	20.7
India	−33.6	−34.4	−34.2	−32.8	−33.7
Indonesia	3.1	1.3	−2.1	−4.7	−7.9
Korea	18.8	20.3	22.4	23.7	24.5
Malaysia	23.7	24.6	26.5	29.1	31.7
Singapore	22.4	24.1	24.9	25.2	25.8
Taipei,China	30.9	34.5	37.5	41.8	45.4
Thailand	7.7	6.9	6.3	5.9	6.1
Viet Nam	−9.7	−9.7	−8.7	−8.0	−7.3
GCC[a]	148.6	203.4	238.4	257.7	272.4
Japan	105.6	129.2	120.3	101.8	89.4
United States	−324.7	−393.6	−457.7	−454.4	−475.2
Euro area	−36.4	−17.3	10.2	31.4	62.3
Other advanced	13.2	7.2	16.2	41.4	61.0
Other EMDEV[b]	−42.8	−25.4	0.7	12.2	12.2
World (error)	381.9	497.7	606.7	723.7	813.4
Memo:					
Germany	120.2	139.5	155.4	165.9	179.4
Russia	62.0	78.5	81.8	77.0	62.3
Spain	−69.0	−64.1	−61.9	−62.0	−62.0
United Kingdom	−45.8	−44.2	−54.7	−58.2	−58.7

Source: IMF, *World Economic Outlook,* October 2009.

a. GCC (Gulf Cooperation Council) includes Bahrain; Kuwait; Oman; Qatar; Saudi Arabia; and UAE.

b. Newly industrialized Asian economies (Hong Kong, China; Korea; Singapore; Taipei,China) are classified under the EMDEV (emerging markets and developing economies) group.

the IMF *WEO* projections are essentially built up from individual country projections, conducted by the country desks, having to assume essentially fixed exchange rates. There is no general equilibrium model at work that would force global consistency. The surplus with "outer space" projected in October of 2009 by the IMF *WEO* reflected the strengthening of a tendency that took root after the Asian crisis of 1997–98 for many emerging and developing countries, particularly in Asia, to pursue an export-oriented growth strategy and to try to self-insure against volatile international capital flows by accumulating large amounts of foreign exchange reserves. These strategies were mostly successful, with emerging and developing countries adding $4,693 billion to their foreign exchange reserves in the ten years between 1999 and 2008.[31] Emerging Asia accounts for most of this accumulation.[32]

What "allowed" that reserve accumulation in emerging and developing economies was, to a great extent, the increasing current account deficit of the U.S. economy during the same period. The cumulative current account deficit of the United States over the same 1999–2008 period was $5,712 billion.[33] It is broadly possible to view the EA surplus and the U.S. deficit as mirror images of one another, although other parts of the world did of course also have current account surpluses and deficits, and both the United States and EA traded with a multitude of other countries in other regions.[34] It should also not be overlooked that reserve movements reflect both current account and capital account positions, and it is possible to "borrow" reserves by importing capital. Reserve accumulation in the PRC, for example, has been larger than its cumulative current account surpluses, because the PRC also has had a cumulative capital account surplus.[35] Nonetheless, the big part of the story in the 1999–2008 period has indeed been the complementary nature of the East Asian surpluses and the U.S. deficit. The PRC and the other surplus countries in Asia could not have run those current account surpluses had the United States not run its large current account deficits. For example, if the net savings rate in the United States had gone up significantly, the general equilibrium interactions of the world economy would have produced a decline in the EA surpluses. Conversely, if the net savings rate had fallen in the EA region, general equilibrium interactions would have led to a decline in the U.S. current account deficit. The causal chains would have involved shifts in demand and supply for the goods and services produced by all countries, as well as changes in relative prices, reflected in real exchange rates. It is also important to stress that one cannot say that the EA surpluses

31. IMF Currency Composition of Official Foreign Exchange Reserves (COFER) database, March 31, 2010; and IMF Balance of Payments Statistics, June 2010.
32. Note that the Asian NICs (newly industrialized countries: Hong Kong, China; Korea; Singapore; Taipei,China) are included in our EA grouping as well as in the EMDEV total; the IMF includes them in the advanced economies group.
33. IMF Balance of Payments Statistics, June 2010.
34. This complementarity has been called a new Bretton Woods system by Dooley, Folkerts-Landau, and Garber (2004) and Eichengreen (2004).
35. Cumulative, 1999–2008, capital account surplus of $386 billion, current account surplus of $1,421 billion, reserve accumulation of $1,800 billion. (IMF Balance of Payments Statistics, June 2010).

"caused" the U.S. deficits, any more than one can say that the U.S. deficit "caused" the EA surpluses. The savings and investment behavior in both the United States and EA, complemented by the savings and investment behavior in the rest of the world, led to a particular constellation of current account surpluses and deficits, "causing each other." But in that complex picture, the savings and investment propensities in the large U.S. and PRC economies have indeed played a predominant role.

During the crisis year of 2009, as reflected in table 2-8, the global current account imbalances diminished significantly. In the United States, net domestic savings rose despite strong expansionary fiscal policy, because investment declined sharply, by more than 3 percentage points of GDP. Household savings rose significantly, with corporate savings also rising modestly, leading to a 1.9 percent of GDP increase in net domestic savings and hence a 1.9 percentage point decline in the current account deficit.[36] In the PRC, it is essentially the massive fiscal stimulus that led to a decline in net savings, leading to a smaller current account surplus, which continued to decline in the first months of 2010.

Looking forward, there is widespread agreement that the United States cannot go back to current account deficits of 6 percent or more of GDP. There are several mutually reinforcing reasons for this consensus. Various sectors of the economy have to continue to deleverage and in the process augment their savings rate. This is particularly true for the household sector. Moreover, the United States has become a significant net debtor with respect to the rest of the world, and a large current account deficit would tend to increase this net debt status rapidly, which in turn would affect variables such as the exchange rate and set in motion forces that would reduce the current account deficit.[37] So it is reasonable to project a lower U.S. current account deficit than in the boom years of 2004–07, even if there is a fairly vigorous economic recovery in the United States. How much lower it will be is more difficult to say. The fiscal deficit is going to

36. Bureau of Economic Analysis (www.bea.gov).
37. One cannot say that the current account deficit alone determines net debt status. The relative returns a country makes on its foreign investments compared to the returns foreigners make on their investments also influence net debt positions. Indeed for many years the United States was able to earn significantly more on its foreign investments than investors in the United States made on theirs. This "allowed" the United States to run large current account deficits with much less worry about its debtor status than would otherwise have been the case. But in the longer run, large current account deficits will reassert the tendency toward increasing net debtor status. See Hausmann and Sturzenegger (2007) and Gourinchas and Rey (2007).

TABLE 2-10. Current Account Projections, Spring 2010,
for the Period 2010–2015
Billions of U.S. dollars

	2010	2011	2012	2013	2014	2015
Emerging Asia	468.8	519.4	588.7	666.5	768.0	886.4
People's Republic of China	334.7	391.0	461.0	544.6	644.2	759.5
Hong Kong, China	27.0	23.3	23.2	21.2	21.2	21.8
India	−29.7	−30.4	−32.4	−35.8	−39.8	−42.7
Indonesia	9.5	2.8	−2.3	−6.9	−9.8	−13.2
Korea	15.9	24.0	25.7	23.6	24.9	26.6
Malaysia	32.8	33.7	34.7	35.8	36.6	38.0
Singapore	42.9	46.2	49.5	51.1	53.5	53.4
Taipei,China	35.5	34.7	37.5	40.8	45.1	51.0
Thailand	7.4	1.1	−0.8	−0.1	0.1	0.7
Viet Nam	−7.1	−7.0	−7.4	−7.7	−8.2	−8.6
GCC[a]	132.9	175.5	211.1	225.2	228.9	238.3
Japan	149.7	131.1	116.9	108.3	109.5	113.8
United States	−487.2	−523.9	−571.3	−603.1	−623.1	−638.2
Euro area	−4.7	13.1	4.2	4.1	0.6	−7.4
Other advanced	72.0	17.3	27.8	12.2	15.1	21.3
Other EMDEV[b]	−60.4	−75.6	−90.1	−115.9	−149.0	−202.9
World (error)	234.8	271.1	272.8	289.0	341.0	395.4
Memo:						
Germany	181.9	189.5	168.7	158.9	148.8	132.8
Russia	77.6	80.3	69.5	54.2	24.0	−13.4
Spain	−75.0	−73.0	−73.6	−74.9	−76.9	−79.1
United Kingdom	−37.0	−37.1	−39.2	−39.3	−38.8	−40.2

Source: IMF, *World Economic Outlook,* April 2010.
a. GCC (Gulf Cooperation Council) includes Bahrain; Kuwait; Oman; Qatar; Saudi Arabia; and UAE.
b. Newly industrialized Asian economies (Hong Kong, China; Korea; Singapore; Taipei,China) are classified under the EMDEV (emerging markets and developing economies) group.

decline only slowly and will tend to limit the overall increase in savings.[38] A U.S. current account deficit in the range of 2 to 4 percent of GDP is likely for the next few years. This is indeed what the IMF *World Economic Outlook* projects in both the October 2009 forecast referred to in table 2-9 and in the revised April 2010 forecast presented in table 2-10.

38. Note that there is no simple link between the fiscal deficit and the current account deficit, in theory or in history. Other things equal, a widening fiscal deficit (public dissaving) leads to an increase in the current account deficit. But other things are not equal and private savings can and have moved either to reinforce or to counteract changes in public savings. The U.S. current account deficit, for example, widened in the late 1990s despite a significant improvement in public savings.

Such a reduction in the U.S. current account deficit will reduce aggregate world effective demand from pre-crisis levels and require a decline in the aggregate current account surplus of the rest of the world for global effective demand to be maintained. This is a point that has been strongly stressed by many observers and policymakers and that is at the heart of the debate between the PRC and the United States on macroeconomic and exchange rate policies, as well as of the discussions taking place within the framework of the G-20 mutual assessment process.

A few points need to be stressed in this context.

First, given overall worldwide flows, even a 4 percentage point *once-and-for-all* reduction in the current account deficit of the United States would be significant, but not overwhelming. It would represent a "demand withdrawal" of about 1 percent of world GDP. It would be different if such a demand withdrawal were to be an *ongoing cumulative process*. But that is most unlikely to be the case since nobody is predicting that the U.S. current account will turn into a significant surplus.

Second, there are other countries besides the PRC with the potential of helping world demand. While the PRC surplus has been the most important surplus in absolute terms and even more so as a percentage of own GDP in the pre-crisis years, the PRC is by no means the only country that can increase world demand through a reduction in its surplus. The Gulf oil exporters, Germany, Japan, Russia, and some of the other EA countries have all run significant current account surpluses. Germany, in particular, developed a strange status in 2010: it has a large and increasing current account surplus with a *depreciating* currency! As the euro is dragged down by worries about debt sustainability and competitiveness in several southern European countries, Germany becomes more and more competitive and accumulates larger and larger surpluses. So the attention should shift, partially at least, from the PRC to Germany.[39]

Finally, the reduction of the U.S. current account deficit could also be partially offset by what happens in other emerging and developing countries, notably in Latin America and, within EA, by developments in India. In the aggregate, other emerging and developing countries, excluding

---

39. The existence of the euro zone means that the exchange rate implications of the German and PRC surpluses are quite different, of course. The euro zone as a whole is not in surplus.

India, which is included in EA, have run small surpluses in their current accounts in the immediate pre-crisis period. Including India in the "Other EMDEV" category reduces this surplus, but still leaves these developing countries without much capital imports. Given the huge needs for infrastructure and other investments in these countries, and the much improved macroeconomic frameworks in many of them, it would seem reasonable that they be net capital importers and run a moderate current account deficit in the aggregate. This is what was expressed in the Per Jacobsson lecture at the annual meetings of the IMF and the World Bank in Istanbul in October 2009.[40]

In April 2010, the IMF revised its October 2009 WEO forecast somewhat in the direction described above and along the lines suggested in the Per Jacobsson lecture. Table 2-10 describes these revised IMF forecasts. The fundamental problem remains, however. The PRC surplus grows a little less rapidly than before, and the other emerging and developing countries are now projected to run a small but significant deficit. The U.S. deficit is revised upward. As a consequence of these revisions, the "error" term (surplus with outer space) is reduced a little, but is still large and increasing over time.

There is no substantial "rebalancing" of the structure of world investment and savings foreseen in the Spring 2010 IMF projections of a type that would allow global imbalances to become much smaller. Moreover, the large positive error term indicates that the individual country projections from which the aggregates are derived still include an excess of "ex ante" savings over "ex ante" investment, imparting a deflationary bias to the world economy.

Global imbalances were one of the factors that led to financial instability, thereby contributing to the making of the crisis, and they are projected to remain significant. The "rebalancing" debate is therefore going to remain central to the policy discussions taking place within the frame-

---

40. "As policy frameworks in these countries have improved, it is desirable and should be natural for them to be net capital importers rather than run balanced or surplus current accounts, without this leading to the types of balance of payments crises that these countries experienced in the 1980 and 1990s. And given the very high Chinese savings rate, some of these flows could and should come, directly or indirectly, from China. . . . The average return on those investments in the developing countries will surely be higher than what China can earn in U.S. Treasury bills." Derviş (2009a).

work of the G-20 process. Against this background, how can one summarize the challenges faced by policymakers?

Conclusion

Globalization and the increasing integration of markets may well in the long run lead to more sustainable current account surpluses and deficits, reflecting a reduction in home bias in the allocation of savings, different age structures of populations, and differences in the returns to capital. Ideally these "imbalances" should reflect capital flowing from lower-return to higher-return areas and activities, thereby increasing world GDP and real income as a whole. Despite this long-term trend and its fundamentally desirable nature, many other factors are in play, some of them working in opposite directions. Concerns about the volatility of private capital flows, as well as worries about insufficient effective demand, lead countries to want to accumulate foreign exchange reserves and run current account surpluses even when the underlying structure of rates of return to capital would warrant capital imports. Private capital flows are much more volatile than what would be the case in a world of perfect markets and foresight, and these flows respond to short-term bubbles as well as panics. Partly reflecting these imperfections, governments and central banks intervene, at times heavily, in capital markets, manage their exchange rates, and accumulate reserves. The large current account imbalances we observe are due more to the behavior of the official sector than to the functioning of capital markets per se, and they are both a reflection of and a source of uncertainty and instability. These imbalances do deserve, therefore, the attention of policymakers.

Emerging Asia, and the PRC in particular, has been a key source of current account surpluses and therefore a significant cause of potential deflationary bias in the world economy insofar as these surpluses cannot be matched by sustainable and "healthy" deficits elsewhere. After the crisis, there is much greater consensus that the United States should not and cannot continue to run very large current account deficits. Yet the April 2010 IMF *WEO* projections foresee a return to almost pre-crisis levels of U.S. deficits on its current account, despite the fact that there remains an "adding up" problem, as desired surpluses again seem to exceed desired deficits.

Instead of focusing exclusively on the U.S. and PRC current accounts, it would be useful for policymakers to focus on the overall structure of savings and investment globally when trying to "rebalance" the world economy. It would be particularly desirable if more capital could safely flow to capital-poor developing countries, where savings rates are low but average rates of return to investment are high, although the variance of these returns is still higher than elsewhere. This should happen, however, in a way that does not again lead to the stop-and-go cycles and to the very high indebtedness levels most often coupled with short maturities of the past. There can be too much of a good thing! The quality of these capital flows, in terms of maturity and inherent volatility, should improve. Part of these flows should and will come from the high EA savers themselves. Multilateral development banks should play a larger role, not only through traditional lending, but also through various forms of public-private partnerships and investment guarantees. The IMF should provide greater amounts of truly precautionary finance. All this could lead to a more "gentle" rebalancing than one that would be achieved bilaterally by the United States and the PRC alone.[41]

Exchange rates are part, but only part, of the desirable adjustment mechanisms. What leads to the EA current account surpluses is the excess of savings over investment. As long as that excess persists, the current account surpluses will persist. An appreciation of the renminbi, for example, will only lead to a reduction of the PRC surplus if it leads to a reduction of the excess of PRC savings over investment. For this to happen, the terms of trade and internal reallocation effects of the appreciation must lead to higher consumption demand, partly due to a higher real wage and higher labor income, without this being more than offset by possibly lower investment due to a decrease in profit rates. Exchange rate appreciation in the PRC can be helpful as part of an overall policy package that sustains GDP growth but allows it to be driven somewhat more by investment in the nontradable sectors and domestic consumption. It is important, therefore, that the potential investment and growth-depressing effects of a real appreciation be counteracted by appropriate compensating macroeconomic policies.[42] The history of Japan in the 1980s and the early 1990s,

---

41. Quite a bit of progress has been made by the multilateral institutions in this direction. The IMF's lending capacity has increased substantially, and the Flexible Credit Line (FCL) constitutes a new source of precautionary finance. The World Bank and the regional development banks have also increased their lending and are working more effectively in various partnerships, including with sovereign wealth funds. Nonetheless, the volume of these activities remains small in comparison with the needs and the potential of overall capital flows. For an analysis of precautionary finance, see Derviş (2009b).

42. For a historical analysis of reversals in current account surpluses, see IMF (2010).

when current account surpluses persisted despite a massive appreciation of the yen, should be a reminder that there is no automatic and inevitable correlation between exchange rates and current accounts. Having said that, one should add, however, that it is of course possible that without the appreciation, the Japanese surpluses would have been even larger.

In this rebalancing debate it is important to correctly appreciate the role of "net" exports. It is often reported that the contribution of net exports to the growth of a current account surplus country has been "small." The contribution of net exports is obtained by multiplying the growth of exports minus imports by the "share" of these net exports in total final demand and comparing the result to overall growth. Performing this calculation for the PRC in the period from 1998 to 2008, one finds that net exports accounted for 0.62 percentage points of real growth, on average, compared to a growth average of 9.8 percent.[43] A sentence is then often added to the reporting of these results stating that the growth of net exports is not an important factor in explaining PRC growth. In an accounting sense this is of course true, although the overall expansion of trade, both exports and imports, may have been a major channel for technological innovation and diffusion. Moreover, one should remember that the growth of net exports for the world as a whole *has to sum to zero*, which is of course not the case for other elements of final demand such as consumption or investment. Continuous positive contributions to growth from net exports, even if they are small, in the case of a particular country, imply continuous increases in its trade surplus. Over any substantial period of time, therefore, the contribution of net exports to the demand for a country's output should be expected to be very small, particularly if it is a large country![44]

Finally, it is important to stress that the debate about "rebalancing" is linked to the debate about the international monetary system and the role of reserve currencies. Part of the global imbalances problem reflects the demand for dollar reserves that the United States has been supplying over the past four decades by essentially running its large current account

43. IMF, International Financial Statistics and authors' calculations.
44. Net exports made very large contributions to real GDP growth in the PRC for a few years, in 2005, 2006, and 2007, ranging from 3.5 percentage points in 2005 to 2 points in 2007. Such contributions are clearly exceptional and would be unsustainable. In India, over the same period, net exports accounted for negative 1 percentage point of growth: exports contributing positively at 1.4 percentage points and imports decreasing growth by about 2.4 points, on average.

deficit. If the demand for reserves continues to grow, they must be supplied. It stands to reason, therefore, that if there could be an agreement to
supply reserves by periodic allocations of special drawing rights (SDRs),
this would reduce the demand for dollars and, all other things equal, reduce
the "need" for a U.S. current account deficit. As has been pointed out,
notably by José Antonio Ocampo,[45] an allocation of SDRs according to the
current quota at the IMF would not help much, as the demand for reserves
comes from many countries with small quotas. Nonetheless, over time, the
existence of a widely used international reserve asset other than the dollar
would help weaken the link between the U.S. deficit and the demand for
foreign exchange reserves. An allocation of SDRs more tilted toward countries with strong demand for reserves would speed up the process. It is not
clear, however, what such an allocation formula would be and how it
could best reflect some overall equity or distribution principle.

   How can one summarize the various components of the "rebalancing"
debate? There is indeed a problem rooted in the large savings surplus of
EA, primarily due to the very high level of PRC savings. These are significantly larger than the level of investment and therefore a potential source
of deflationary bias in the world economy. The very low level of U.S. savings that helped compensate for the excess savings of EA is unlikely to persist. The rate of return to investment in the United States was artificially
inflated by the housing and other asset bubbles as well as partly fictitiously
manufactured in the financial sector. A more sustainable flow of capital
would reflect somewhat lower returns in the United States, a smaller U.S.
current account deficit, a smaller EA current account surplus, and a somewhat higher aggregate current account deficit of the other emerging and
developing countries. The Gulf oil exporters will continue to run a large
surplus, reflecting absorptive capacity constraints and high oil prices.
Europe as a whole would continue to be in balance, although some internal European rebalancing is certainly desirable, with a reduction of the
Mediterranean deficits and a significant reduction of the German surplus.

   Such a rebalancing would improve the worldwide allocation of capital.
It would also benefit the EA countries as they would reduce the risk of
incurring large capital losses on huge dollar balances and avoid protectionist backlash against their exports. Note, however, that the relative
magnitudes involved in such "rebalancing" should not be exaggerated.
Once-and-for-all shifts in the structure of world demand should not be

45. See Ocampo (2010).

confused with ongoing changes. A large reduction of the U.S. current account deficit of say, 3 percentage points of GDP, is equivalent to about three quarters of a percentage point reduction in global demand, and it would be a once-and-for-all reduction. In the year after the reduction, there would be no further deflationary impulse coming from the reduced level of the U.S. current account if it stays at the same level. A reduction in the PRC surplus from about 10 percent of GDP to, say, 5 percent of GDP adds about 0.40 percentage points to world demand. These are not insignificant magnitudes, but they are not long-run determinants of world growth. The popular worry that the U.S. consumer as "the engine of world growth" is now "disappearing" often seems to mix up *once-and-for-all* with *ongoing* changes. There was and continues to be the need for a rebalancing of the structure of world demand. An "ex ante" excess of savings over investment worldwide rooted in an "ex ante" current account surplus with "outer space" imparts a deflationary bias to the world economy. But the analysis of current accounts should not make us forget that the real drivers of growth are aggregate *domestic* demand and supply factors. On the supply side, the pace of technical progress, the rate at which it is diffused, and the national savings and investment rates are going to be the prime determinants of growth. On the demand side, real disposable income and expectations about the future are going to be the prime determinants of effective demand. In that context, while EA may have been saving more than it was able to invest domestically, the fact that it was able to invest "so much" and "so productively" has been a major driver of its own growth, as well as of world growth. EA growth does not just lead to a once-and-for-all change in world demand, but to an *ongoing process* of world demand expansion that benefits the world as a whole. Moreover, while there may be serious adjustment problems, particularly if the adjustments occur over a short period, EA can continue to grow rapidly with much lower current account surpluses.

Looking to the next decade, it is likely that the combination of high investment and savings rates with continued technological diffusion and continued absorption of lower productivity labor by higher productivity sectors, as well as continued improvements in factor allocation within sectors, will allow EA to continue to grow at impressive rates, well above the world average. Growth may also increase in other developing countries, if they manage to increase their investment rates without running into macroeconomic instability, likely resulting in high overall world growth even if the advanced economies expand very slowly.

The ensuing structural transformation is unprecedented and no doubt needs to be managed, from a political economy perspective. It does not have to imply some kind of impoverishment of the advanced economies, but a closing of the huge gap in incomes that opened up centuries ago. If the transition is well managed, it is compatible with a growth of prosperity overall, but at very different relative rates. But it will imply a serious shift in the economic and financial weight of countries and thereby in their political influence and power.

Looking toward the longer run, other factors such as natural resource scarcities and climate constraints may come into play. This chapter has focused on the 1990–2020 period. What lies beyond 2020 is surely more difficult to analyze.

COMMENT BY
JOSÉ ANTONIO OCAMPO

The chapter by Kemal Derviş and Karim Foda makes an important contribution to the analysis of the growth of Emerging Asia and its impact on the global economy. In the words of the authors, "Emerging Asia's growth performance is *transforming* in a very fundamental way the overall structure of the world economy and *relocating its center of gravity*." There is no question that this statement is correct. The chapter also analyzes in depth the role of Emerging Asia in the rebalancing of the world economy, in the context of the broader debate on what that rebalancing implies for other parts of the world economy.

Derviş and Foda present an optimistic view of the capacity of Emerging Asia to continue on its path of rapid growth over the next decade. This is based on two major observations. The first is that supply factors will continue to play a favorable role. Again, to quote the authors, growth will continue to be "based on continued high investment rates, availability of both unskilled and skilled labor in most economies, particularly in the People's Republic of China (PRC) and India, and decent total factor productivity performance based on continued rapid diffusion of technology, increases in intrasector efficiency of resource allocation and continued reallocation of resources, notably labor, from low- to higher-productivity activities." The second is that, although demand factors associated with global rebalancing may be a constraint, it would not be a strong one. According to their view, it would not be a major problem for the world economy either. The last point comes most clearly in the concluding section, where Derviş and Foda estimate that even a large rebalancing of the U.S. current account deficit and the Chinese surplus represent only small fractions of world aggregate demand.

One implication of this optimistic scenario is that the rest of the developing and emerging world can count on Emerging Asia to continue growing fast. This is what Sub-Saharan Africa and South America, among other regions, are already betting on. An important development would be for countries in these regions to comfortably start running current account deficits, avoiding, however, again in the words of the authors, "the stop-and-go cycles and the very high indebtedness levels most often coupled with short maturities of the past." Current account deficits by low-saving developing countries would furthermore make a desirable contribution to the correction of global imbalances, a point that was forcefully made by Derviş in the 2009 Per Jacobsson Lecture delivered at the annual meetings of the IMF and the World Bank in Istanbul. This would also allow the excess savings of Emerging Asia to contribute to the growth of the developing world at large. I would add that the PRC is also making a major contribution to those parts of the developing world that have natural resource–based export structures through its effects on commodity prices, which have continued to be high relative to the last two decades of the twentieth century, due in particular to the very high demand by this country for energy and minerals.[1]

By way of caution, I want to present a few skeptical notes on this optimistic scenario. My notes or cautions are based on three basic points: (1) the complications raised by *domestic* dynamics of high savings and investment, particularly in the PRC; (2) the dynamics of international trade and the implications of the weakening of the "center-periphery" nature of Emerging Asia trade patterns; and (3) some unpleasant dimensions of global rebalancing, which are not sufficiently emphasized by Derviş and Foda. In the section on global imbalances, I want to reinforce one of the points made by the authors: the limited role of exchange rate adjustments in this process.

Most of my comments relate to the PRC, for one obvious reason: it is an economy that has strong regional and global links, as reflected in particular in its large share in world trade due to its position at the center

---

1. World Bank (2009).

of the East Asian production network, plus its increasingly active participation as a global investor. This is not true of India, which has a much
smaller share in world trade and investment. Thus, although India will
have implications for global growth because of its sheer size, its multiplier
effects at the regional and world level will be much weaker.

The major implication of my analysis is that the Chinese engine will
continue to run fast—though probably somewhat more slowly than
Derviş and Foda think—but it is unlikely to serve as an alternative world
engine to the United States and western Europe, which will almost certainly grow weakly in the foreseeable future.

The Domestic Dynamics of High Savings and Investment

One note of skepticism is prompted by two parallel observations by analysts of the Chinese situation. The first, from the work of Yilmaz Akyüz,
relates to savings: the extremely high and rising savings rate of the PRC
since the late 1990s is associated with the massive increase in the share of
profits in value added (over 10 percentage points of GDP) and, as a mirror, a falling share of wages and private consumption.[2] This relates to an
old point, which is certainly true for East Asia in general: in a comparative perspective, high savings are associated with household savings, but
even more with the share of profits in GDP, as savings from profits tend
to be high. This observation is part of a long tradition of macroeconomics associated with Michal Kalecki and Nicholas Kaldor, among others,
but is generally ignored in the mainstream macroeconomic literature. An
implication of it is that a high profit share may generate problems of
underconsumption.

The second point, from the work of Yongding Yu, is expressed in terms
of the major challenges that the PRC has faced during the recent crisis and
the investment based stimulus package that it put in place, possibly the
largest adopted by any national authority.[3] Because there was excess
capacity in many parts of the industrial sector, there was a bias toward
investments in infrastructure and real estate. The first led, however, to a
rush to projects that reduced the quality of investments. The second led
to a housing price bubble. Both are already leading to an increasing share
of nonperforming loans in the domestic financial system.

2. See Akyüz (2010a and 2010b).
3. See Yu (2010).

The major implication of this is that the PRC may face a reduction in its investment rate for purely domestic reasons and should reduce its savings rate to encourage more private consumption, and possibly more government consumption (social programs). This is why the best news that the world has received in recent months is the rising wage pressure in the PRC. Whether this will be a smooth process in economic (and political) terms is a good question. My own personal bet is that this, together with the factors that I mention below, implies that the PRC will grow at a rate that, though still high by international standards (say in the vicinity of 6–7 percent annually) is significantly lower than in its recent historical record. Put in other terms, the PRC has already started the process of slowing down from fast rates of growth, a transition that Japan and the Asian Tigers experienced earlier. In any case, the PRC's share in the world economy will continue to increase rapidly, not only due to its fast rate of growth but also to the currency appreciation it is likely to face over the next few years.

The Dynamics of International Trade

A second note of skepticism relates to international trade. It may be true that supply factors are important, but trade links are also relevant. Indeed, in the Keynesian tradition, supply factors, particularly investment, are dependent on aggregate domestic demand and external conditions. Trade factors are particularly relevant for East Asia, which has relied for its development process on strong links with the world economy, first through the "flying geese" pattern—an essential part of the "waves" of Asian development that the authors mention at the beginning of their chapter—and later through what can be described as a PRC-centered East Asian production network. Problems here may come from two different fronts.

The first one relates to the dynamics of international trade. Economic historians have observed that the collapse of world trade during the recent Great Recession was initially faster than during the Great Depression of the 1930s, despite the fact that protectionist forces were weaker this time.[4] And despite its rapid recovery since mid-2009, world trade had not returned to pre-crisis levels as of mid-2010. In particular, the latest available estimates by the CPB Netherlands Bureau for Economic Policy Analysis indicate that, in May 2010, world imports in volume terms continued to be 5.6 percent below those of the first semester of 2008, and those from

4. See O'Rourke (2009).

industrial countries 7.2 percent below.[5] In value terms, the levels are even lower. Due to these trends, I am inclined to think that we have experienced a historical break in the long-term relation between world trade and world GDP. In other words, the high elasticities of world trade to world GDP are unlikely to return. This, I acknowledge, is merely a personal guess, though other analysts concur.

The second problem is related to the "center-periphery" character of the East Asian production network. In a sense, the PRC has been the last actor (we might say the "assembler," but it certainly goes beyond that) in a network to which other East Asian countries are linked, the most advanced of them producing equipment and intermediate goods for the network. The "center-periphery" element is associated with the fact that goods are at the end destined to the industrial country markets. So, if the latter continue to grow at a slow pace, so will the growth dynamics associated with this network.

This has major implications. One is that growth, to continue, will have to be more domestically based than in the past, particularly in larger economies. Another is that the pattern of growth will have to be different. Structural change will imply that many of the regional links in the PRC-centered production network are likely to weaken. As we will see below, the implications of global rebalancing reinforce this trend. This is not a major problem for India, which is a more inward-oriented economy, and not even perhaps for the PRC, which can succeed in its structural transformation toward a more inward-oriented economy, perhaps as indicated with somewhat lower dynamics; but it is bad news for growth in the rest of East Asia.

Exchange Rates and Global Rebalancing

Before I mention my last note of caution, I want to underscore my agreement with the authors on the essential role that savings-investment balances have in determining the current account surpluses of East Asia, and thus on the important but limited role of exchange rate adjustments as a mechanism in global rebalancing. As Derviş and Foda indicate, this has already been reflected in previous adjustments of the Japanese economy, which experienced massive exchange rate adjustment in the 1980s but still ended up with a high current account surplus.

5. CPB Netherlands Bureau for Economic Policy Analysis (2010).

The major issue here is that exchange rate variations have broad macroeconomic effects, and therefore this variable is not simply a relative price that adjusts external accounts. One link comes from the close connections between the exchange rate, financial stability, investment, and economic activity. China no doubt has in mind the Japanese experience of the 1980s when it resists the strong pressure to appreciate its currency. Many have argued that this was one of the factors that led to the Japanese financial crisis and its "lost decade" in terms of economic growth. The problems could have been even more severe in the case of the PRC, due to the vulnerabilities of its domestic financial system, which have not been fully resolved and may be increasing again.

Furthermore, a sharp appreciation of the renminbi also would have other major macroeconomic effects on the PRC, as well as global implications. It could have contractionary effects on domestic economy activity. If this effect prevails, it would tend to reduce the demand for imports and might actually encourage exports by reducing the domestic market for some goods and services. This effect thus would run counter to the direct effect of the exchange rate on the trade balance, and helps to illustrates a point that was emphasized by Joan Robinson, among others, more than half a century ago: that when we take into account variations in aggregate demand, there is in fact no one "equilibrium" exchange rate; it would depend on the level of economic activity. Another way to see this problem is again through the savings-investment balance. If, for example, an appreciation in the value of the currency discourages investment (a likely effect in an export-oriented economy), it would tend to *increase* rather than reduce the current account surplus.

The major implication of this is that the problems associated with the Chinese current account surplus can only be solved through global macroeconomic policy coordination and not through narrow changes in Chinese exchange rate policy. Elsewhere, I have argued that this process is closely linked to the reform of the global reserve system.[6]

Rebalancing the Chinese economy also has strong regional implications that are worth emphasizing. This implies looking more inward for the sources of demand, but also, as pointed out, to domestic consumption in particular. The major problem here, as again emphasized by Akyüz, is that consumption is much less import-intensive in the PRC than investment and exports. So, the PRC may be able to avoid a strong slowdown

6. See, for example, Ocampo (2010).

while correcting its current account deficit by encouraging consumption. But this process will also reduce the links between the PRC and the world economy and will significantly affect other East Asian countries that are closely linked to the PRC-centered production network. It would make the PRC look more like India: a still dynamic economy, but one that is less capable of spreading its growth to other countries (except perhaps through commodity markets). It also implies that in terms of global dynamics, the PRC is unlikely to replace in the immediate future the "old" Western center as the dynamic pole of the world economy.

APPENDIX A. Country Contributions to Real GDP Growth (Expenditure Based), 1998–2008

Year	GDP growth	Government consumption	Private consumption	Investment	Exports	Imports	Net exports
People's Republic of China[a]							
1998	7.83	1.67	3.68	2.33	0.39	−0.05	0.34
1999	7.63	2.18	4.98	3.36	1.79	−3.04	−1.24
2000	8.42	1.79	3.31	1.31	4.49	−5.00	−0.51
2001	8.30	1.68	2.41	4.20	1.01	−1.13	−0.12
2002	9.09	1.24	2.81	5.09	4.36	−3.82	0.53
2003	10.02	0.81	2.36	7.50	7.03	−7.41	−0.38
2004	10.08	0.80	2.11	6.44	6.65	−6.49	0.16
2005	10.43	1.54	3.02	5.38	7.38	−3.86	3.52
2006	11.65	1.32	3.46	5.61	6.49	−3.67	2.83
2007	13.04	1.21	3.04	4.05	4.07	−2.07	2.00
2008	8.95	1.07	2.87	5.26	−0.03	−0.26	−0.29
Average	9.59	1.39	3.10	4.59	3.97	−3.34	0.62
India							
1998	6.12	1.65	4.76	0.12	0.04	−0.88	−0.84
1999	7.33	1.61	4.88	4.53	0.57	−1.01	−0.44
2000	4.30	0.20	2.22	−0.83	1.59	−1.12	0.47
2001	5.26	0.41	4.06	1.33	0.38	0.04	0.41
2002	3.74	−0.07	1.19	2.01	1.37	−1.17	0.20
2003	8.50	0.37	3.74	3.47	0.83	−2.10	−1.27
2004	8.09	0.62	2.33	7.83	1.63	−2.84	−1.21
2005	9.27	0.91	4.19	5.05	2.23	−4.62	−2.38
2006	9.45	0.48	4.93	4.94	2.25	−3.67	−1.42
2007	9.51	1.01	4.77	5.13	0.81	−2.00	−1.18
2008	4.42	1.82	3.38	−0.67	3.25	−7.04	−3.79
Average	6.91	0.82	3.68	2.99	1.36	−2.40	−1.04

APPENDIX A. Country Contributions to Real GDP Growth (Expenditure Based), 1998–2008

Year	GDP growth	Government consumption	Private consumption	Investment	Exports	Imports	Net exports
United States							
1998	4.36	0.32	3.38	1.35	−0.13	−0.57	−0.70
1999	4.83	0.70	3.78	1.45	0.24	−1.34	−1.10
2000	4.14	0.56	3.66	1.11	0.86	−2.06	−1.20
2001	1.08	0.64	1.61	−1.37	−0.89	1.08	0.19
2002	1.81	0.87	1.67	−0.24	−0.40	−0.08	−0.48
2003	2.49	0.75	1.88	0.48	0.15	−0.77	−0.62
2004	3.57	0.47	2.27	1.71	0.96	−1.83	−0.88
2005	3.06	0.45	2.10	1.18	0.70	−1.38	−0.68
2006	2.67	0.39	1.66	0.80	0.95	−1.12	−0.18
2007	2.14	0.45	1.72	−0.59	1.04	−0.47	0.56
2008	0.44	0.87	0.65	−1.23	0.97	−0.82	0.15
Average	2.78	0.59	2.22	0.42	0.40	−0.85	−0.45
Hong Kong, China							
1998	−6.03	0.21	−3.23	−6.89	−10.64	14.51	3.87
1999	2.56	0.70	0.39	−3.38	7.08	−2.23	4.85
2000	7.95	0.37	3.25	4.79	26.33	−26.80	−0.47
2001	0.50	0.85	1.59	−2.01	−3.89	3.96	0.07
2002	1.84	0.55	−0.60	−2.07	13.60	−9.65	3.95
2003	3.01	0.58	1.46	−0.25	26.62	−25.40	1.22
2004	8.47	0.15	6.17	1.76	35.24	−34.86	0.38
2005	7.08	−0.45	2.90	0.19	22.62	−18.18	4.44
2006	7.02	0.14	4.42	2.68	21.27	−21.50	−0.23
2007	6.38	0.25	5.48	0.54	15.70	−15.59	0.11
2008	2.15	0.43	2.18	−0.05	9.19	−9.60	−0.41
Average	3.72	0.34	2.18	−0.42	14.83	−13.21	1.62
Indonesia							
1998	−13.13	−1.90	−2.80	−17.18	18.16	−9.41	8.75
1999	0.79	0.96	6.75	−5.32	−17.17	15.57	−1.60
2000	4.92	0.25	−9.26	11.97	7.48	−4.53	2.95
2001	3.64	0.61	3.80	1.11	−0.52	−1.42	−1.95
2002	4.50	0.69	7.51	−0.17	−4.87	3.18	−1.69
2003	4.78	1.26	3.77	5.42	−0.75	2.15	1.39
2004	5.03	0.61	1.99	−0.33	3.36	−5.79	−2.43
2005	5.69	0.25	1.26	2.45	3.79	−4.08	−0.29
2006	5.50	0.99	1.75	1.72	−1.33	2.89	1.56
2007	6.28	0.25	4.89	1.11	0.26	−1.38	−1.11
2008	6.06	0.58	1.08	4.54	2.12	−4.96	−2.84
Average	3.10	0.41	1.89	0.48	0.96	−0.71	0.25

(continued)

APPENDIX A. Country Contributions to Real GDP Growth (Expenditure Based), 1998–2008 (Continued)

Year	GDP growth	Government consumption	Private consumption	Investment	Exports	Imports	Net exports
Republic of Korea							
1998	−6.85	0.37	−6.71	−12.69	10.61	1.98	12.59
1999	9.49	0.67	7.52	6.89	−3.39	−2.15	−5.55
2000	8.49	0.66	7.49	4.03	2.77	−6.36	−3.59
2001	3.97	1.30	3.37	−0.24	−1.40	0.90	−0.50
2002	7.15	0.78	4.86	2.12	−0.25	−0.44	−0.68
2003	2.80	0.79	−0.43	1.53	3.23	−2.38	0.86
2004	4.62	0.89	0.28	1.43	7.40	−5.32	2.08
2005	3.96	1.10	3.31	0.93	−0.06	−1.29	−1.35
2006	5.18	1.40	3.49	1.47	2.47	−3.71	−1.24
2007	5.11	0.93	2.70	1.31	4.38	−4.18	0.20
2008	2.22	0.91	1.28	2.68	12.11	−14.89	−2.78
Average	4.19	0.89	2.47	0.86	3.44	−3.44	0.00
Malaysia							
1998	−7.36	−1.72	−6.84	−18.26	13.94	5.53	19.46
1999	6.14	1.89	2.57	−2.92	13.01	−8.42	4.59
2000	8.86	0.08	6.05	6.87	9.11	−13.25	−4.14
2001	0.52	1.94	2.61	−2.34	−8.84	7.15	−1.68
2002	5.39	1.62	1.31	1.71	3.74	−3.00	0.74
2003	5.79	0.76	2.15	−0.70	4.83	−1.25	3.58
2004	6.78	0.47	2.41	1.85	16.26	−14.19	2.06
2005	5.33	0.43	3.23	−2.00	8.36	−4.68	3.68
2006	5.85	0.29	2.76	1.66	5.90	−4.77	1.13
2007	6.18	1.05	3.62	2.57	0.82	−1.87	−1.06
2008	4.63	0.87	1.58	−1.67	−2.12	5.97	3.85
Average	4.37	0.70	1.95	−1.20	5.91	−2.98	2.93
Thailand							
1998	−10.51	−0.18	−6.20	−15.37	4.68	8.12	12.80
1999	4.45	0.95	4.30	0.96	2.01	−4.77	−2.76
2000	4.75	0.37	2.83	3.42	11.65	−15.18	−3.53
2001	2.17	0.23	2.41	1.78	0.51	−2.51	−2.00
2002	5.32	0.35	2.99	0.97	1.75	−1.19	0.56
2003	7.03	0.39	3.93	2.87	5.97	−5.41	0.55
2004	6.17	1.06	3.05	3.84	9.35	−11.12	−1.77
2005	4.46	1.24	2.77	5.93	6.41	−12.67	−6.26
2006	5.57	0.64	1.96	−1.75	4.02	1.14	5.17
2007	4.93	0.98	0.28	−0.55	3.41	1.90	5.31
2008	2.46	0.56	3.00	3.16	4.99	−10.56	−5.58
Average	3.35	0.60	1.94	0.48	4.98	−4.75	0.23

APPENDIX A. Country Contributions to Real GDP Growth (Expenditure Based), 1998–2008 (Continued)

Year	GDP growth	Government consumption	Private consumption	Investment	Exports	Imports	Net exports
Viet Nam							
1998	5.76	−0.07	3.21	2.42	4.33	−3.92	0.41
1999	4.77	−0.51	1.04	−0.10	7.50	−3.19	4.31
2000	6.79	0.07	2.32	3.99	8.80	−8.58	0.22
2001	6.89	0.35	2.87	3.71	3.34	−3.32	0.02
2002	7.08	0.34	4.85	4.40	6.20	−9.45	−3.25
2003	7.34	0.55	6.03	4.83	6.86	−10.66	−3.81
2004	7.79	0.57	3.89	2.78	11.56	−11.34	0.22
2005	8.44	0.28	3.81	3.11	9.48	−6.46	3.02
2006	8.23	0.37	5.03	4.27	10.30	−11.06	−0.76
2007	8.46	0.54	6.88	9.97	9.79	−22.42	−12.63
2008	6.31	0.45	6.90	−0.91	5.94	−6.26	−0.31
Average	7.08	0.27	4.26	3.50	7.65	−8.79	−1.14
Brazil							
1998	0.04	0.75	−0.52	−0.39	0.11	0.08	0.20
1999	0.25	−0.29	0.56	−0.61	2.50	−1.91	0.59
2000	4.31	−0.30	2.39	2.66	1.00	−1.43	−0.43
2001	1.31	0.91	−0.04	0.01	2.36	−1.93	0.43
2002	2.66	1.30	−0.11	−1.40	2.29	0.58	2.87
2003	1.15	−0.96	0.92	−0.24	1.06	0.37	1.43
2004	5.71	0.94	1.26	2.32	2.38	−1.19	1.19
2005	3.16	1.31	2.40	−0.40	−0.82	0.66	−0.15
2006	3.97	0.92	2.42	1.22	−0.19	−0.40	−0.59
2007	6.08	1.45	3.24	2.69	−0.19	−1.10	−1.29
2008	5.14	0.33	3.52	2.61	1.13	−2.45	−1.32
Average	3.07	0.58	1.46	0.77	1.06	−0.79	0.27
Mexico							
1998	5.03	1.01	6.48	−0.32	1.92	−4.06	−2.14
1999	3.76	1.04	2.22	0.04	1.24	−0.78	0.46
2000	6.59	0.87	4.35	1.88	2.24	−2.75	−0.51
2001	−0.03	0.60	2.54	−2.96	−3.41	3.19	−0.22
2002	0.77	0.46	−0.01	−0.06	−0.52	0.90	0.38
2003	1.39	−0.14	−1.41	2.60	−1.13	1.47	0.34
2004	4.01	−0.64	2.22	2.81	2.37	−2.76	−0.38
2005	3.28	0.35	2.48	0.18	1.42	−1.15	0.27
2006	5.04	0.21	1.57	3.11	2.28	−2.14	0.14
2007	3.43	0.48	2.73	0.59	1.21	−1.58	−0.37
2008	1.25	−0.12	0.96	1.07	0.33	−0.98	−0.65
Average	3.14	0.38	2.19	0.81	0.72	−0.60	0.13

(continued)

APPENDIX A. Country Contributions to Real GDP Growth (Expenditure Based), 1998–2008 (Continued)

Year	GDP growth	Government consumption	Private consumption	Investment	Exports	Imports	Net exports
Turkey							
1998	3.22	−1.68	0.58	−2.28	−2.56	9.56	7.00
1999	−3.37	1.56	−0.29	−3.63	−2.55	1.54	−1.01
2000	6.78	0.29	6.79	3.05	2.02	−5.37	−3.35
2001	−5.70	−0.04	−6.01	−6.54	5.78	1.11	6.89
2002	6.16	1.12	3.82	3.62	−0.67	−1.72	−2.39
2003	5.27	0.11	6.98	0.91	−1.01	−1.72	−2.73
2004	9.36	0.87	6.72	3.61	2.76	−4.60	−1.84
2005	8.40	0.83	6.45	2.28	0.14	−1.30	−1.16
2006	6.89	1.39	3.67	3.59	2.38	−4.13	−1.75
2007	4.67	1.05	4.11	0.00	0.70	−1.19	−0.49
2008	0.66	0.10	−1.00	0.86	1.74	−1.04	0.70
Average	3.85	0.51	2.89	0.49	0.79	−0.81	−0.01

Source: IMF International Financial Statistics and authors' calculations.

a. A small statistical discrepancy exists between "exports-imports" and "net exports" for China, since the data reported by the *IFS* were reported at different frequencies and in different currencies.

References

Akyüz, Yilmaz. 2010a. "Global Economic Prospects: The Recession May Be Over but What Next?" Research Paper 26. Geneva: South Centre (March).

————. 2010b. "Export Dependence and Sustainability of Growth in China and the East Asian Production Network." Research Paper 27. Geneva: South Centre (April).

Asian Development Bank. 2009. "Key Indicators for Asia and the Pacific 2009." 40th ed. Manila.

————. "Asian Development Outlook 2010: Macromanagement beyond the Crisis." 41st ed. Manila.

Atkinson, A. B. 1969. "The Timescale of Economic Models: How Long Is the Long Run?" *Review of Economic Studies* 36, no. 106: 137–52.

Balassa, Bela. 1964. "The Purchasing Power Parity Doctrine: A Reappraisal." *Journal of Political Economy* 72: 584–69.

Barro, R. J., and J. W. Lee. 2010. "A New Data Set of Educational Attainment in the World, 1950–2010." Working Paper 15902. Cambridge, Mass.: National Bureau of Economic Research. (Accompanying data are available at www.barrolee.com.)

Bergsten, C. Fred. 2010. "Beijing Is Key to Creating More U.S. Jobs." *Foreign Policy*, April 14 (www.foreignpolicy.com/articles/2010/04/14/china_the_job_killer).

Bosworth, Barry, and Susan M. Collins. 2008. "Accounting for Growth: Comparing China and India." *Journal of Economic Perspectives* 22: 45–66.

Chong-En Bai, Chang-Tia Hsieh, and Yingyi-Qian. 2006. "The Return to Capital in China." *Brookings Papers on Economic Activity* (Fall): 61–88.

Cline, William. 2010. "Exports of Manufacturers and Economic Growth: The Fallacy of Composition Revisited." In *Globalization and Growth: Implications for a Post-Crisis World,* edited by Michael Spence and Danny Leipzinger, pp. 195–234. Washington: Commission on Growth and Development, World Bank.

CPB Netherlands Bureau for Economic Policy Analysis. 2010. *World Trade Monitor: May 2010* (July 26) (www.cpb.nl/eng/research/sector2/data/trademonitor.html).

Dadush, Uri, and Bennett Stancil. 2010. "Policy Outlook: The World Order in 2050." Washington: Carnegie Endowment for International Peace (February).

Derviş, Kemal. 2009a. "Growth after the Storm." The Per Jacobsson Lecture. Delivered at the Annual Meetings of the IMF and the World Bank. Istanbul, Turkey (www.brookings.edu/speeches/2009/1004_global_economy_dervis.aspx).

———. 2009b. "Precautionary Resources and Long-Term Development Finance: The Financial Role of the Bretton Woods Institutions after the Crisis." The Fourth Annual Richard H. Sabot Lecture. Delivered at the Center for Global Development, Washington (www.cgdev.org/content/publications/detail/1423582).

Dooley, Michael, David Folkerts-Landau, and Peter Garber. 2004. "An Essay on the Revived Bretton-Woods-System." *International Journal of Finance and Economics* 4: 307–13.

Eichengreen, Barry. 2004. "Global Imbalances and the Lessons of Bretton Woods." *Economie Internationale* 100: 39–50.

G-20 Finance Ministers and Central Bank Governors. 2009a. Communiqué. St. Andrews, UK (November 7) (www.g20.org/Documents/2009_communique_standrews.pdf).

G-20 Leaders Statement. 2009b. Pittsburgh, Penn., September 24–25 (www.g20.org/Documents/pittsburgh_summit_leaders_statement_250909.pdf).

Gourinchas, P., and H. Rey. 2007. "From World Banker to Venture Capitalist: U.S. External Adjustment: The Exorbitant Privilege." In *G7 Current Account Imbalances: Sustainability and Adjustment,* edited by R. Clarida, pp. 11–55. University of Chicago Press.

Greenspan, Alan. 2007. "Balance of Payments Imbalances." The Per Jacobsson Lecture. Delivered at the Annual Meetings of the IMF and the World Bank. Washington (www.perjacobsson.org/lectures/102107.pdf).

Greenwald, Bruce, and Joseph Stiglitz. 2010. "A Modest Proposal for International Monetary Reform." In *Time for a Visible Hand,* edited by Stephany Griffith-Jones, José Antonio Ocampo, and Joseph Stiglitz, pp. 314–44. Oxford University Press.

Griffith-Jones, Stephany, José Antonio Ocampo, and Joseph E. Stiglitz, eds. 2010. *Time for a Visible Hand.* Oxford University Press.

Hanushek, Eric A., and Ludger Woessmann. 2009. "Do Better Schools Lead to More Growth? Cognitive Skills, Economic Outcomes, and Causation." Discussion Paper 4575. Bonn: Institute for the Study of Labor (IZA).

Hausmann, Ricardo, and Federico Sturzenegger. 2007. "The Missing Dark Matter in the Wealth of Nations and Its Implications for Global Imbalances." *Economic Policy* 22, no. 51: 469–518.

Hsieh, Chang-Tai. 2002. "What Explains the Industrial Revolution in East Asia? Evidence from the Factor Markets." *American Economic Review* 92, no. 3: 502–26.

Hsieh, Chang-Tai, and Peter J. Klenow. 2009. "Misallocation and Manufacturing TFP in China and India." *Quarterly Journal of Economics* 124, no. 4.

International Monetary Fund. 2010. "Getting the Balance Right: Transitioning out of Sustained Current Account Surpluses." In *World Economic Outlook* (April).

"Joint Letter from G-20 Leaders." 2010. Office of the Press Secretary, The White House. (March 30) (www.whitehouse.gov/the-press-office/joint-letter-g20-leaders).

Kharas, Homi. 2010. "The Emerging Middle Class in Developing Countries." Working Paper 285. OECD Development Centre. Brussels: OECD, January (www.oecd.org/dataoecd/12/52/44457738.pdf).

King, Mervyn. 2010. Speech by Mervyn King, Governor of the Bank of England. University of Exeter (January 19) (www.bankofengland.co.uk/publications/speeches/2010/speech419.pdf).

Lewis, W. Arthur. 1954. "Economic Development with Unlimited Supplies of Labor." *Manchester School of Economic and Social Studies* 22: 139–91.

Michaud, Michael, and Timothy Ryan. 2010. "130 Members of Congress Push for Action on China Currency Manipulation." Office of Congressman Mike Michaud. (March 15) (www.michaud.house.gov/index.php?option=com_content&task=view&id=969&Itemid=76).

Minami, Ryoshin. 1968. "The Turning Point in the Japanese Economy." *Quarterly Journal of Economics.* 82, no. 3: 380–402.

Mussa, Michael. 2008. "Massive and Persistent Resistance to Substantial and Necessary Appreciation of the Renminbi by the Chinese Authorities: A Comment on McKinnon and Schnabl." Presented at the Seventh BIS Annual Conference. Lucerne, Switzerland, June 26–27, 2008 (www.bis.org/events/conf080626/mussa.pdf).

Ocampo, José Antonio. 2007. "The Instability and Inequities of the Global Reserve System." *International Journal of Political Economy* 36, no. 4: 71–96.

———. 2010. "Reforming the Global Reserve System." In *Time for a Visible Hand,* edited by Stephany Griffith-Jones, José Antonio Ocampo, and Joseph Stiglitz, pp. 289–313. Oxford University Press.

Ofer, Gur. 1987. "Soviet Economic Growth: 1928–1985." *Journal of Economic Literature* 25, no. 4: 1767–833.

O'Rourke, Kevin H. 2009. "Government Policies and the Collapse in Trade during the Great Depression." November 27 (www.voxeu.org/index.php?q=node/4267).

Petri, Peter A., and others. 2009. "Inclusive, Balanced, Sustained Growth in the Asia-Pacific." Singapore: Pacific Economic Cooperation Council, Taskforce on the Global Economic Crisis.

Samuelson, Paul A. 1964. "Theoretical Notes on Trade Problems." *Review of Economics and Statistics* 46: 145–54.

Spence, Michael, and Danny Leipziger, eds. 2010. "Globalization and Growth: Implications for a Post-Crisis World." Washington: Commission on Growth and Development, World Bank.

Subramanian, Arvind. 2010. "The Weak Renminbi Is Not Just America's Problem." *Financial Times,* March 17 (www.ft.com/cms/s/0/0ad03172-3205-11df-a8d1-00144feabdc0.html).

World Bank. 1993. *The East Asian Miracle: Economic Growth and Public Policy.* Policy Research Report. Washington.

———. 2009. *Global Economic Prospects 2009: Commodities at the Crossroads.* Washington.

Wyplosz, Charles. 2010. "Is an Undervalued Renminbi the Source of Global Imbalances?" *VoxEU.org.,* April 30 (www.voxeu.org/index.php?q=node/4866).

Yiping, Huang, and Jiang Tingsong. 2010. "What Does the Lewis Turning Point Mean for China? A Computable General Equilibrium Analysis." Working Paper E2010005. China Center for Economic Research, Peking University) (March 17).

Yu, Yongding. 2010. "Asia: China's Policy Response to the Global Financial Crisis." *Journal of Globalization and Development* 1, no. 1, article 12.

THREE

Large Asian Economies and the United States: Is Rebalancing Feasible?

RAJIV KUMAR and DONY ALEX

Factors such as lax financial sector regulation, regulatory capture by major financial players, and an intellectual climate that saw markets as fully self-correcting and market agents as perfectly rational on the basis of complete information, as well as global macroeconomic imbalances have been identified as the major drivers of the financial crisis and the subsequent global economic slowdown. These factors characterized the "great recession" of 2007–09. Some analysts, however, have cited global macroeconomic imbalances as the root cause of the financial crisis and the subsequent global recession.[1] The debate on the nature and role of global imbalances has focused largely on the U.S. and Chinese macro-balances. Essentially the argument has been that the United States was able to run the huge deficits, both fiscal and external, principally because the Chinese surpluses allowed it to do so at minimal cost and in an apparently riskless manner.[2] In this chapter we first examine the nature

1. See Caballero (2009); Portes (2009); and Vines (2009).
2. The root of the present macroeconomic imbalances has been succinctly captured by Obstfeld and Rogoff (2009, pp. 2–3): "The United States' ability to finance macroeconomic imbalances through easy foreign borrowing allowed it to postpone tough policy choices (something that was of course true in many other deficit countries as well). Foreign banks' appetite for assets that turned out to be toxic provided one ready source of external funding for the U.S. deficit. Not only was the United States able to borrow in dollars at nominal interest rates kept low by a loose monetary policy. Also, until around the autumn of 2008, exchange rate and other asset-price movements kept U.S. net foreign liabilities growing at a rate far below the cumulative U.S. current account deficit.

At the same time, countries with current account surpluses faced minimal pressures to adjust. China's ability to sterilize the immense reserve purchases it placed in U.S. markets

and magnitude of the global macro-imbalances, then look at some possible scenarios for redressing them, and finally discuss the role that Asian economies, particularly the three large economies of the People's Republic of China (henceforth, PRC), India, and Japan, can play to achieve a more balanced global economic growth that can be sustained in the coming period.

To preempt our conclusion, we find that, individually, the Asian economies, including the PRC, which is by far the fastest growing, cannot be expected to compensate for the likely decline in U.S. demand as it moves to a more sustainable growth path in the coming decades. While a switch in the Chinese growth strategy to more domestic demand–driven growth is clearly essential, an increase in the demand for regional public goods like regional power grids, highways, and improved telecom connectivity in Asia would contribute significantly to achieving a more balanced global growth in the future. Asian leaders should therefore be giving far greater attention to the factors that impede progress toward greater pan-Asian economic integration, which is a necessary condition for expanding the supply of regional public goods in Asia, and bring these to the same level as in Europe and North America.

Macro-imbalances are not a new phenomenon. They have almost always been a feature of the modern global economy.[3] Macroeconomic imbalances were seen to facilitate faster growth by permitting a creditor country, generating a current account surplus, to park its excess saving in safe assets (like U.S. Treasury bills) for possible use in financing a future external account deficit.[4] However, large macroeconomic imbalances can be seen as a symptom of deeper underlying distortions in the financial and monetary systems of the concerned economies. As the recent crises have demonstrated, imbalances, when allowed to persist, can threaten the stability of the global economy, as well as its attendant financial and monetary systems. Macroeconomic imbalances can be attributed to many

---

allowed it to maintain an undervalued currency and defer rebalancing its own economy. Complementary policy distortions therefore kept China artificially far from its lower autarky interest rate and the U.S. artificially far from its higher autarky interest rate. Had seemingly low-cost postponement options not been available, the subsequent crisis might well have been mitigated, if not contained."

3. Frieden (2009).

4. Dooley, Folkerts-Landau, and Garber (2005); Cooper (2007); and Caballero, Farhi, and Gourinchas (2008).

factors, such as a shift in saving behavior, productivity changes, the accumulation of foreign exchange reserves, movements in commodity prices, and also a shift in investors' attitude toward risk.[5]

In the 1920s, the first major macroeconomic imbalance involved an erstwhile great power, the United States, and a militarily defeated but rising economic power, Germany. This period ended with the most dramatic and disastrous interwar macroeconomic imbalance that the world had witnessed.[6] One factor that has been found to intensify global imbalances is the manipulation or devaluation of the exchange rate by the creditor country to retain its competitive advantage in trade. In the U.S.-German case during the 1920s, the United States, at the time a creditor economy, brought about a substantial devaluation after it took the dollar off the gold standard and later enacted the Smoot-Hawley tariff in June 1930 to restrict imports. The Great Depression, with its terrible and drawn-out consequences, which included the second Great War, followed.

Two contrasting explanations have been given for the present state of global imbalances. The first has been put forward mainly by Barry Eichengreen.[7] This view attributes imbalances to a savings deficit in the United States, which translates into a current account deficit that is met by an inflow of capital from the rest of the world. Capital was attracted to the United States because it offered similar or even higher rates of return, along with greater liquidity of its markets and lower perceived risks on investment.[8] The second view, whose chief proponent has been present Federal Reserve Chairman Ben Bernanke, argues that high savings rates in countries like the PRC, and perhaps Germany, have made huge surpluses available, which, by lowering the cost of borrowing, have contributed to the huge current account deficit in countries such as the United States.[9] According to this view, the onus of correcting global imbalances falls on surplus economies, which should be implementing policies to lower their domestic savings and raising their domestic consumption as

---

5. Blanchard and Milesi-Ferretti (2009).

6. See Frieden (2009).

7. Eichengreen (2009).

8. Gruber and Kamin (2008) found that the U.S. bond yields were comparable to those prevailing in other advanced economies, especially in Europe, contradicting the view that they were the most attractive. It has also been noted that outflows from the United States have been larger than from other advanced economies (Portes 2009).

9. Bernanke (2005).

a share of GDP. This is in contrast to those who see the U.S. deficits as the primary cause of imbalances and recommend policies designed to raise household and public savings in the United States, as well as greater reliance on external demand to push up U.S. economic growth rates. Both these arguments, it is worth pointing out, confine themselves to macro-imbalances in the external account. They do not refer to the inter-country imbalances that have characterized global economic growth in the past few decades or to the intra-country imbalances captured by rising Gini coefficients in many of the larger emerging economies.[10]

While the debate on global imbalances is ongoing, it appears that these imbalances are beginning to be redressed by market behavior. In the period ending in 2009, the latest for which data are available, U.S. private savings rose by around 34.5 percent from their level a year earlier; household savings led the change with an increase of 62.5 percent between 2008 and end of 2009. At the same time, the Chinese current account surplus, which was 9.8 percent of GDP in January 2009, declined to 7.8 percent, effectively switching nearly US$55 billion from external to domestic demand in sustaining the Chinese GDP growth. This was largely a result of the massive fiscal stimulus of US$570 billion, announced by the Chinese government immediately after the Lehman crisis, which has principally been focused on infrastructure capacity expansion. The German current account surplus came down rather sharply, from 6.4 percent to 2.9 percent over the twelve months of 2009. A cause for worry and a possible exacerbation of global imbalances remains the persistence of the U.S. government fiscal deficit, which is expected to rise to 9 percent of GDP (US$1.36 trillion) by the end of 2010,[11] leading to an increase in the U.S. public debt of $1.7 trillion over two years. If the surplus countries are successful in reducing their surpluses, as they are being encouraged to do, there will be less capital available to finance U.S. deficits and interest rates on U.S. Treasury bills will eventually rise. This will further raise the debt-

---

10. For example, it is reported that per capita incomes in Sub-Saharan Africa were one seventeenth of those in the United States in 1980 and worsened to one fortieth in 2008. Nearly all major emerging economies experienced worsening income inequalities during this period. These imbalances have generated significant anti-globalization sentiments both within individual countries and worldwide. While these "development imbalances" are perhaps more important from the emerging economy point of view, we restrict ourselves to the global macro-imbalances in this chapter and leave the latter for future research, as their causes and the policies to redress them are quite different.

11. Congressional Budget Office (2010).

servicing burden for the United States, which would exert significant downward pressure on the dollar. This could be advantageous for U.S. exports and redress the trade deficit with its major trading partners, including the PRC, Japan, and Germany. The key question is whether the rest of the global economy can generate sufficient demand to allow the expansion of U.S. exports and the reduction of its trade and overall current account deficit, without leading to a global recession.

In the above context, we discuss the possible means by which the existing imbalances can be further and more quickly reduced. In the next sections we provide some stylized facts regarding global imbalances and project optimal saving and consumption rates for the United States and the PRC, respectively, which would help to reduce the imbalances. Finally, we look at measures that surplus economies could take to increase domestic demand and raise the share of consumption in GDP.

Economic Trends

To understand the origins of this latest phase of macroeconomic imbalances, the starting point has to be the Asian crisis of the late 1990s.[12] This crisis left the Asian economies bitter about not getting timely or adequate financial assistance from the IMF and consequently suffering huge welfare losses.[13] This in turn propelled them toward taking more contingent measures for the future. Such measures largely focused on achieving a degree of self-insurance by raising the stockpile of foreign exchange reserves as insurance against a future financial crisis. This process of accumulating reserves in turn changed the current account of some countries from deficit to surplus.

Total foreign exchange reserves in these Asian economies, excluding Japan, which had large reserves of about US$217 billion before the Asian crisis in 1996, rose from US$329 billion at the end of 1998 to US$2.3 trillion by early 2008, the period before the Lehman collapse (see figure 3-1). That nearly all Asian economies emerged virtually unscathed from the Lehman financial crisis is perhaps testimony to the success of this

12. Blanchard and Milesi-Ferretti (2009) argue that the imbalances that emerged in the period from 1996 to 2000 were not due to the Asian crisis but were driven primarily by the buoyant U.S. prospects relative to Asia. This argument however does not seem convincing, as the data point to a sharp rise in imbalances after 1997 (see figure 3-4).

13. See the chapter by Domenico Lombardi in this volume.

FIGURE 3-1. Foreign Exchange Reserves, 1995–2009

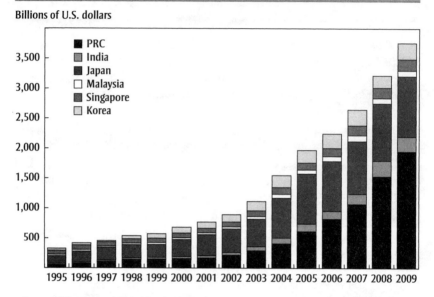

Billions of U.S. dollars

Source: IMF, International Financial Statistics (2010).

strategy.[14] However, it can be argued that the cost of accumulating these reserves, for the individual countries and for the global economy, has been far too high and incommensurate with the benefits of achieving a degree of self-insurance against the crisis.

In terms of rate of growth in reserve holdings, the PRC leads the pack with annual quarter-on-quarter growth of around 33 percent, followed by India, which registered growth of around 28 percent during the period from 2000Q1 to 2008Q4. For countries like the PRC and some other East Asian economies, net exports play an important role in sustaining high GDP growth rates.[15] This has been achieved by keeping a fixed exchange

14. The notable exception was Singapore, with its strong dependence on external demand. It suffered negative GDP growth of (–2 percent) in 2009, but has since staged a sustained recovery, achieving positive GDP growth of 5.6 percent in 2010 (IMF 2010b).

15. Net exports contributed as much as 10 percent to overall GDP growth in the PRC in the years from 2001 to 2009. Expectedly, the PRC's exports and total trade—after its accession to the WTO in 2001—have grown at a substantially higher rate than its GDP (Prasad 2009).

rate with the U.S. dollar to maintain export competitiveness and in turn has led to huge accumulation of reserves to prevent the currency from appreciating.[16] So as a growth-enhancing process to make exports competitive,[17] these countries had to keep their exchange rate undervalued and in that process their foreign exchange reserves grew to unprecedented levels.[18]

Figure 3-2 clearly substantiates the point that PRC exports were made competitive by undervaluing the exchange rates through the process of sterilization, which eventually led to bulging foreign exchange reserves. As figure 3-2 shows, the PRC also undertook a large sterilization operation after 2002, which led to a sharp rise in the foreign exchange reserves from 2001 while the monetary base remained flat.

As Simon Johnson has argued, "These reserves are accumulated through arguably the largest ever sustained intervention in a foreign exchange market—that is, through The People's Bank of China buying dollars and selling renminbi, and thus keeping the renminbi-dollar exchange rate more depreciated than it would be otherwise."[19] This is substantiated by noting that the net purchase of U.S. securities by the PRC rose sharply from US$84.3 billion in 2005 to around US$276.8 billion in 2008. The main components of these purchases were U.S. Treasury bills. In 2008, net purchases by the PRC of U.S. Treasury bills galloped to around

16. It has been argued by Rodrik (2010) that this was more necessary once the PRC joined the WTO in 2001. Before joining the WTO, it had other industrial policies for enhancing its growth process hinging on industrialization and trade. As Rodrik (2010, p. 6) argues, "China's manufacturing industries were promoted by a wide variety of inducements, including high tariff barriers, investment incentives, export subsidies, and domestic content requirements on foreign firms."

17. "Partial correlation between my index of (log) undervaluation and annual growth rate is 0.026 for developing nations. (For reasons explained in that paper, I am inclined to think of this relationship as causal.) However, in the case of China this estimate rises to 0.086, a much bigger number that may be due to the large reservoir of surplus labour and the huge gap in the productivity levels of modern and traditional parts of the economy" (Rodrik 2010, p. 91).

18. Corden (2009) argues that the PRC has two parts to its exchange rate policy. One is the "exchange rate protectionism" for which it had to keep its exchange rate undervalued with the intention of maintaining profitability and employment in the export sector. The second is to keep its exchange rate stable by keeping it fixed or pegged to the dollar.

19. Simon Johnson, "Should We Fear China?" testimony submitted to U.S.-China Economic and Security Review Commission hearing, "U.S. Debt to China: Implications and Repercussions," Panel I: China's Lending Activities and the U.S. Debt, February 25, 2010. Excerpts taken from Simon Johnson's blog: Baseline Scenario.

FIGURE 3-2. Change in Foreign Exchange Reserves and Monetary Base in the PRC, 2000–09

Annual growth rate (percent)

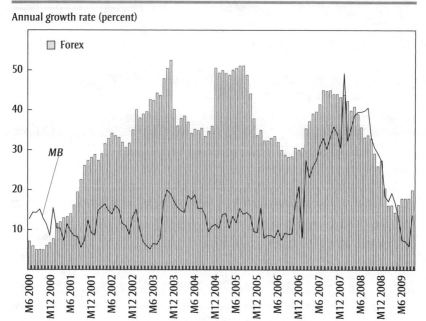

Source: IMF, International Financial Statistics (2010).

US$133.8 billion from just US$16.6 billion in 2007. In May 2009, Chinese holdings of U.S. Treasuries peaked at US$801 billion and have been hovering around US$755.4 billion since December 2009.

The contribution of net exports to overall Chinese GDP growth increased sharply between 2000 and 2009 (see figure 3-3). The PRC's surplus on the trade account as a percentage of GDP jumped from 2 percent in 2000 to 9.3 percent in 2007.[20]

The United States has been the single largest export destination for the PRC, absorbing as much as 18.3 percent of the PRC's total exports in 2008. On the other hand, Chinese imports were higher than Japan's, which supplied about 12.5 percent of total Chinese imports in 2008. Dur-

20. Prasad (2009).

FIGURE 3-3. PRC Exports to India, Japan, and the United States, 1990–2008

Billions of U.S. dollars

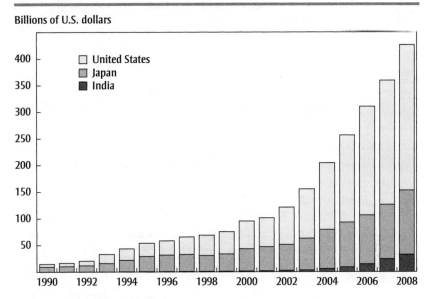

Source: Asian Development Bank (2009).

ing the period from 2000 to 2008, Chinese exports to the United States, Japan, and India grew, on average, by about 23 percent, 16 percent, and 46 percent, respectively. Surprisingly and largely unknown is the fact that the sharpest rate of growth for exports from the PRC has been to India: Chinese exports to India grew by around 29 percent during the 1990s (1991–99) and by 46 percent annually in the period 2000–08. Table 3-1 shows the U.S. bilateral trade balance with Japan, the PRC, and India. The U.S. trade deficit with the PRC is around five times its deficit with Japan, which not so long ago was a major trading partner of the United States. India's deficit with the PRC, though worrisome to India, is minuscule in comparison with both Japan's and the PRC's deficit with the United States.

The PRC's absolute increase in its trade balance can also be corroborated by the growth of its current account surplus. Figure 3-4 shows the current account balance for the PRC and some other emerging markets that generated small current account deficits in 1996 and became current account surplus countries thereafter. From figure 3-4 it can be seen quite clearly that after the 1997–98 Asian crisis, the PRC saw sustained and

T A B L E   3 - 1 .   U.S. Bilateral Trade Balance, 1998–2009
Billions of U.S. dollars

Country	1998	2007	2008	2009
Japan	−64	−84	−74	−45
PRC	−56	−258	−268	−226
India	−5	−9	−8	−5

Source: U.S. Census Bureau.
Note: Numbers are rounded to the nearest billion.

large-scale growth in its current account surplus. This is reflected on the opposite side by the steady increase in the U.S. current account deficit. However, there is not a one-to-one correspondence between Chinese surpluses and U.S. deficits. As figure 3-4 shows, the years in which the United States suffered from the largest current account deficits (2006 and 2007) were not the same as those in which either the PRC or the whole of East Asia earned their largest current account surpluses.

F I G U R E   3 - 4 .   Current Account Balances, 1996–2010

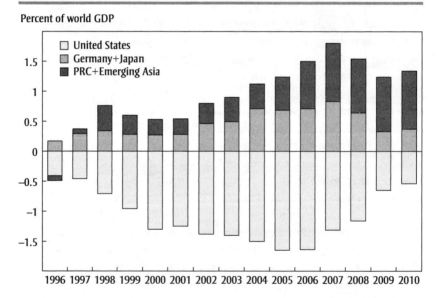

Percent of world GDP

Source: IMF (2010b).

FIGURE 3-5. Change in Current Account Surpluses of Oil-Exporting Countries, 1996–2010

Percent of GDP

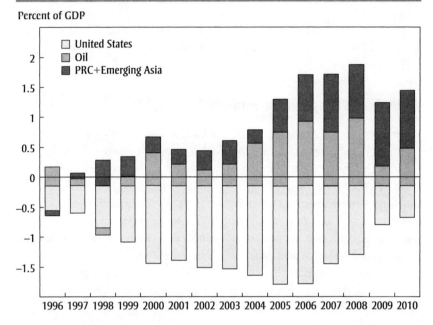

Source: IMF (2010b).

Thus it may not be entirely fair to argue that the PRC was mainly responsible for the global macroeconomic imbalances. Other countries, such as the oil-exporting economies, were perhaps equally responsible. The emergence of large trade and current account surpluses in most of Asia was also a result of the dot-com bubble and spiraling commodity prices. The commodity price hikes especially helped the oil-exporting countries in the Middle East with their exports; their burgeoning export earnings eventually made them large current account surplus countries (see figure 3-5).

Thus the oil-exporting countries were also major contributors to global macro-imbalances during 2004 and 2008. They contributed more in terms of current account surpluses (0.66 percent of world GDP) than the combined current account surpluses of the PRC and other East Asian emerging economies (0.54 percent of world GDP). In a clear trend after 2004, it can be seen that most advanced economies, especially the United

States, saw a substantial increase in their current account deficits. Con-tributors to the sharp increase in the U.S. current account deficit included factors such as equity price appreciation and the rise in real estate prices spurred by speculative investment. Maurice Obstfeld and Kenneth Rogoff argue that the resulting asset price bubble was a crucial factor in the United States in high consumer spending and borrowing.[21]

The Role of Savings and Investments in Global Macro-Imbalances

During the 1990s and until 2001, the PRC had an average gross savings rate of around 38 percent of GDP, which jumped to above 52 percent in 2008. The United States, on the other hand, saw its savings rate decline from 18 percent in 2001 to 13 percent of GDP in 2008. Japan has not seen much movement, with its savings rate hovering around the same rate of 28 percent of GDP as was seen in 2000. India, somewhat like the PRC, has also seen a sharp increase in its savings rate, from 25 percent of GDP in 2000 to 37 percent in 2008.

As figure 3-6 shows, the PRC quite distinctly has the highest savings rate among the four countries, followed by India. Commentators have blamed the PRC's high savings rate for contributing to the consumption orgy in the United States. They argue that the high rates of saving led to persistent lowering of global interest rates as savings outstripped invest-ment demand. Corporate savings have been the main driver of savings growth in the PRC. The corporate savings rate in the PRC is high because of the government subsidies and the repressed financial markets, which do not permit households to look for alternative investment opportunities and force them to park their massive savings in state-owned banks. These savings earn very low rates of interest, and banks are able to make capital available to state-owned and other enterprises at relatively low interest rates. This also explains the high level of profitability of Chinese corpo-rations.[22] Chinese firms have ploughed the higher earnings into savings and investments, thereby pushing up the overall national savings rate. Some scholars argue that the high domestic savings in the PRC reflect insufficient social welfare arrangements, as well as a lack of financial inter-

---

21. Obstfeld and Rogoff (2009). U.S. deficit-financing requirements, which were around $1.4 trillion in 2009, are expected to rise to $9 trillion over the next decade, leading to uncer-tainty in currency and bond markets (Prasad 2009).

22. See Prasad (2009) and Lin (2009).

FIGURE 3-6. Gross National Savings, 1992–2009

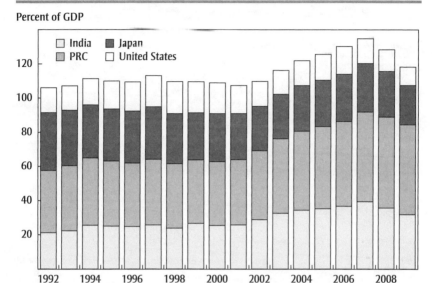

Source: ADB (2010); IMF (2010b).

mediation and pension facilities.[23] Demographic factors in the PRC, such as its one-child policy, have also been cited as a factor in the high savings rate of domestic households.[24]

Figure 3-7, which contrasts the world private savings rate with U.S. long-term real interest rates for the period 2003–09, provides the empirical basis for the "savings glut" view that the main cause of the U.S. external deficit is the increase in world savings. The savings glut hypothesis asserts that the high levels of saving in the world reduced real interest rates and led to the asset price bubble and the consumption binge in the United States.

If we compare the investment rates in the United States, Japan, the PRC, and India, we find that the PRC again stands out, with an average rate of growth of 40.5 percent from 1992 to 2008 (figure 3-8). India has also maintained a reasonably high growth rate in investment, an average

23. See Woo (2008) and Cordon (2009).
24. Guonan Ma and Zhou Haiwen (2009) also find that that a pronounced decline in youth dependency is a major reason the PRC is one of the world's largest creditors.

FIGURE 3-7. World Savings Rate and U.S. Interest Rates (TIPS)
Compared, 2003–09

Percent

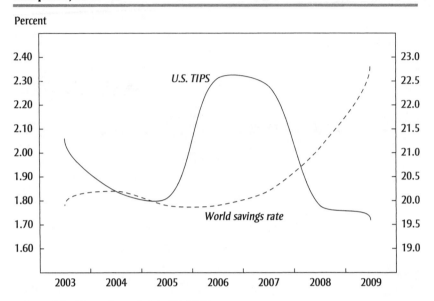

Source: Federal Reserve Economic Data; IMF (2010b).
Note: TIPS: Treasury Inflation-Protected Securities.

of 28 percent over the same period. Table 3-2 shows that, for both the
PRC and India, investment contributes around 50 percent to GDP,
whereas in the United States and Japan the contribution of investment
is a mere 4.3 and 13.3 percent, respectively.

In contrast, aggregate consumption (of private households and government) accounted for nearly the entire GDP growth in the United States.
In the PRC, consumption's contribution was only 40 percent in the years
from 2000 to 2008. India has maintained a more balanced demand composition, with consumption contributing 57 percent to GDP growth. This
share is unlikely to change as domestic demand in India seems to be picking up smartly in the post-crisis period.

Among the deficit countries, the United States has the largest current
account deficit in the world. Studies have characterized the post 1990s
macro-imbalances scenario from the U.S. deficit side as happening in
three phases.[25] The first phase is "Differences in Perceived Profitability,

25. See Blanchard and Milesi-Ferretti (2009).

FIGURE 3-8. Gross Domestic Investment, 1992–2008

Percent of GDP

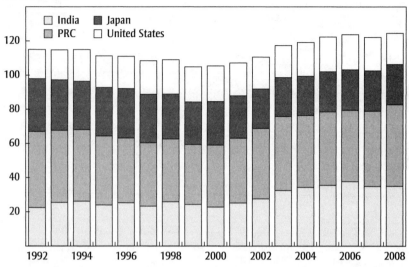

Source: IMF (2010b).

1996–2000"; the second is "Declining U.S. Saving, 2001–04"; and the last is "Asset Booms and Busts, 2005–08." The first or "good" phase (from 1996 to 2000) saw a peak in U.S. capital expenditures due to the technology boom and reflecting expectations of higher productivity. The expectations for a productivity surge were overly optimistic, but productivity differences in a way led to a high current account deficit with an

TABLE 3-2. Contribution to GDP, 2000–08

Percent

Country	Total consumption	Private consumption	Government consumption	Investment	Net exports
United States	100	87	13	4.3	–4.3
Japan	66.6	40	26.6	13.3	33.3
PRC	40.1	27.4	12.7	49	10.8
India	57	48.6	7	50	–4.15

Source: Prasad (2009).
Note: Totals may not add to 100 because contribution of employment to GDP growth has not been included.

appreciating U.S. dollar. This was also the period when Japan was in a contractionary phase (its "lost decade") and, in Asia, investment was low in the aftermath of the 1997–98 crisis. Still, this was considered the "good" phase of the macroeconomic imbalances, with excesses emerging on the back of a "relatively profitable story" linked to the productivity surge. In the second or "bad" phase, 2001–04, the U.S. current account deficit was fueled by fiscal deficits and low private savings. This period included the dot-com bust, with the prolonged expansionary monetary policy stance of the U.S. leading to very low interest rates, which may be seen to have ultimately precipitated the financial crisis of 2007–09. The third phase, 2005 to 2008, showed the typical pre-crisis components of the asset price bubble, high capital flows, and investment. On the surplus side, apart from the high saving rates in the PRC, there are sharp increases in commodity and oil prices leading to a surplus in the oil-exporting countries, especially in the Middle East.

To sum up, global macro-imbalances can be seen as a combined result of high U.S. current account deficits, which were financed by rising savings in the PRC and the oil-exporting economies. But it is plausible to argue that the rising savings in the PRC driven by high corporate savings also contributed to a lowering of global interest rates, which allowed U.S. households to finance their consumption and acquisition of assets, especially real estate. It is perhaps impossible to identify any single cause of these imbalances, which were even seen as positively driving high rates of global GDP growth. But in hindsight it is clear that these imbalances ultimately proved unsustainable, and the key task going forward is to minimize them with coordinated action.

Reducing Macroeconomic Imbalances

The literature on measures that can be taken to tackle global imbalances identifies two distinct approaches. One argues that imbalances are just a manifestation of a short-term disequilibrium in an otherwise equilibrium setting and that this will automatically adjust itself after some time.[26] Recent reductions in the PRC's current account surplus and the increase in household savings in the United States support this argument.[27] How-

26. See Antràs and Caballero (2007) and Caballero, Farhi, and Gourinchas (2008).
27. The improvements in current account balances that have occurred across the world recently have been mainly due to the reduction in trade balances, reflecting a temporary

ever, other commentators, led by scholars such as Obstfeld and Rogoff, argue that these imbalances are the result of severe economic distortions that have to be rectified with coordinated and conscious policy action.[28] They think that leaving the disequilibrium to be corrected by the markets can make things worse. Figure 3-9 shows the contribution of the current account balance of some major countries and regions to the world GDP in 2008. The United States is the biggest contributor to the macroeconomic imbalances, with a current account deficit of around 1.16 percent of world GDP. The PRC, with its large surpluses, is second with a contribution of around 0.70 percent. It is worth noting that, in 2004, the PRC current account surplus was just one tenth of the U.S. current account deficit.[29] But its surplus increased sharply starting in 2005, and from just US$68 billion in 2004 it peaked at US$426 billion in 2008. Current account surpluses in Japan and deficits in India contribute around 0.26 and 0.04 percent to the world GDP. Developing Asia and Middle East current account balances represent around 0.70 and 0.57 percent of world GDP, respectively.[30] Therefore it is clear that in the Asia-Pacific region measures to correct the macro-imbalances have to focus on a possible restructuring of the U.S. and Chinese external accounts.

As figure 3-10 shows, the U.S. trade deficit with the PRC saw a marked increase during the period from 1998 to 2007, whereas, throughout the same period, the U.S. trade deficit with the rest of East Asia declined sharply. Thus the pattern of Asian-U.S. trade flows did not change significantly over this ten-year period. The important change was that the PRC emerged as the most important Asian exporter to the United States while

---

adjustment due to the financial crisis. The imbalances that were contributed by oil-exporting countries were due to highly inflated world oil prices, which will most likely stay lower in the coming years. There are forecasts that estimate that "the direct effect of lower oil prices *would be* to reduce the U.S. current account deficit in 2009 by over 1 percent of GDP in 2009 relative to 2008, and *reduce* the surplus of oil exporters by some 8 percent of their GDP (over 0.5 percent of world GDP)" (Blanchard and Milesi-Ferretti 2009). So, in a sense, the imbalances from the oil-exporting countries, which contributed around 0.6 percent of global GDP, should not be a major concern for the near future.

28. See, for example, Obstfeld and Rogoff (2007).

29. The trade balance between the United States and the PRC also widened during this period, with the U.S. trade deficit reaching US$268 billion in 2008, as compared with just US$162 billion in 2004.

30. Germany is also one of the largest contributors to global imbalances with its current account surpluses accounting for as much as 0.39 percent of global GDP. In this chapter, however, we are looking only at the imbalances in the Asia-Pacific region.

FIGURE 3-9. Current Account Balances, 2008

Percent of world GDP

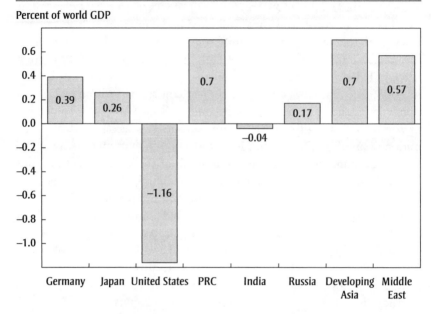

Source: IMF (2010b, WEO database).

FIGURE 3-10. U.S. Global Trade Deficit, 1998 and 2007

Percent

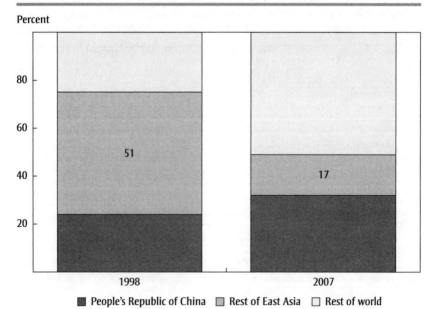

Source: U.S. Department of Commerce; U.S.-China Business Council (2009).

TABLE 3-3. **Global Current Account Balances**

Country or region	Current account balance (% of GDP)	Current account balance (% of world GDP)	Share in world GDP (%)	Gross saving (% of GDP)
PRC	9.79	0.70	7.26	52
United States	−4.9	−1.16	23.43	13
Japan	3.97	0.26	8.09	28
India	−3.07	−0.04	1.98	35.8
Germany	6.40	0.40	4.10	25.5
Middle East[a]	18.3	0.60	3.10	42
Developing Asia[b]	5.90	0.70	11.7	47.6

Source: IMF database.

Note: Data are in 2008 prices.

a. The Middle East is composed of fourteen countries: Bahrain, Egypt, Iran (Islamic Republic of), Iraq, Jordan, Kuwait, Lebanon, Libya, Oman, Qatar, Saudi Arabia, Syrian Arab Republic, United Arab Emirates, and Yemen.

b. Developing Asia is composed of twenty-six countries: Afghanistan, Republic of Bangladesh, Bhutan, Brunei Darussalam, Cambodia, PRC, Fiji, India, Indonesia, Kiribati, Lao People's Democratic Republic, Malaysia, Maldives, Myanmar, Nepal, Pakistan, Papua New Guinea, Philippines, Samoa, Solomon Islands, Sri Lanka, Thailand, Timor-Leste, Democratic Republic of Tonga, Vanuatu, and Viet Nam.

importing larger volumes of basic inputs from the rest of Asia. But it is unreasonable to expect the PRC to remain merely an efficient and cost-effective intermediary for Asian exports to the United States. It will have to absorb some of these imports from the rest of Asia, in an enlarged domestic market driven by rising domestic demand. If the PRC has to fill this deficit alone, then it will need to increase its consumption levels by around 10 percent of GDP, which would lead to a gross national consumption level of around 46 percent of GDP.[31] This required increase in PRC domestic demand sustained for a minimum of five years hardly looks feasible.

As table 3-3 shows, the $14 trillion U.S. economy (23.4 percent of the global economy) is about three times the size of either the PRC or Japanese economy and nearly twelve times that of India. Thus, to match a reduction in the U.S. current account deficit, the PRC and Japan would have to reduce their surpluses by a magnitude that would imply an unacceptable negative impact on their economies. For example, for the U.S.

31. We have taken 2009 current prices from IMF (2009). The U.S. economy stood at about US$14.1 trillion; the PRC's economy at around US$4.7 trillion; and the world economy at around US$58 trillion.

current account deficit to come down to a more sustainable rate of 3 percent of GDP would imply a reduction of U.S. aggregate demand, with a
corresponding impact on its GDP of $420 billion. A compensating reduc-
tion in the PRC's current account surplus would imply a decline of around
9 percent in its GDP. Such a large increase in domestic demand in the PRC
would be infeasible. A reduction in aggregate demand in the United States
would have to be made up by a combined increase in all three major surplus economies: the PRC, Japan, and Germany. This is hardly conceiv-
able. It is perhaps more practical for the Asian economies to try and boost
domestic demand, as has happened in the PRC and Japan, and buttress
this with efforts to promote demand for regional public goods that are not
yet adequately provided for in the region.

Measures for Enhancing Domestic Demand in Asia

In all likelihood, the advanced economies will take much more time to
recover than the emerging economies, which are already experiencing
sharper recoveries from the crisis-induced slowdown. Thus, for the global
economy to revert to pre-crisis growth rates would require that the demand
shortfall in the U.S. and major European economies be compensated by
higher demand growth in large emerging economies like Brazil, the PRC,
India, Indonesia, and South Africa. The Asia-Pacific region, with three of
the largest emerging economies, and the ASEAN sub-region would be best
placed to generate the additional aggregate demand required to compensate for the likely demand slowdown in advanced economies. This would
of course also imply a further shift in global economic gravity from the
Atlantic to the Asia-Pacific region.

   The thirteen largest Asian economies[32] have a total GDP of US$13.9 tril-
lion, which is similar in size to the U.S. economy of about US$14.1 trillion
at 2009 prices. According to a recent IMF study, U.S. private sector
demand declined by about 3 percentage points of GDP from the pre-crisis
(2003–07) average.[33] This decline in private sector demand led to an
increase in private savings from near zero before the crisis to around 5 percent of disposable income in 2009. If the falloff in U.S. demand has to be
accommodated by the thirteen largest Asian economies, then they would

   32. Japan; the PRC; Korea; India; Taipei,China; Indonesia; Thailand; the United Arab
Emirates; Singapore; Pakistan; Malaysia; Sri Lanka; and Saudi Arabia.
   33. See Lee, Rabanal, and Sandri (2010).

FIGURE 3-11. Composition of Asian Economic Growth, 2008

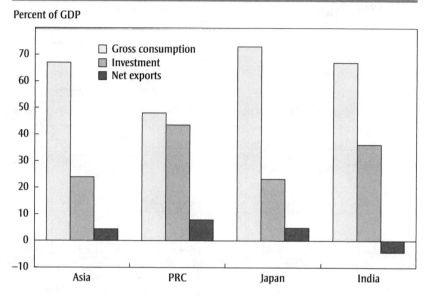

Percent of GDP

Source: IMF (2010b, WEO database); Prasad (2009).

need to increase their aggregate demand by a similar amount, about 3 percent of their GDP.[34] The question is where this additional demand would be generated within Asia.

Most of the Asian economies have consumption levels averaging around 60 percent of their GDP (figure 3-11). The only exception seems to be the PRC, where total consumption in 2008 contributed to only 48 percent of total GDP growth, with private consumption contributing a mere 35 percent compared with 71 percent in the United States. In India, total consumption accounts for 67 percent of annual GDP growth, with private consumption contributing around 57 percent. Investment demand

34. There has been an increase in the potential gap in the GDP of advanced economies, mainly due to a demand shortfall. The IMF (2009) projected the output gap of advanced economies in 2009 and 2010 to be around 4.1 percent and 3.7 percent of their overall GDP. This would amount to around US$1.5–1.6 trillion. The thirteen largest Asian economies would have to raise their overall consumption level by around 10 percent of their total GDP in order to accommodate such a gap. The fiscal stimulus due to the financial crisis has temporarily led to higher consumption patterns in the region. However, structural reforms will need to be undertaken in order to raise consumption levels and sustain them.

FIGURE 3-12. Middle East Current Account Balance and Savings, 1997–2010

Percent of GDP

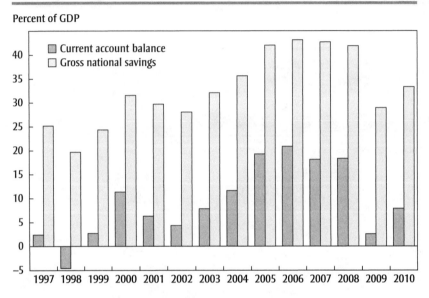

Source: IMF, International Financial Statistics (2010b).

accounted for 40 percent of total GDP growth in developing Asia in 2008 (43.5 percent in the PRC, 23.8 percent in Japan, and 36.2 percent in India). These are already significantly high levels of capacity formation, and so domestic investment demand in individual Asian economies can hardly be expected to contribute to the higher aggregate demand required to boost overall global economic activity.

Net exports contributed, on average, 4.4 percent of GDP growth in Asia in 2008. Their share in the case of the PRC and Japan for the period 2000 to 2008 was 11 percent and 33 percent, respectively. India, whose growth paradigm is a contrast to that of the East Asian economies, saw net exports contribute a negative 4.6 percent to GDP growth during the same period. Thus, except in India, net exports could also not be expected to lead to higher economic growth in Asia.

There are three possible routes to raising aggregate demand in Asia. The first is to raise domestic private consumption demand, especially in the PRC and Japan, and also in the ASEAN region. This would enable relevant countries, including the United States, to take greater advantage of external demand and rebalance their own economies.[35] While this would have some positive impact, especially in reducing the PRC's dependence on external demand to sustain its double-digit GDP growth, it would not fully compensate for the demand deficiency in advanced economies.

The second way forward would be for the oil-rich West Asian or Middle Eastern (these terms are used interchangeably here) economies to reduce their savings-investment gap (in other words, their current account surpluses) to push up aggregate demand. Apart from the PRC, the countries of the Middle East are the second largest current account surplus group in the world (figure 3-12).[36] In the last few years, high oil prices have generated high export earnings for these countries, leading in turn to high current account surpluses. This is in contrast to the 1990s when, owing to the low global oil prices, the majority of oil-exporting countries of West Asia experienced current account deficits.

The oil price surge that peaked in July 2008 led to current account surpluses in this region of around 18 percent of GDP in the period from 2004 to 2008, from less than 5 percent in the 1990s. But these surpluses have not been converted into higher spending by these countries.[37] Demand in these oil-exporting economies, taking marginal propensity to import as a proxy, did not rise to even one third of the increase in additional oil revenues. While savings rates rose from 28 percent of GDP in 2002 to 42 percent in 2008, investment rates languished at around 23–24 percent, generating current account surpluses of 18 percent. These economies need to feel certain of their future revenues in order to expand their domestic demand by building the necessary infrastructure and, for instance, improving temporary immigration of workers from other Asian economies.

---

35. See the chapter by Kemal Derviş and Karim Foda in this volume.

36. The countries of the Middle East or West Asia as included here include twenty countries: Algeria, Bahrain, Djibouti, Egypt, Islamic Republic of Iran, Iraq, Jordan, Kuwait, Lebanon, Libya, Mauritania, Morocco, Oman, Qatar, Saudi Arabia, Sudan, Syrian Arab Republic, Tunisia, United Arab Emirates, and Republic of Yemen. West Asian countries constitute the bulk of imbalances (current account surplus) in the Middle East and North Africa. In 2008, the Middle East group had current account balances of around US$345 billion, of which West Asia constituted around US$290 billion.

37. IMF (2006). The IMF study found that the countries of the Gulf Cooperation Council (GCC) the major oil-exporting countries in Asia, spent around 15 percent of their additional oil revenues on imports. In the case of OPEC, the world's largest oil-exporting group, it was found that the additional revenue spent on imports was around 31 percent. Considering non-oil revenues, the composition changes somewhat for the GCC (34 percent) but not much for OPEC countries (36 percent).

Apart from increasing immigration and imports to meet additional domestic consumption demand, financial sector development can also contribute to raising demand in oil-exporting countries by reducing their revenue volatility. Therefore, financial sector reforms designed to deepen the financial markets and promote more efficient operations should become a priority in the West Asian oil-exporting economies. However, the implementation of necessary reforms in their financial sectors will come about only in the medium to long term. Therefore, these oil-exporting countries cannot be relied upon at present to make up for the shortfall in global aggregate demand.

The third modality would be to boost regional economic activity by accelerating the process of pan-Asian economic integration and establishing institutional mechanisms for designing and financing regional infrastructure projects. Two specific modalities that could be considered for shoring up regional demand would be: (1) to complete the process of trade and economic integration between the ASEAN+4,[38] which would contribute to greater dynamism in regional economic activity; (2) to establish an Asian Investment Bank (AIB), which would supplement the efforts of the Asian Development Bank (ADB) and other national development banks to finance infrastructure and connectivity in Asia at levels comparable to those in Europe and the United States.

The ASEAN+4 nations constitute around 96 percent of GDP in Asia in purchasing power parity (PPP) terms and more than 80 percent of exports and imports. The rationale of a grouping like ASEAN+4 is to remove barriers to intra-regional trade and allow the smooth flow of goods and services between countries in Asia. Regionally, exports within ASEAN increased from 18.9 percent of world exports in 1990 to 24.9 percent of world exports in 2006, and imports from 15.2 percent to 22.5 percent in the same period. Further, the ASEAN countries decided in 2009 to form a new trade forum called ATIGA (ASEAN Trade in Goods Agreement) to work toward greater trade integration within the region.[39] However, the level of intra-regional trade should be seen in comparison with that in the

38. ASEAN+4 includes the ten countries of ASEAN (Association of Southeast Asian Nations) plus the PRC, Japan, Korea, and India.

39. The main features of ATIGA are the following: (1) To create a new comprehensive framework for enhancing the trade in goods in the region, taking into consideration all the other trade initiatives by ASEAN; (2) to enhance the ASEAN legal framework by improving transparency and accountability within the region; and finally, (3) to improve the ASEAN free trade area's rule-based system.

European Union (EU) and the North American Free Trade Agreement (NAFTA), where in 2006 exports contributed 67.6 percent and 53.8 percent and imports 63.2 percent and 34.3 percent of world trade, respectively. There is clearly a long road ahead for further expansion of intra-regional trade in Asia.

Several studies undertaken by the Research and Information System for Developing Countries (RIS), New Delhi, have shown that admitting India into the existing ASEAN+3 formation would significantly enhance welfare gains accruing to member countries.[40] Similarly, studies conducted under the aegis of the Comprehensive Economic Partnership in East Asia (CEPEA) process showed that an ASEAN+6 formation that included Australia and New Zealand would generate higher welfare gains and boost economic activity in Asia significantly more than that achieved under the ASEAN+3 process.[41] These alternative proposals should therefore be mainstreamed and promoted to achieve a rebalancing of economic growth in the Asia-Pacific region. They would significantly enhance intra-regional trade within Asia and reduce its dependence on exports to other regions.

One of the major bottlenecks for low intra-regional Asian trade is the lack of proper infrastructure in Asia as compared with that in Europe and the United States. To enhance intra-regional trade, a more developed infrastructure that improves connectivity should include better roads, railways, airways, seaways, fiber optic cable networks, and the like. The investment requirements for such infrastructure development are simply gigantic. In a flagship study undertaken by the ADB, it is estimated that, between 2010 and 2020, developing Asia would need to invest around US$8 trillion in national infrastructure capacity and an additional US$287 billion in regional infrastructure projects. Nationally, the study determined that, it would need to spend around 68 percent on new infrastructure investment and the remainder on maintaining and replacing existing infrastructure. Regionally, the study determined that approximately 1,077 bilateral, subregional, and pan-Asian infrastructure projects would need to be undertaken by 2020. This would amount to an overall infrastructure investment of approximately US$750 billion per year and would generate real income gains of around US$13 trillion over the next decades.[42]

40. The formation is called JACIK and includes India along with ASEAN, the PRC, Korea, and Japan. See Kondo (2006).
41. See Urata and Okabe (2007) and Urata and Terada (2008).
42. ADB (2009).

Although these are almost mind-boggling figures, they could be achieved. The investment in infrastructure could be undertaken by creating an Asian Investment Bank.[43] The AIB would not in any way diminish the role and importance of the ADB, as the needs are enormous enough for both to co-exist and supplement each other. A similar circumstance exists in Europe, for example, where both the European Investment Bank (EIB) and the European Bank for Reconstruction and Development (EBRD) have co-existed for more than three decades. Moreover, the ADB could then devote greater attention to the development of longer-term sustainable development paradigms for Asia that take into account the changing global realities and ecological concerns. AIB, like its well-established counterpart in Europe, based in Luxembourg, would be managed independently of extra-regional interests and could focus on more efficient utilization of savings generated within Asia. It would also help facilitate the development of Asian financial markets. The proposal for an AIB has been prepared by the United Nations Economic and Social Commission for Asia and Pacific (UNESCAP) and has received wide support. It would be useful to add it to the agenda of the G-20 for two reasons. First, it could be presented as an Asian effort to correct the existing global macro-imbalances, which is a key G-20 issue. Second, discussing it at the G-20 would help to overcome the resistance that it faces from Japan and a few other G-20 members.

A globally comparable physical infrastructure would also contribute to achieving higher productivity levels in, and expansion of, the manufacturing sector in Asia. This is one of the more urgent and important tasks in countries like India where the manufacturing sector has lagged behind (see figure 3-13). The growth of the manufacturing sector would enable a higher absorption of entrants to the workforce, which in India's case is as high as 12 million annually. The expansion of the manufacturing sector to primarily cater to demand within Asia would ensure that the region actually benefits from its demographic advantage and also reinforce current trends in intra-regional trade. Greater regional connectivity and more efficient physical infrastructure would also permit a rise in service sector productivity levels. These have generally been falling in Asia, except in India and Singapore, as compared to productivity levels in advanced economies.[44]

43. See Kumar (2005 and 2007).
44. IMF (2010).

FIGURE 3-13. Asian Productivity Levels Relative to the United States, 1996–2008

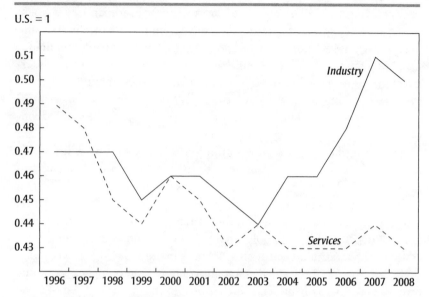

Source: IMF (2010a).

Conclusion

The rebalancing required in the Asia-Pacific region can be achieved in three ways. First, structural reforms would have to be undertaken in major economies such as the PRC to boost domestic demand and reduce their dependence on external demand and net exports. Second, the oil-exporting countries could be expected to spend their savings from sudden surges in oil prices if they could be assured of more stable future income streams. This would be achieved through reforms in the Asian financial sector that would ensure that such savings could be suitably invested and generate a stable income stream. A rise in domestic investment demand in these countries would help absorb skilled labor from labor-surplus Asian economies and also strengthen intra-regional economic activity in general. Third, and perhaps the most important modality for rebalancing, would be to enhance intra-regional trade and investment flows by promoting pan-Asian economic integration and addressing the tasks of preparing a shelf of needed regional and national infrastructure projects and mobilizing financing for them.

This chapter has argued that a formation like the ASEAN+4 and the establishment of an Asian Investment Bank would be most appropriate for achieving the full potential of intra-regional trade and investment activity. The creation of a world-class physical infrastructure in Asia and in its individual economies would, on the one hand, help expand manufacturing activity in South Asian countries where it is relatively underdeveloped. On the other hand, it would help raise productivity levels in the service sector in East Asian economies. Both would enhance intra-regional economic activity in Asia, which is necessary for the global economy to return to the pre-crisis growth trend.

The strengthening of regional economic activity in Asia will provide necessary external demand stimulus for the U.S. economy. The phase of providing fiscal stimulus in the United States will have to be wound down in the coming years as the rising debt-to-GDP ratio tests market confidence. The United States cannot sustain the current levels of fiscal and external account deficits. This will imply a reduction in its domestic demand, especially in U.S. consumption. Rising Asian demand would compensate for the declining U.S. domestic demand and help it achieve higher economic growth and employment. Thus it is critical in the context of Asia-Pacific rebalancing that intra-regional economic activity in Asia be bolstered through higher demand for regional public goods supplemented by rising domestic demand in the current surplus economies.

COMMENT BY
YIPING HUANG

Large Asian current account surpluses, especially those of the PRC and Japan, were an important part of the growing global imbalance problem in the years preceding the 2007–09 global financial crisis. Economists and policymakers continue to debate whether insufficient saving in the United States or too much saving in Asia was a more fundamental cause of the imbalance. But most share the view that rebalancing is critical for achieving more sustainable growth of the world economy. And structural adjustments by Asian economies, especially the large Asian economies of the PRC, Japan, and India, must be a part of that global process.

Rajiv Kumar and Dony Alex suggest three fundamental approaches to rebalancing the Asian economies. First, large economies like the PRC should embark on more structural reforms in order to reduce their reliance on external markets. Second, oil-exporting countries should find ways to invest their surpluses when oil prices spike in order to generate steady future income streams. And, third, Asian economies as a whole should promote regional integration in order to boost intra-regional trade and investment flows. Specifically, Kumar and Alex propose an ASEAN+4 framework to enhance regional cooperation and an Asian Investment Bank to facilitate the development of the region's physical infrastructure.

The authors argue that these measures could boost domestic consumption and investment and thereby reduce Asia's reliance on external markets. They may also have the added bonus of providing a stronger external market for U.S. exports. Therefore, these measures, if successfully implemented, should help rebalance the regional and global economies.

My main comments can be summarized in three points. First, the causes and forms of the external imbalances among the large Asian economies such as the PRC, Japan, and India are different. It may require very different policy packages to resolve the imbalance problems in different countries. Second, not only the PRC but also many other Asian economies should make exchange rate policy adjustments to deal with the imbalances. And finally, of the three recommendations made by Kumar and Alex, structural reforms are probably the most critical for boosting domestic demand and reducing external surpluses in Asia. Here, then, I focus on the needed structural reforms for the PRC, arguably the most important surplus country in Asia.

While it is useful to analyze the large Asian economies as a group, it is critical to recognize the differences among them. The PRC and Japan, now the second and third largest economies of the world, have very large current account surpluses. However, domestic demand is driven mainly by consumption in Japan and by investment in the PRC. India's domestic demand is relatively more balanced between consumption and investment. But India actually has a current account deficit. And for understandable reasons, the authors did not look more closely at the other large Asian economies such as the Republic of Korea and Indonesia, which again differ in their economic structure and external account positions.

As the authors correctly point out, exchange rate policy was one important factor behind the external imbalances of the region, especially those of the PRC. However, they do not include exchange rate policy adjustment as an explicit policy recommendation for global rebalancing. Most Asian economies have adopted an export-led development strategy to promote economic growth. Conservative exchange rate policy has been a part of that policy strategy, which was largely responsible for the current account surpluses in Asia. Therefore, realignment of exchange rates, not only in the PRC but also in many other Asian economies, should form a part of the rebalancing efforts.

Of the three policy recommendations put forward by Kumar and Alex, structural reform is probably the most important one. Oil exporters' high savings at times of high oil prices may be difficult to eliminate. Oil exporters' total absorption is often fundamentally influenced by income expectations. In fact, domestic demand in oil-exporting countries picked up steadily in the years before the global financial crisis, following a period of sustained high oil prices. But oil prices are volatile in nature, and it is probably impossible to stabilize their income flows. While it is useful to consider some policy measures to limit oil exporters' current account surpluses or deficits, the external balances of these countries will likely continue to swing violently.

Of all the Western Pacific surplus countries, the PRC is probably the most important player in the global imbalance dynamic. The PRC's current account surpluses surged from about 3 percent of GDP in 2004 to 10.8 percent in 2007. However, they began to shrink in relative terms after that and accounted for only 3.5 percent of GDP during the first quarter of 2010. But it is too early to conclude that the PRC has successfully rebalanced its external account. The latest improvement in the PRC's external imbalance was probably a result of both structural and cyclical factors. Therefore, resolution of the PRC's external imbalance is a critical step toward successful global rebalancing.

What were the fundamental causes of the PRC's growing current account surpluses in the years leading up to the global financial crisis? As Kumar and Alex note, the literature has already offered a number of explanations, including an undervalued currency, demographic transition, and boosting saving and growth-centered economic policy. All of these factors contributed in one way or another to the PRC's structural imbalances. But the fundamental cause lies in the PRC's asymmetric liberalization approach during the reform period: complete liberalization of product markets but continued heavy distortions in factor markets.

Despite more than thirty years of market-oriented reforms, the PRC's markets for labor, capital, land, and other resources are still subject to restrictions by government policies and institutions. In the labor market, the household registration system continues to discriminate against rural residents and depress wages for migrant workers. Land is still owned by the state in the cities and by collectives in the countryside. Local government still offers substantial discounts on land use fees to manufacturing investors. Repressive financial policies include heavily regulated interest rates (often negative real interest rates), state influences on commercial banks' credit allocation, and strict capital account controls. The government still directly intervenes in the pricing of water, oil, electricity, and other resources.

Some of these distortions, such as the household registration system, are transitional phenomena and will eventually disappear as reforms continue. Others, such as low energy prices, are introduced deliberately by the government in order to support domestic economic activity. These distortions generally depress the prices of production factors and therefore reduce production costs. These distortions reached the highest level in 2006, above 10 percent of GDP. Such distortions are producer- or investor-subsidy equivalents. They artificially raise profits from production, increase returns to investment, and improve the competitiveness of Chinese exports. With such "subsidies" to production, investment, and exports, the PRC managed to temporarily boost economic growth but at the same time suffered structural imbalances.

One natural consequence of such distortions is depressed household income. The share of household income in GDP declined by more than 10 percentage points during the first decade of the twenty-first century. Over the same period, income shares of the corporate sector and the government rose significantly. Such changes in the broad income distribution pattern were probably a more fundamental explanation of the PRC's weak domestic consumption and high corporate saving in recent years. The combination of these two factors naturally results in large current account surpluses.

When the Wen Jiabao government took office in 2003, it immediately recognized the risks of structural imbalances, including large current account surpluses, for growth prospects. Over the next seven years, the government adopted various measures to reduce these imbalance problems. It eliminated agricultural taxes, provided income supports for both the rural and urban poor populations, and strengthened the social security systems in order to boost consumption. It relied on administrative tools of the National Development and Reform Commission to control the pace of investment growth. It also adjusted export tax rebates and appreciated the currency modestly to narrow external imbalances.

Unfortunately, after seven years of policy efforts, all the imbalance problems became worse: the consumption share is lower, the investment share is higher, and the current account surplus is larger. The key reason for this fantastic policy failure is that the government relied mainly on administrative measures. Adjustments to the incentive structure were quite limited. If incentives for producers, investors, and exporters remain extraordinarily high, it is hard to expect changes in their behavior or changes in the economic structure.

Therefore, while I agree with Kumar and Alex that structural reforms are key for rebalancing the Chinese economy, reducing the PRC's current account surpluses requires a comprehensive package, including a change in the government's overemphasis on the growth target and reform of the exchange rate policy. But liberalization of the factor markets should form a core part of that policy package.

Fortunately, the government has already started its efforts to liberalize the factor markets. In late 2009, it began to let market forces play a greater role in determining water and energy prices. It also began experimenting with reform of the household registration system in various cities. Financial liberalization, including capital account liberalization, also accelerated. In June 2010, the People's Bank of China restarted its efforts to allow greater exchange rate flexibility, although so far moves in the bilateral exchange rate against the U.S. dollar remain very limited.

Some changes in economic fundamentals also accelerated adjustments of production costs. The demographic transition, for instance, is pushing the economy rapidly toward the Lewis turning point, where the economy transitions from labor surplus to labor shortage. In early 2010, most provinces raised their minimum wage by between 15 and 20 percent. Raising wages has been an ongoing process since 2004, disrupted only briefly by the global financial crisis in 2007–09. A rapid increase in labor costs could substantially reduce the implicit "subsidy" to producers and exporters. It also will put more income into household budgets and therefore should be favorable for future consumption growth. In fact, in 2009 the consumption share of GDP saw its first uptick in many years.

Like liberalization of the product markets, liberalization of the factor markets could take years to complete. But as long as the Chinese government stays on this reform path, it should be able to remove one very important cause of the PRC's external imbalance and contribute to the much-needed global rebalancing.

References

Agarwala, Ramgopal. 2008. "Towards an 'Asian Bretton Woods' for Restructuring of the Regional Financial Architecture." Research and Information System for Developing Countries (RIS) Discussion Paper 133. New Delhi (March 2008).

Aiyar, Swaminathan, and S. Anklesaria. 2009. "An International Monetary Fund Currency to Rival the Dollar?" Washington: Cato Institute.

Antràs, Pol, and Ricardo J. Caballero. 2007. "Trade and Capital Flows: A Financial Frictions Perspective." Working Paper 13241. Cambridge, Mass.: National Bureau of Economic Research.

Asian Development Bank. 2009. *Asian Development Outlook 2009.* Manila, Philippines.

Asian Development Bank (ADB) Institute Report. 2009. "Infrastructure for a Seamless Asia." ADB Institute, Tokyo.

Bagnai, Alberto. 2009. "The Role of China in Global External Imbalances: Some Further Evidence." *China Economic Review* 20: 508–26.

Bergsten, C. Fred. 2007. "How to Solve the Problem of the Dollar." Op-ed in the *Financial Times,* December 11, 2007.

———. 2009a. "The Dollar and the Deficits." *Foreign Affairs* 88 no. 6 (November/ December).

———. 2009b. "The Dollar and the Budget Deficit." November 27, 2009 (VoxEu.org).

———. 2010. "How Best to Boost U.S. Exports." Op-ed in the *Washington Post,* February 3, 2010.

Bernanke, Ben S. 2005. "Remarks by Governor Ben S. Bernanke: The Global Saving Glut and the U.S. Current Account Deficit." The Sandridge Lecture. Virginia Association of Economists, Richmond, Va., March 10.

Blanchard, Olivier. 2009, "Sustaining a Global Recovery." *Finance and Development* 46 (September): 9–12.

Blanchard, Olivier, and Gian Maria Milesi-Ferretti. 2009. "Global Imbalances: In Midstream?" Washington: IMF Staff Position Note (December).

Caballero, Ricardo J. 2009. "The 'Other' Imbalance and the Financial Crisis." Bank of Italy's Paolo Baffi Lecture, December 10.

Caballero, Ricardo J., Emmanuel Farhi, and Pierre-Olivier Gourinchas. 2008. "An Equilibrium Model of 'Global Imbalances' and Low Interest Rates," *American Economic Review* 98 no. 1 (March): 358–93.

Congressional Budget Office (CBO). 2010. "The Budget and Economic Outlook: Fiscal Years 2010 to 2020." Washington.

Cooper, Richard N. 2007. "Living with Global Imbalances." *Brookings Papers on Economic Activity* 2: 91–110.

Corden, W. Max. 2009. "China's Exchange Rate Policy, Its Current Account Surplus, and the Global Imbalances." *Economic Journal* 119, no. 541: 103–19.

Dooley, Michael P., David Folkerts-Landau, and Peter Garber. 2004. "The Revived Bretton Woods System: The Effects of Periphery Intervention and Reserve Management on Interest Rates and Exchange Rates in Center Countries." Working Paper 10332. Cambridge, Mass. National Bureau of Economic Research.

Eichengreen, Barry. 2004. "Global Imbalances and the Lessons of Bretton Woods." Working Paper 10497. Cambridge, Mass.: National Bureau of Economic Research.

———. 2006a. "The Development of Asian Bond Markets." In *Asian Bond Markets: Issues and Prospects,* BIS Papers 30: 1–12. Basle: Bank for International Settlements.

———. 2006b. "Global Imbalances and the Asian Economies: Implications for Regional Cooperation." Working Paper on Regional Economic Integration 4. Manila, Philippines: Asian Development Bank.

———. 2006c. "The Blind Men and the Elephant." *Issues in Economic Policy* 1 (January 2006). Washington: Brookings.

———. 2009. "The Dollar Dilemma: The World's Top Currency Faces Competition." *Foreign Affairs* 88, no. 5.

Frieden, Jeffry A. 2009. "Global Imbalances, National Rebalancing, and the Political Economy of Recovery." Working Paper. New York: Council on Foreign Relations, Centre for Geopolitical Studies and International Institutions and Global Governance Program.

Gruber, Joseph W., and Steven B. Kamin. 2008. "Do Differences in Financial Development Explain the Global Pattern of Current Account Balances?" International Finance Discussion Paper 923. Washington: Federal Reserve.

Henning, C. Randall. 2009. "The Future of the Chiang Mai Initiative: An Asian Monetary Fund?" Policy Brief PB09-5. Washington: Peterson Institute for International Economics.

International Monetary Fund (IMF). 2006. "Oil Prices and Global Imbalances." Chapter 2 in *World Economic Outlook (WEO).* Washington (April).

———. 2009. *World Economic Outlook.* Washington.

———. 2010a. "Does Asia Need Rebalancing?" Chapter in *Regional Economic Outlook (REO), Asia and Pacific.* Washington (April).

———. 2010b. *World Economic Outlook.* Washington.

Ito, Hiro. "U.S. Current Account Debate, with Japan Then, with China Now." *Journal of Asian Economics* 20: 294–313.

Kondo, Masanori. 2006. "Japan and an Asian Economic Community." RIS Discussion Paper 106. New Delhi: Research and Information System for Developing Countries.

Kumar, Nagesh. 2005. "Towards a Broader Asian Community: Agenda for the East Asian Summit." RIS Working Paper 100. New Delhi: Research and Information System for Developing Countries.

———. 2007. "Towards Broader Regional Cooperation in Asia." RCC Discussion Paper. Colombo, Sri Lanka: UNDP Regional Centre in Colombo.

Lee, Jaewoo, Pau Rabanal, and Damiano Sandri. 2010. "U.S. Consumption after the 2008 Crisis." Washington: IMF Staff Position Note SPN/10/01 (January).

Lin, Justin Y. 2009. "Global Financial Crisis and Paradigm Shift in Both Sides of the Global Imbalance." Edward K. Y. Chen Distinguished Lecture Series. University of Hong Kong.

Ma, Guonan, and Zhou Haiwen. 2009. "China's Evolving External Wealth and Rising Creditor Position." Working Paper 286. Basle: Bank for International Settlements.

Mundell, Robert. 2005. "The Case for a World Currency." *Journal of Policy Modeling* 27: 465–75.

———. 2009. "Financial Crises and the International Monetary System." Paper presented at Columbia University, March 3.

Obstfeld, Maurice, and Kenneth Rogoff. 2009. "Global Imbalances and the Financial Crisis: Products of Common Causes." Paper prepared for the Federal Reserve Bank of San Francisco Asia Economic Policy Conference, Santa Barbara, Calif., October 18–20.

Persaud, Avinash. 2004. "When Currency Empires Fall." Gresham College Lecture Series, London, July 10.

Portes, R. 2009. "Global Imbalances." In *Macroeconomic Stability and Financial Regulation: Key Issues for the G20,* edited by M. Dewatripont, X. Freixas, and R. Portes (www.voxeu.org/G20_ebook.pdf).

Prasad, Eswar S. 2009a. "Is the Chinese Growth Miracle Built to Last?" *China Economic Review* (Elsevier) 20, no. 1 (March): 103–23.

———. 2009b. "Rebalancing Growth in Asia." Working Paper 15169. Cambridge, Mass.: National Bureau of Economic Research (July).

Prasad, Eswar, and Grace Gu. 2009. "An Awkward Dance: China and the United States." IZA Policy Paper 13. Bonn: Institute for the Study of Labor (IZA).

Rodrik, Dani. 2010. "Making Room for China in the World Economy." *American Economic Review,* Papers and Proceedings (May 2010): 89–93.

Sundaram, P. 2009. *ASEAN Economic Community.* ASEAN Annual Report 2008–09.

Urata, Shujiro, and Misa Okabe. 2007. "The Impacts of Free Trade Agreements on Trade Flows: An Application of the Gravity Model Approach." Discussion Paper 07052. Tokyo: Research Institute of Economy, Trade, and Industry (RIETI).

Urata, Shujiro, and Takashi Terada. 2008. "Japan and East Asian Integration: ASEAN+3 or ASEAN+6?" Paper presented at the annual meeting of the ISA's 49th Annual Convention, San Francisco.

U.S.-China Business Council (USCBC). 2009. "The U.S. Trade Deficit: Is China the Problem?" Washington: USCBC.

Wadhwa, Deepika. 2009. "Assessing the Potential for Growth of Intraregional Trade in South Asia." In *Challenges and Opportunities of Trade and Financial Integration in Asia and the Pacific.* Bangkok: UNESCAP.

Wei, Shang-Jin. 2010. "The Mystery of Chinese Saving." February (voxeu.org).

Wolf, Martin. 2009. "Why China's Exchange Rate Policy Concerns Us." *Financial Times,* December 8.

Williamson, John. 2009. "Why SDR Could Rival the Dollar." Policy Brief PB09-20. Washington: Peterson Institute for International Economics.

Yongding, Yu. 2007. "Global Imbalances: China's Perspective." Prepared for the International Conference "European and Asian Perspectives on Global Imbalances." Beijing, July 12–14, 2006.

FOUR

G-20 Financial Reforms and Emerging Asia's Challenges

MASAHIRO KAWAI

One important lesson of the global financial crisis that began in 2007 is that a systemic crisis that affects a country's overall financial system is very costly, not only in terms of fiscal resources—mobilized to counteract the economic downturn and support the financial system—but also in terms of output and employment lost. Policymakers should therefore make every effort to avoid a systemic financial crisis and maintain financial stability by pursuing sound macroeconomic and regulatory policies, identifying systemic risks when they emerge, and acting on them to reduce the likelihood of a crisis.

The crisis devastated the economies of the United States and Europe, and severely affected the Asian economies through the trade channel. Global economic recovery is under way at this writing in late 2010. However, the continuation of the recovery is not certain, and there is a risk of a "double dip" due to the sovereign debt crises in Greece, Ireland, and a few other southern European countries in the euro zone, as well as high unemployment, subdued household consumption, and a sluggish commercial real estate sector in the United States. The bright side of the global economy is that a solid recovery is taking hold in emerging Asia, particularly in the People's Republic of China (PRC, henceforth), India, and the Association of Southeast Asian Nations (ASEAN) countries.

Most Asian financial systems have not been significantly affected by the global financial crisis for three reasons. First, Asian authorities undertook significant supervisory and regulatory reforms in the wake of the 1997–98 financial crisis to improve their banks' balance sheet quality—

as exemplified by low nonperforming loans, high capital ratios, and low leverage—and risk management practices. Second, Asian economies have reduced short-term external debt while accumulating sizable foreign exchange reserves, which has helped enhance their capacity to respond to external shocks. Third, Asian financial firms have taken a conservative approach to risk taking and business—such as eschewing the use of sophisticated derivatives, expanded securitization businesses, and the origination and sale of complex structured instruments to investors. This is partly due to the authorities' prudent—but often tight—regulation and supervision.

Nevertheless, Asian monetary and financial authorities need to respond to new challenges posed by the global financial crisis and the recent regulatory reforms pursued in the G-20 process. With the further liberalization of financial market activities and opening up of financial markets to foreign firms, emerging Asia's financial services and business activities are expected to become more sophisticated and complex, which will pose additional challenges. Authorities need to continuously upgrade their technical and analytical capacity to effectively regulate and supervise financial firms and markets so as to promote both financial innovation and stability.

In the rest of this chapter I summarize the progress on financial system reforms achieved as a result of the G-20 process and argue that emerging Asia benefits from such progress but should properly balance the need to develop financial markets and promote financial stability. I then discuss the challenges of further developing and deepening emerging Asia's financial sectors and upgrading financial regulation and supervision. Finally, I address the issue of managing capital inflows and maintaining macroeconomic and financial stability under volatile global financial conditions.

Progress on Financial System Reform through the G-20 Process

The G-20 process has focused on the reform of the global regulatory environment for financial systems including, but not limited to, the following issues:

—building stronger capital, liquidity, and leverage standards;
—addressing "too-big-to-fail" problems;
—improving regulation of the shadow banking system;

—designing macroprudential supervisory and regulatory frameworks; and

—strengthening international coordination of financial supervision and regulation.

There is some concern about the relevance of these specific issues for Asia's financial systems since their market structures, practices, and thus their needs are somewhat different from those of advanced Western economies. Nonetheless, these developments in the G-20 process will have significant implications for Asia as the region's financial systems evolve.

Capital Adequacy, Liquidity, and Leverage Standards

At the G-20 meeting in Seoul in November 2010, leaders endorsed the landmark agreement reached by the Basel Committee on Bank Supervision (BCBS) on the new bank capital and liquidity framework (see box on next page). The agreement intends to increase the resilience of the global banking system by raising the quality, quantity, and international consistency of bank capital and liquidity, constrain leverage and maturity mismatches, and introduce capital buffers above the minimum requirements that can be drawn upon in bad times.

The agreed capital standards are complex, but changes in the capital adequacy rules are expected to introduce a fair amount of counter-cyclicality into the capital rules. Once fully in place, the new rules effectively establish a required minimum range of Tier 1 capital of 6 percent to 11 percent, with a central point of 8.5 percent. In periods of strong credit growth, banks will need to achieve at least an 11 percent total capital ratio. In cyclical downturns, they can draw down their total capital ratio to 6 percent. The liquidity ratio will also reduce pro-cyclicality by capping maximum leverage.

Leverage standards have the benefit of being simpler and more transparent than capital requirements. Given that excessive reliance on short-term funding during booms—particularly when interest costs and margins were low—contributed to the fragility of the financial system, a capital charge on the maturity mismatch from the funding of asset-liability growth could help dampen banks' reliance on short-term funds and pro-cyclicality. That is, banks with medium- to long-term assets that have low market liquidity—and those that funded these assets with short-term liabilities—must hold additional capital. The additional

Main Elements of New Capital and Liquidity Requirements

Beginning on January 1, 2013, banks will be required to meet the following new minimum requirements for risk-weighted assets (RWAs): 3.5 percent common equity; 4.5 percent Tier 1 capital; and 8.0 percent total capital. On January 1, 2014, the requirements will be 4 percent common equity and 5.5 percent Tier 1 capital. On January 1, 2015, the requirements will be 4.5 percent common equity and 6 percent Tier 1 capital.

The capital conservation buffer will be phased in between January 1, 2016, and year-end 2018, becoming fully effective on January 1, 2019. It will begin at 0.625 percent of RWAs on January 1, 2016, and increase each subsequent year by an additional 0.625 percentage point, to reach its final level of 2.5 percent of RWAs on January 1, 2019.

The use of existing public sector capital injections as capital will be grandfathered until January 1, 2018. Capital instruments that no longer qualify as non-common equity Tier 1 capital or Tier 2 capital will be phased out over ten years beginning January 1, 2013.

Capital instruments that do not meet the criteria for inclusion in common equity Tier 1 will be excluded from common equity Tier 1 as of January 1, 2013.

After an observation period beginning in 2011, the liquidity coverage ratio (LCR) will be introduced on January 1, 2015. The revised net stable funding ratio (NSFR) will move to a minimum standard by January 1, 2018.

BCBS also changed the definitions of risk-weighted capital, which effectively increased the amount of required capital for a given portfolio of assets.

Source: Basel Committee for Banking Supervision (2010).

capital charge would then force banks to recognize and reserve against risks from maturity mismatches that give rise to funding liquidity risks. Thus, leverage combined with clear requirements for higher levels of equity capital will likely contribute to financial stability. The Basel III standards, as summarized in the box, will also introduce an overall leverage ratio limit by 2015.

Asia's banks would be less affected than their U.S. and European counterparts by these new capital, liquidity, and leverage requirements. This is primarily due to the fact that Asian banks' balance sheets were less damaged by the global financial crisis and would require fewer changes to meet the new standards—and partly reflects the progress achieved by reforms following the Asian financial crisis of 1997–98. Nevertheless, as Asian economies across the region grow and banks increase lending, there will be a need to increase capital in the future.

The Too-Big-to-Fail Problem and Systemically Important Financial Institutions (SIFIs)

Dealing with SIFIs   The global financial crisis demonstrated that large financial firms—because of their size, interconnectedness with other financial firms, global nature, or complexity of their business operations—can be a source of vulnerabilities or spread contagion, creating systemic risks to financial stability. In dealing with such systemically important financial institutions (SIFIs), international discussions have focused on how to (1) define SIFIs, (2) best modify regulations governing SIFIs, (3) regulate financial groups (especially cross-border groups) and close regulatory gaps and inconsistencies, and (4) resolve internationally active SIFIs with cross-border businesses.

First, it is not always clear what constitutes a SIFI that could pose systemic risk to financial markets because of size or market influence. Therefore, a set of criteria for determining classification as a SIFI would be helpful. Efforts are being made to develop indicators of systemic importance based on size, interconnectedness, and complexity at international as well as national levels.

Second, some regulatory modifications may be needed to either discourage excessive risk taking or introduce larger cushions against its consequences. For example, capital charges on large financial firms based on the nature of their business operations and their size could be introduced to rebalance incentives within firms away from an excessive concentration on riskier activities.

Third, "supervisory colleges" to aid regulators in monitoring major internationally active financial institutions have been established and now help to strengthen oversight of the largest cross-border financial firms. These colleges are addressing issues related to regulatory cooperation and information sharing (through memorandums of understanding), living wills, and contingency planning.

Fourth, it is crucial to establish a special resolution mechanism for SIFIs so that damage to the financial system and the economy can be mitigated should they fail. This is the most fundamental approach to the too-big-to-fail problem. An important challenge is to establish an internationally agreed resolution mechanism for SIFIs with significant cross-border operations.

The G-20 Decision   Leaders at the G-20 meeting in Seoul reaffirmed the view that no firm should be too big or too complicated to fail and that taxpayers should not bear the costs of resolution. They endorsed the Financial Stability Board (FSB) proposal to reduce the moral-hazard risks posed by SIFIs and address the too-big-to-fail problem. This requires a multipronged framework combining:

—a resolution framework and other measures to ensure that all financial institutions can be resolved safely, quickly, and without destabilizing the financial system and exposing taxpayers to the risk of loss;
—a requirement that SIFIs—initially in particular financial institutions that are globally systemic (G-SIFIs)—should have greater capacity to absorb losses (due to required contingency capital) to reflect the greater risk that the failure of any of these firms poses to the global financial system;
—more intensive supervisory oversight;
—a robust core financial market infrastructure to reduce contagion risk from individual failures; and
—other supplementary prudential requirements as determined by the national authorities, which may include, in some circumstances, liquidity surcharges, tighter large exposure restrictions, levies, and structural measures.

The G-20 agreed to conduct rigorous risk assessment on SIFIs through international supervisory colleges and to explore possible institution-specific crisis cooperation agreements for crisis management. Regular peer reviews will be conducted by the FSB on the effectiveness and consistency of national policy measures for these firms.

Given that major global financial firms are actively operating in many parts of Asia, the region's authorities face the challenge of how best to supervise and regulate them. Several Asian authorities have opted to require them to incorporate locally so that the host authorities can exercise their own supervisory and regulatory powers over the local operations of these large global firms. In addition, large local financial firms, particularly banks, may be important nationally or regionally but relatively small globally. Most Asian financial systems are bank-centric and concentrated in a small number of financial firms, and there is often a strong state-owned presence in their banking systems. Although these banks do not necessarily pose global risks, they may pose domestic and/or regional risks. Hence there is merit in identifying local SIFIs and applying specific regulatory and supervisory oversight.

Regulating the Shadow Banking System

One of the major regulatory and supervisory deficiencies exposed by the global financial crisis was that the scope of regulation and supervision had been narrowly focused on insured deposit-taking banks and had failed to cover all financial firms and activities that were outside of such banking systems. This "shadow banking" system grew among investment banks, mortgage brokers and originators, special investment vehicles, insurance companies writing credit default swaps, hedge funds, and other private asset pools, which had long been lightly regulated by a patchwork of agencies and generally not supervised prudentially.[1] Shadow banks were not subject to the same rigorous regulations as deposit-taking banks and thus were able to avoid maintaining as much liquidity or reserves. As a result, they created a high level of financial leverage. In addition, they conducted an enormous amount of trading activity in the over-the-counter (OTC) derivatives market, which grew exponentially in the decade before the 2007–09 financial crisis.

The G-20 process has attempted to broaden the scope and increase the consistency of both global and national regulation in order to capture shadow banks within the borders of financial regulation and supervision. In the United States, all major investment banks have been converted into bank holding companies so that they are now under central bank supervision. New regulations would also require other large nonbank financial

---

1. Adrian and Shin (2009) estimated that the "shadow banking" system was as large as US$10.5 trillion, comprising US$4 trillion in assets of the large investment banks, US$2.5 trillion in overnight repos, US$2.2 trillion in structured investment vehicles, and another US$1.8 trillion in hedge fund assets. This should be compared with US$10 trillion in assets held in the conventional U.S. banking system, which meant that system leverage was at least double what was reported.

U.S. regulators could not detect the growth of the "shadow banking system" owing to the highly fragmented nature of the U.S. regulatory and supervisory framework; bank supervision was divided among five federal agencies (Federal Reserve, Federal Deposit Insurance Corporation, Office of the Comptroller of the Currency, Office of Thrift Supervision, and National Credit Union Administration) and the states; insurance companies were supervised at the state level; investment banks were supervised by the Securities and Exchange Commission; and derivatives trading in organized exchanges was supervised by the Commodity Futures Trading Commission; over-the-counter derivatives were under no agency supervision.

firms to be placed under tighter regulation and closer supervision. Other efforts have been undertaken, with reforms made to increase transparency and improve coordination among the relevant authorities.

These efforts include measures to improve transparency and regulatory oversight of hedge funds and OTC derivatives in an internationally consistent and nondiscriminatory manner, recognizing the importance of a level playing field. More specifically the G-20 leaders reaffirmed the commitment to trade all standardized OTC derivative contracts on exchanges or electronic trading platforms, where appropriate, and clear through central counterparties (CCPs) by the end of 2012.

However, these efforts are in no way sufficient, and the potential for regulatory gaps remains, which would allow the shadow banking system to continue without significant changes in its activities or its oversight. Recognizing this, the G-20 leaders called on the FSB to work in collaboration with other international standard-setting bodies to develop recommendations to strengthen the regulation and oversight of the shadow banking system by mid-2011.

Emerging Asia does not have many examples of the sophisticated types of shadow banks that have plagued the financial stability in advanced economies. Nonetheless, there are many nonbank financial firms that operate outside the formal banking system, including finance companies (which played an important role in the Thai financial crisis in 1997), merchant banks (which played a key role in the Korean financial crisis in 1997), real estate finance companies, and consumer credit firms, in addition to securities firms and insurance firms. Asia has to be fully aware that regulatory balkanization and gaps in oversight could create risks to financial stability, and it needs to construct new regulatory regimes that are capable of overseeing the entire financial system in a broad and integrated manner.

Macroprudential Supervision and Regulation

The global financial crisis revealed that the financial authorities had failed to identify where the ultimate financial risks in the system lay because the use of various risk-shifting instruments made them difficult to track. They overestimated the system's ability to withstand a large adverse shock. This reflected two problems. First, authorities appeared to assume—incorrectly—that the traditional "bottom-up" approach of microprudential regulation and supervision of individual firms was sufficient. Second, regulators focused on their specific areas of responsibility, and no central organization was in charge of either assessing risks to the entire financial system or economy, or monitoring areas outside of the regulatory boundary, such as the shadow banking sector. After the crisis erupted, a third problem emerged: the authorities did not have the legal authority and tools to respond to the crisis promptly and adequately, either preemptively or ex post. For example, the U.S. Federal Reserve did not have the authority to resolve nonbank SIFIs. Finally, there was no organizational structure in place for coordinating information, assessing financial vulnerabilities, and deciding on and implementing regulatory actions. Those responsible for macroeconomic stability have claimed that they can do little more than warn the government and the financial system of emerging dangers, given their lack of legal power to intervene.

The aim of macroprudential supervision and regulation is to remedy these shortcomings. Macroprudential supervision attempts to provide a "top-down" framework for identifying risks in the financial system as a whole, and for regulating the system through an organizational framework and process to manage those risks in a timely way.

In the United States and Europe, undetected systemic risks arose for a number of reasons, including the widespread use of sophisticated derivative financial products that transferred risks around the system; the development of the inadequately regulated shadow banking system; an excessive reliance on wholesale funding by banks; under-capitalization of banks; and a lack of understanding of the riskiness of complex financial products. These factors, on the whole, did not apply to Asian financial systems during the crisis, and, on the whole, this explains why those economies did not suffer financial crises and recovered relatively quickly.

In theory, the ideal approach to macroprudential supervision and regulation would be to assign responsibility for managing systemic risk to a "systemic stability regulator," whose tasks would include:

—monitoring systemic risks—such as large or growing credit exposure to real estate across firms and markets;

—assessing the potential for deficiencies in risk-management practices, broad-based increases in financial leverage, or changes in financial markets/products;

—analyzing possible spillovers among financial firms or between firms and markets—for example, through the mutual exposure of highly interconnected firms;

—identifying possible regulatory gaps, including gaps in the protection of consumers and investors;

—curtailing systemic risks across the entire financial system—through legislative action, prudential measures, advising on monetary policy, and intervention in individual institutions; and

—issuing periodic reports on the stability of the financial system.

In practice, although the method of managing systemic risk would be driven by existing institutional arrangements, success would require significant inputs from the central bank, financial regulators, and the finance ministry. The stability regulator needs to be adequately funded and staffed, and should be supported by political and legal authority (see Kawai and Pomerleano 2010). It needs the legal power to collect information about systemic risk, as well as discretionary tools that can be used to supplement automatic countercyclical stabilizers. Such tools could include standards for loan-to-value ratios for lending, reserve requirements, increased margin and collateral calls, and restrictions on capital flows. Many Asian authorities have long intervened actively in the financial markets in a macroprudential way, without having systematic frameworks. Therefore, the main challenge for them is to systematize these practices and craft a comprehensive structure for managing them.

International Coordination of Financial Regulation and Supervision

As financial activity becomes increasingly global, there is a stronger need for international coordination of financial regulation and supervision. While creating a World Financial Organization (Eichengreen 2009) may be a difficult task, it is becoming increasingly important to establish a global framework that will mandate across jurisdictions minimum consistency in regulatory principles that would apply to similar markets, institutions, services, and products. The International Monetary Fund (IMF) and the FSB, in cooperation with regional financial and other bodies, can play an important role in such coordination.

International Coordination of Macroeconomic-Financial Surveillance and Macroprudential Policies   A key area of international coordination is the prevention of systemic crisis through concerted macroeconomic-financial surveillance and implementation of macroprudential policies.

Some of the challenges emerging today are to reduce both the procyclicality of financial market activities and the risks from boom and bust cycles in the credit and other financial markets. Credit cycles and business cycles tend to be associated with each other within a country, and they are also increasingly synchronized around the world as a result of rising international trade and capital flows. Policies to "lean against the wind" with countercyclical regulation in one country, or even one region, would be more effective if such actions were coordinated across major economies with similar cycles (Atlantic Council 2010).

It is important to strengthen macroeconomic-financial surveillance at the country level, as well as internationally, so as to detect the emergence of systemic financial risks like credit booms and asset price bubbles. For this purpose, IMF surveillance should be enhanced to focus on both national and international systemic risks and vulnerabilities. Its analytical capacity needs to be enhanced to assess domestic macroeconomic and financial links and international spillover effects of economies' shocks and policies. IMF efforts should be closely coordinated with the work of the FSB, which is best positioned to coordinate national macroprudential supervision in order to achieve global financial stability.

Need for Internationally Aligned Insolvency Regimes for Cross-Border Firm Failures   Delays and uncertainties of policy actions during the height of the global financial crisis added market uncertainty and exacerbated contagion. For example, measures and processes for dealing with insolvent financial firms, managing creditor claims on collateral assets, or unwinding financial transactions are often designed for domestic operations. An effective resolution framework would also help forestall unilateral actions like financial ring fencing.[2] There is a clear need for better information sharing and cross-border burden sharing on losses—for example, in the case of restructuring operations, mergers, or liquidation of cross-border financial businesses.

It is encouraging that the G-20 leaders agreed that globally systemically important financial institutions (G-SIFIs) should be subject to a sustained process of mandatory international recovery and resolution planning, and reaffirmed the commitment made in June 2010 at the Toronto G-20 summit to national-level implementation of the BCBS's cross-border resolution recommendations.

Financial System Reforms in Emerging Asia

Emerging Asia faces the significant challenge of maintaining the momentum of reform efforts—starting from the post–Asian financial crisis period—to further develop and deepen the region's financial systems, while at the

2. Financial "ring fencing" means the legal walling off of specific assets or liabilities within a jurisdiction or a financial firm.

same time upgrading regulatory and supervisory frameworks to maintain financial stability. The region's underdeveloped financial systems remain an important hurdle to funding development objectives and achieving sustained growth, especially for infrastructure investment and small- and medium-sized enterprise (SME) activity.

Financial Market Development in Emerging Asia

One primary cause of the Asian financial crisis of 1997–98 was financial sector weakness across the Asian economies. This weakness included: the predominance of the banking sector in the financial system and the underdevelopment of markets for long-term funding, such as local-currency bond markets; inadequate regulatory and supervisory frameworks and risk management culture on the part of banks; and poor corporate governance of both banks and their corporate borrowers. As a result, authorities in the region have been focusing on strengthening the banking sector, developing capital—particularly local-currency bond—markets, upgrading financial regulatory and supervisory frameworks, and improving corporate governance.

It is noteworthy that the global financial crisis that originated in the United States barely dented Asian banking systems' balance sheets. This is partly due to the fact that Asian authorities had undertaken significant supervisory and regulatory reforms over the previous ten years that helped improve the quality of balance sheets and risk management practices of their banks; in addition, Asian financial firms have taken a conservative approach to risk taking—illustrated by their not utilizing sophisticated derivatives, expanding securitization businesses, or providing complex structured instruments to investors.[3]

Key indicators of the quality of banks' balance sheets suggest that these efforts have been successful. As shown in figure 4-1, the ratios of nonperforming loans (NPLs) to total loans by the banking systems in emerging Asia and Japan dropped significantly from high levels in 2000 to below 5 percent in 2009. For some economies, such as Indonesia, the PRC, and the Philippines, the fall in the NPL ratio was dramatic. Other banking soundness indicators also show that Asia's banking system is healthy (see

---

3. Another reason for the limited impact of the global financial crisis on Asia's financial systems was that Asian economies had reduced their short-term external debt while accumulating sizable foreign exchange reserves, which helped enhance their capacity to respond to external shocks.

FIGURE 4-1. Nonperforming Loan Ratios of Asian Economies, 2000–09

Percent of total loans

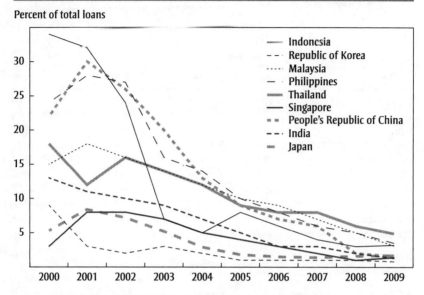

Source: IMF, *Global Financial Stability Report*, various issues; and national authorities.

table 4-1). The ratio of bank regulatory capital to risk-weighted assets remained above 10 percent for all Asian economies, except for Taipei, China. The Republic of Korea (Korea, henceforth) and Thailand reported a healthy improvement, with its bank capital ratio rising from less than 8 percent in 2000 to more than 11 percent in 2009. The ratios of bank provisions to NPLs also rose significantly over the period 2000–09.

Authorities in the region have paid attention to the development of their capital markets. As a result, both stock market capitalization and the total stock of bonds outstanding expanded rapidly, and Asia is achieving a more balanced financial system than in the past (see table 4-2). Nonetheless, the banking sector remains larger than the non-bank financial sector or the bond market in all Asian economies, while in Hong Kong, China; India; and Indonesia stock market capitalization exceeds banking sector assets.

One aspect of capital market development emphasized over the past decade is the provision of adequate protection to investors. Authorities in the region have promoted good corporate governance by introducing

TABLE 4-1. Banking Soundness Indicators, 2000 and 2009
Percent

Economy	Ratio of nonperforming loans to total loans		Ratio of bank regulatory capital to risk-weighted assets		Ratio of bank provisions to nonperforming loans	
	2000	2009	2000	2009	2000	2009
People's Republic of China	22.4	1.6	13.5	10.0	4.7	115.0
Hong Kong, China	7.3	1.3	17.9	16.8	—	—
India	12.8	2.4	11.1	13.2	—	52.6
Indonesia	20.1	3.3	21.6	17.4	36.1	127.4
Republic of Korea	6.6	0.8	6.7	11.4	81.8	125.2
Malaysia	8.3	1.8	11.3	13.5	57.2	95.6
Philippines	15.1	3.0	16.2	16.0	43.6	112.3
Singapore	3.4	2.5	16.4	13.5	87.2	91.0
Taipei,China	5.3	1.2	10.8	8.6	24.1	95.7
Thailand	17.7	4.8	7.5	11.7	47.2	99.4
Mean	11.9	2.3	13.3	13.2	47.7	106.0
Median	10.5	2.1	12.4	13.3	45.4	99.4
Memo						
Euro zone	—	2.4	—	8.3	—	—
Japan	5.3	1.9	11.7	15.8	35.5	27.1
United States	1.1	5.4	9.4	11.7	146.4	58.3

Source: IMF, *Global Financial Stability Report,* various issues; and national authorities. Adapted from Arner and Park (2010).

guidelines that listed companies must follow. Some countries have strengthened their laws and regulations to enhance protection of retail investors. For example, Thailand passed the Class Action Act, which enables retail investors to sue financial institutions for misconduct and illegal activities. Singapore regulates real estate–related financial instruments to protect less-educated retail investors. The PRC has developed a monitoring and early warning system for the capital market. In addition, it regulates the risk exposure of securities companies and sets the qualifications for players in the innovative financial market.

Banking Sector Reform

Implementation of Basel II A major reform undertaken by financial authorities in Asia to strengthen their banking systems is the adoption of the Basel II framework. More specifically, they are in the process of imple-

TABLE 4-2. Size and Composition of Financial Systems
Percent of GDP

	Financial sector assets							
	Deposit-taking financial institutions		Nonbank financial institutions		Stock market capitalization		Total bonds outstanding	
Economy	2000	2009	2000	2009	2000	2009	2000	2009
People's Republic of China	157.2	200.6	5.1	5.8	48.9	82.7	16.9	52.3
Hong Kong, China	505.5	651.7	188.3	459.0	368.3	1,093.9	35.8	68.4
India	64.5	103.5	15.6	29.0	69.9	205.2	24.6	48.8
Indonesia	63.6	34.7	8.7	11.4	16.2	39.8	31.9	18.2
Republic of Korea	130.5	158.6	41.9	67.3	27.8	100.3	66.6	122.7
Malaysia	154.2	211.5	41.4	99.9	120.6	149.5	73.3	96.5
Philippines	99.2	83.1	23.9	20.0	33.3	53.6	27.6	39.2
Singapore	646.3	643.7	76.6	83.9	167.3	271.7	48.0	84.7
Taipei,China	256.0	295.6	29.4	92.2	75.9	173.5	37.7	57.5
Thailand	132.3	146.6	10.7	41.1	23.8	67.1	25.3	67.0
Mean	221.0	253.0	44.2	92.0	95.2	223.7	38.8	65.5
Median	143.2	179.6	26.6	54.2	59.4	124.9	33.8	62.2
Memo								
Euro zone	230.9	315.6	157.8	214.5	79.6	56.5	87.9	114.4
Japan	510.8	541.8	274.7	291.3	67.6	69.7	97.4	189.6
United States	79.6	107.9	279.3	314.1	152.1	105.8	138.0	175.8

Source: IMF, *Global Financial Stability Report*, various issues; and national authorities. Adapted from Arner and Park (2010).

menting Pillar 1 of Basel II to control the risks of failure of individual banks. Some countries, such as the PRC, the Philippines, Indonesia, and Malaysia, have gone further by implementing Pillar 2 (a supervisory review process) and Pillar 3 (market discipline) of Basel II.

The time frame for the implementation of Pillar 1 varies across Asian countries (table 4-3). Japan and Singapore are substantially ahead of other Asian economies in implementing this pillar. The authorities have not only required their banks to implement a credit risk management system to reduce the probability of losses from future NPLs, but have also formulated plans to address both operational risk and market risk.

On the issue of managing credit risk, all Asian countries listed in the table except the PRC are expected to fully implement either the standardized approach or the internal rating based (IRB) approach not later than

TABLE 4-3. Timetable for the Implementation of Pillar 1 of Basel II

	Credit risk			Operational risk		
Country	Standardized approach	Foundation IRB	Advanced IRB	Basic indicators approach	Standardized approach	Advanced measurement approach
People's Republic of China	Not permitted	2010–13	2010–13	Undecided	Undecided	Undecided
India	2008–09	2012–14	2012–14	2008–09	2012–14	2012–14
Indonesia	2009	2010	2010	2009	2010	2011
Japan	2007	2007	2008	2007	2007	2008
Republic of Korea	2008	2008	2009	2008	2008	2009
Malaysia	2008	2010	2010	2008–10	2008–10	Undecided
Singapore	2008	2008	2008	2008	2008	2008
Thailand	2008	2008	2009	2008	2008	Not permitted

Source: Bank for International Settlements; Federal Reserve Bank of San Francisco.
Note: IRB = internal rating based.

2010. India implemented the standardized approach in 2009 and plans to implement the IRB approach between 2012 and 2014. Unlike other countries, the PRC does not permit its banks to apply the standardized approach, but it plans to implement the IRB approach between 2010 and 2013.

On the issue of managing operational risk, all Asian countries except the PRC are expected to adopt the basic indicators approach not later than 2010. All except India, Indonesia, and the PRC are expected to implement the standardized approach and advanced measurement approach not later than 2010. The PRC has not yet decided which approach it will adopt to address operational risk.

In addition, many Asian economies have also started to monitor certain types of risks that their banking systems might face. For example, the PRC has set up a mechanism for monitoring foreign investment assets, while Korea has established a bureau to control foreign exchange risk and address future problems of new NPLs. Viet Nam has focused on addressing risk arising from the mismatching of loan and deposit maturities and requires a high proportion of collateral for loans.

Other Reforms　Aside from addressing the risk of failure of an individual bank, the authorities in Asia have adopted measures to prevent systemwide failure. For instance, the PRC, Singapore, and Indonesia are developing or strengthening their financial surveillance systems. Singapore has created the Common Risk Assessment Framework and Techniques (CRAFT) to assess the impact of each individual bank on the rest of the banking system. Authorities in the PRC plan to establish a unit within the People's Bank of China that will monitor and analyze the potential impact of external financial crises and problems on the domestic banking system.

Except for the PRC, all economies in the region have deposit insurance systems, but their coverage limit varies significantly, from a low of an equivalent of US$2,696 in Viet Nam to a high equivalent to US$223,500 in Indonesia. During the height of the global financial crisis in 2008–09, some countries either hiked the deposit insurance coverage limit (the Philippines) or provided a blanket guarantee on deposits but with a timeline for exit (Malaysia, Singapore, and Thailand).

Authorities in the region have introduced reforms to address the liquidity risk that their banking systems may face, especially during times of banking stress. For instance, the PRC, India, Korea, and Singapore have introduced guidelines for liquidity management. Specifically, the PRC has established a framework aimed at maintaining adequate liquidity in commercial banks. India has enhanced its liquidity risk management guidelines based on BCBS principles for liquidity risk management and supervision. Korea requires banks to keep the won liquidity ratio higher than 100 percent. Singapore developed a system to allow banks to improve their day-to-day liquidity management.

Financial Inclusion   Asian authorities have also recognized the need to achieve more inclusive growth by making low-cost financial services accessible to a wider segment of the population so as to reduce poverty and improve the distribution of income. This objective is particularly relevant for Asia, where poverty rates are still high in some countries, and income disparities have grown in recent decades.[4] Improved access to financial services by both households and micro-, small, and medium-sized enterprises (MSMEs) would contribute to alleviating poverty in these areas.[5]

According to the Consultative Group to Assist the Poor (2009), half of the world's adult population—2.5 billion people—does not have access to savings accounts and other formal financial services. Approximately 540 million of these people are estimated to be in Asia, including 260 million in the PRC and 110 million in India. Within developing Asia, only in Thailand, Malaysia, Sri Lanka, Nepal, and Mongolia are more than 50 percent of the adult population estimated to have access to financial services.

There is abundant evidence that financial inclusion promotes economic development and reduces poverty and income inequality.[6] Pande and Burgess (2005) found a strong positive effect on rural poverty, using the "natural experiment" of new branch bank regulations in India that gives banks incentives to expand into underserved markets. However, the high cost of this expansion policy outweighed the aggregate benefits. This result suggests that the benefits from technology-enabled, lower-cost branch expansion would be larger.

---

4. The percentage of the population in poverty remains high in a number of Asian countries, including: Bangladesh (40 percent), Cambodia (30 percent), India (29 percent), and Indonesia (17 percent).

5. Supporting MSMEs is important because: (1) they are more labor-intensive than larger enterprises, and hence their expansion creates more jobs; (2) they often make up the bulk of employment in an economy; (3) they can raise competition and entrepreneurship, and hence boost the economy; and (4) if assisted to overcome credit constraints, they can be as productive as larger firms (Beck, Demirguc-Kunt, and Levine 2005).

6. Beck and others (2008) found a link between financial development, reduced income inequality, and poverty alleviation: the aggregate use of financial services—that is, deeper financial systems—appears to reduce Gini coefficients.

Asia's Framework of Macroprudential Supervision and Regulation

There is an urgent need in Asia both to strengthen microprudential supervision and regulation and to establish an effective macroprudential supervisory framework. In emerging Asia, microprudential supervision and regulation that promotes the soundness and health of individual financial firms—through the monitoring of their capital, assets, earnings, liquidity, leverage, management, and sensitivity to various risks—remains a significant challenge. This is compounded by the need to develop a macroprudential supervisory framework that focuses on economywide systemic risks.

Systemic Stability Regulation An important lesson from the global financial crisis is that monetary and macroprudential policies should play complementary roles in addressing systemic risks—such as the emergence of real estate bubbles—and that the finance ministry should become involved when injecting public funds into weak financial institutions. Specifically, the view that monetary policy should focus only on price stability without regard for asset prices and macroeconomic-financial risks is being questioned. Most Asian central banks seem to take the view that monetary policy should promote financial system stability and thereby avoid boom and bust cycles stemming from credit cycles and asset price movements. This view should be encouraged, and a mechanism should be established that allows central bankers, financial regulators, and finance ministry officials to share information about financial system risks and to coordinate policies in order to prevent the accumulation of systemic risks.

As Kawai and Pomerleano (2010) have argued, a systemic stability regulator—whether as a single entity or in the form of a council—should be created to enable authorities to work together to monitor and respond to emerging systemic risks. The stability regulator should have a clear mandate, as well as the authority, resources, and tools, to achieve the objective of maintaining financial stability.

Real estate loans are an area that the stability regulator should focus on. In Asian economies real estate loans still constitute a small proportion of total bank loans and GDP, except in Korea and Singapore. However, the ratio of real estate loans to total loans has risen as a trend since 2000, which has been associated with rising prices of real estate in most Asian economies except Japan.

Some macroprudential tools already exist, but others still need to be developed by authorities in the region. For instance, all countries in the region already have limits on the loan-to-value ratio (LTVR) for property

TABLE 4-4. Limits on Loan-to-Value Ratios for New Property Lending

Country	Maximum loan-to-value ratio for new loans	Typical loan term (years)	Mortgage type
People's Republic of China	80	10–15 (max. 30)	Adjustable rate
Hong Kong, China	70	20	Adjustable rate
Indonesia	80	15 (max. 20)	Adjustable rate
Japan	80	20–30	Adjustable rate
Republic of Korea	70	3–20	Adjustable rate
Malaysia	80	30	Adjustable rate
Philippines	70	10–20	Adjustable rate
Singapore	80	30–35	Adjustable rate
Thailand	80	10–20 (max. 30)	Adjustable rate

Source: Bank for International Settlements; Organization for Economic Cooperation and Development; Hong Kong Monetary Authority. Adapted from Cruz (2008).
Note: The adjustable rate is typically fixed for one to five years, then floats.

lending to prevent overheating in the property market (see table 4-4). As a countercyclical measure, supervisory authorities should have the power to lower the allowable ratios to contain incipient real estate price bubbles.

Aside from caps on LTVR, some countries have strengthened lending regulations for highly volatile sectors, specifically the real estate sector. For example, the Philippines has imposed a statutory limit of 30 percent on the share of real estate loans in the total loan portfolio of individual banks. India also limits real estate loan ratios but uses a different formula; it has set the maximum exposure for real estate loans at 15 percent of total deposits of individual banks. Some countries have introduced a regulatory loan-to-deposit ratio (LDR), while others have such a measure on the drawing board. For instance, the PRC and the Philippines have limited the LDR to 75 percent. Korea is planning to put a cap on the LDR at 100 percent, and Indonesia is discussing a cap ranging from 75 percent to 102 percent. Statistics suggest that—with the exception of Korea, Thailand, and Viet Nam—the LDRs of the regional economies are heading toward a level below 80 percent.

Bond Market Development

Asian authorities have undertaken initiatives to develop and deepen long-term local-currency bond markets. These markets can contribute to the efficient allocation of savings to long-term investment opportunities. Given the traditional predominance of banks in providing formal financial services, a balanced financial system would require a deep local-currency bond market.

The consequence of having bank-dominant financial systems was that Asia's financial systems could not provide a wide range of financial inter-mediation services, as in the case of advanced economies. For example, the ability of corporations to access long-term local-currency funding, and the household sector to diversify its financial assets through long-term investment opportunities to prepare for retirement, was highly limited.

The Asian financial crisis highlighted the costs of having underdevel-oped local-currency corporate bond markets. Many banks and corpora-tions borrowed short-term funds from abroad, denominated in a foreign currency, to help finance longer-term domestic investment projects. They suffered severely from the so-called "double mismatches"—in maturity and currency—when refinancing these short-term external borrowings abruptly became impossible and currencies sharply depreciated because of the sudden and dramatic withdrawals of foreign-currency-denominated short-term funds. That is, having borrowed in foreign currency with short maturities to finance local long-term investment projects, they were exposed to the risk of rapid liquidation of assets for repayment and losses due to massive exchange rate depreciation. The presence of a local-currency corporate bond market would have provided corporations with a greater opportunity to obtain long-term funds for local projects, thereby elimi-nating both the maturity and currency mismatches.

Recognizing the importance of developing local-currency bond mar-kets, authorities in emerging Asia have attempted to develop such markets by: removing policy distortions; enhancing market infrastructure to sup-port the functioning of bond markets; strengthening the regulation and supervision of capital markets in accordance with international standards and practices; and developing government bond markets that can pro-vide benchmarks for corporate bond markets.

Much progress has been achieved through regional initiatives. The Asian Bond Markets Initiative (ABMI), which was launched by the ASEAN+3 finance ministers in August 2003,[7] has helped enhance the market infra-structure for local-currency bonds and facilitate market access to a diverse issuer and investor base so that robust primary and liquid secondary markets are created in the region. The Asian Bond Fund (ABF) project—launched by the Executives' Meeting of East Asia-Pacific Central Banks

7. ASEAN+3 refers to the ten ASEAN countries plus the PRC, Japan, and Korea.

(EMEAP) in June 2003—attempted to remove impediments to the listing of local-currency bond funds through the mobilization of central bank foreign exchange reserves.[8]

Thanks to domestic reforms and collective regional efforts, emerging Asia's bond markets have deepened and regulatory and market infrastructure has been strengthened significantly since the Asian financial crisis, although liquidity remains limited. The region's share of the global bond market has more than tripled, from a mere 2.1 percent in December 1996 to 6.7 percent in March 2010. Government bonds represent about 70 percent of total bonds issued, while corporate bonds stand at 30 percent (ADB 2010). Notwithstanding the impressive development of emerging Asia's bond markets, most corporate bond markets in Asia remain small compared to the region's equity markets, with the major exception of Korea (and to a lesser extent Malaysia).

As Asia looks beyond the global financial crisis, its new challenge is to rebalance its economies away from an excessive reliance on U.S. and European Union export markets toward more regional demand–driven growth. Better-developed local-currency bond markets could facilitate the mobilization of Asian savings for Asian investment—particularly in infrastructure. They could also provide a better range of instruments for international investors wishing to invest in the region. In this way, they could make an important contribution to the necessary rebalancing of growth.

Recent Trends in Asia's Financial Integration

Although financial sector liberalization and opening have improved financial integration, progress has been slow. The region's massive savings are still largely invested in low-yielding financial assets abroad and intermediated through financial centers outside the region; thus capital allocation is not as efficient as it should be. Decades of bank-dominant financial intermediation and protection of domestic financial markets have left Asia's financial systems less connected with each other. Asia's low degree of intraregional financial integration is also a constraint on financing the region's huge infrastructure needs and SME growth.

A standard approach to assessing the extent of integration among Asian financial markets is to use price- and quantity-based indicators.

---

8. EMEAP members include eight emerging economy members (the PRC; Hong Kong, China; Indonesia; Korea; Malaysia; the Philippines; Singapore; and Thailand) and three advanced economy members (Australia; Japan; and New Zealand).

FIGURE 4-2. Variation Coefficient of Cross-Market Ten-Year Bond Yield Spreads

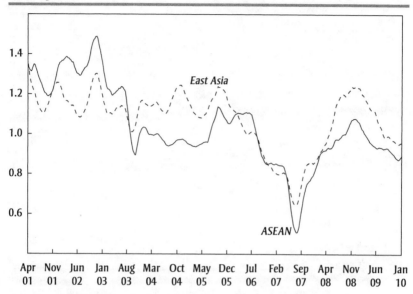

Source: Bloomberg data (accessed in January 2010).
Note: The figure shows the variation coefficient of the cross-market long-term government bond yield spreads over benchmark U.S. Treasury bonds. ASEAN includes Indonesia; Malaysia; the Philippines; Singapore; Thailand; and Viet Nam. East Asia includes the six ASEAN countries, the People's Republic of China; Hong Kong, China; Japan; the Republic of Korea; and Taipei,China.

When assets can be traded freely across a region, after adjusting for risk, prices for similar assets should become more similar: greater financial integration should therefore be accompanied by closer price co-movements. Similarly, closer financial integration implies a higher quantity of—or share of—financial assets being traded within the region and held by regional investors.

Price convergence can be measured from yields on financial assets. Over the past decade, the variation in cross-market yield spreads between long-term government bonds issued by Asian countries and U.S. Treasury bonds has sharply declined, suggesting that financial integration in Asia has deepened. As figure 4-2 shows, after declining over several years since 2001, cross-market yield spreads increased with the start of the subprime loan crisis in 2007, but have since declined. Similarly, figure 4-3 illustrates the somewhat converging trend of equity return across the region since

FIGURE 4-3. **Cross-Market Dispersions in Equity Returns**
(Using the Hodrick-Prescott smoothing technique)

Percent

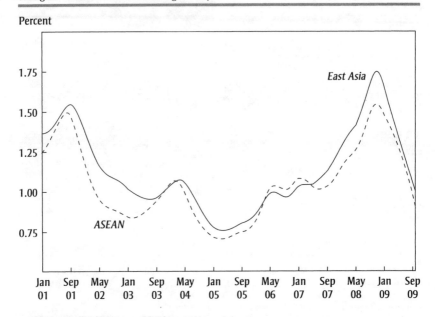

Source: Bloomberg data (accessed in January 2010).
Note: See figure 4-2 for the definitions of ASEAN and East Asia.

2001, although the crisis generated an opposite movement for some time, until convergence was restored in early 2009.

The trend of rising financial integration across Asian economies, although still low, is also shown by quantity indicators. Figure 4-4 details how cross-border portfolio holdings of assets and liabilities evolved between 2001 and 2008. Excluding Japan, the eleven emerging Asian economies for which data are available held approximately 25 percent of their foreign assets within the region in 2008, up from 15 percent in 2001. If Japan is included, the picture changes markedly (see figure 4-4). Since Japanese investors typically hold very few Asian assets (2 percent of their total foreign assets in 2008) and invest heavily in the United States, Asian countries, including Japan, hold a mere 16 percent of cross-border assets within the region (up from 10 percent in 2001) and 34 percent in the United States (down from 39 percent in 2001).

Interestingly, both Asian holdings of U.S. assets and U.S. holdings of Asian assets declined in absolute terms between 2001 and 2008, also as a

FIGURE 4-4. Asia's Cross-Border Portfolio Investments, 2001–08

Percent

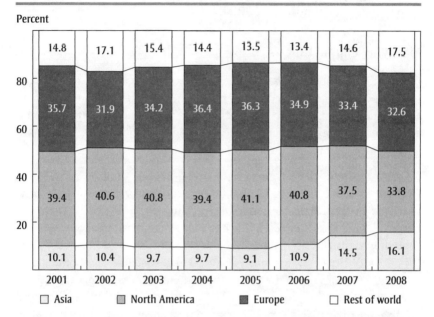

Source: Data are from a geographic breakdown provided in an IMF survey on portfolio investment started in 2001. International Monetary Fund, Coordinated Portfolio Investment Survey (2001 and 2008) (www.imf.org/external/np/sta/pi/datarsl.htm).

Note: Asia refers to twelve economies for which data are available (the People's Republic of China; Hong Kong, China; India; Indonesia; Japan; Republic of Korea; Malaysia; the Philippines; Singapore; Taipei,China; Thailand; and Viet Nam). The People's Republic of China and Taipei,China, are not included on the asset side of the survey.

share of GDP. Unfortunately, these figures for financial assets obtained from the IMF do not cover data for the PRC or Taipei,China, because they do not participate in the assets side of the survey. However, the figures on the liabilities side confirm the trend of low but increasing financial integration suggested by the assets survey.

To conclude, both price and quantity indicators show that financial integration in Asia has risen in recent years but remains low. Asian financial markets are more integrated with global ones than with each other, especially when Japan is included. In part this is due to the underdevelopment of various national markets, a lack of strong institutions and market credibility, and the presence of cross-border barriers to financial transactions. Several studies suggest that the low level of cross-border investments is also due to wide disparities in income and policy variables. To improve the integration of the region's financial markets, regional financial cooperation for market building and cross-border liberalization among Asian economies is essential.

Managing Capital Inflows

Capital inflows provide emerging market economies with invaluable benefits in pursuing economic development and growth by enabling them to finance needed investment, smooth consumption, diversify risks and expand economic opportunities. However, large capital flows, if not managed properly, can expose capital-recipient countries to at least three types of risk (Kawai and Takagi 2010):

—Macroeconomic risk. Capital inflows could accelerate the growth of domestic credit, create economic overheating, goods price inflation, and real exchange rate appreciation, thus threatening sustainable economic growth with price stability.

—Risk of financial instability. Capital inflows could create the maturity and currency mismatches in the balance sheets of private sector debtors (particularly banks and corporations), push up equity and other asset prices, and expose their balance sheets to risks of currency depreciation and asset price declines, thereby contributing to financial fragility.

—Sudden stops and/or reversals of capital flows. Capital inflows could stop suddenly or even reverse themselves within a short period, resulting in rapid reserve decumulation and/or sharp currency depreciation.

These risks are often exacerbated by the pro-cyclicality of global capital flows to emerging and developing economies. It is noteworthy that about 15 percent of the large capital inflow episodes over the past twenty years ended in crisis, with emerging Asia experiencing proportionately more episodes of hard landing (Schadler 2008), the most devastating of which occurred in 1997–98. This history underlines the point that emerging Asian economies need to manage these risks well so that they can fully enjoy the benefits of capital inflows.

Capital Flows in Emerging Asia

Net private capital inflows in the world's emerging economies have been positive over the past twenty years, but they have swung widely during the period. The two years before the Asian financial crisis saw large increases in net private capital flows, followed by a sharp fall in net inflows during

FIGURE 4-5a. Net Private Capital Flows: Emerging and Developing World

Percent of GDP

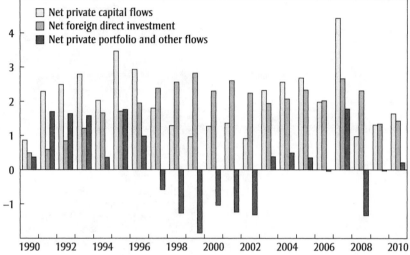

Source: IMF, *World Economic Outlook* Database (October 2010).

the crisis. The same pattern was observed before the global financial crisis, except that the net private capital inflows rose for five years and reached US$690 billion in 2007. In 2008–09, large portfolio capital outflows took place in emerging economies globally, while emerging Asia saw a sizable shift of portfolio capital flows from net outflows in 2008 to net inflows in 2009 (see figures 4-5a and 4-5b). The rapid recovery of emerging Asia from the global financial and economic crisis has made emerging Asia an attractive destination for foreign capital.

Impact of Capital Flows on Emerging Asia

The combination of persistent current account surpluses, rising capital inflows, and accumulation of foreign exchange reserves in Asia—combined with sustained U.S. current account deficits—has exerted upward pressure on the exchange rates in emerging Asia. During the period 2002–07, a clear appreciation trend was observed in many countries. The Korean won and the Thai baht appreciated steadily beginning in 2003. Other currencies in the region started to appreciate in late 2005. However, in 2008 most currencies in the region—except the Japanese yen—experienced

FIGURE 4-5b. Net Private Capital Flows: Emerging and Developing Asia

Percent of GDP

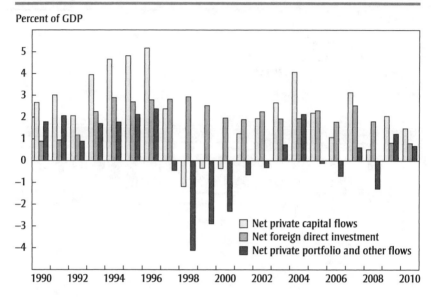

Source: IMF, *World Economic Outlook* Database (October 2010).

sharp drops in their value relative to those of major trading partners when capital flows stopped or reversed. By mid-2009, however, currencies in the region had begun appreciating again as foreign capital returned to the region.

The accumulation of massive foreign exchange reserves is one of the most significant changes in the region's landscape since the Asian financial crisis. Total foreign exchange reserves held by emerging Asian economies and Japan rose from US$268 billion (6 percent of GDP) in 1990 to US$4.1 trillion (34 percent of GDP) in 2007, with the PRC accounting for almost two-fifths of the total (see figure 4-6). The reserve accumulation by emerging Asian economies was the result of intervention in the currency market to stabilize exchange rates with the U.S. dollar. It is to be noted that in 2008 some economies in the region—notably Korea, Singapore, Malaysia, India, and Indonesia—experienced substantial declines in foreign exchange reserves from 2007 levels as a result of reversals in capital flows. The declines in foreign reserves in these economies were, however, more than offset by increases in foreign reserves in the PRC; Japan; Hong Kong, China; and Taipei,China. Foreign exchange

FIGURE 4-6. Foreign Exchange Reserves of Asian Economies, 1990–2010

Billions of U.S. dollars

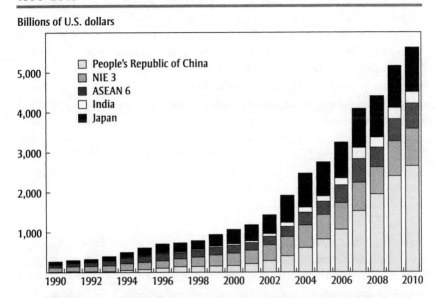

Source: Bloomberg data (accessed on December 7, 2010); IMF, International Financial Statistics.
Note: NIE 3 includes Hong Kong, China; Republic of Korea; and Taipei,China. ASEAN 6 includes Indonesia, Malaysia, the Philippines, Singapore, Thailand, and Viet Nam. Data for 2010 are from September 2010.

reserves of those economies that experienced declines in their reserves in 2008 have quickly recovered while those of other emerging Asian economies including the PRC have continued to rise. As of September 2010, total foreign exchange reserves of Asian economies stood at US$5.6 trillion, with the PRC and Japan recording US$2.6 trillion and US$1.1 trillion, respectively.

Equity prices in most emerging Asian economies increased markedly between 2003 and 2007. Indonesia, India, and the PRC showed strong equity price hikes during this period. Capital inflows to the stock markets of emerging Asia pushed up stock prices. However, there were significant reversals of the stock price booms beginning in October 2008 due to the collapse of Lehman Brothers, which caused a severe global liquidity crunch and increased risk in global equity markets. Sharp declines in equity prices were triggered by foreign investors' withdrawal of substantial investments in the stock markets in these economies. The strong recovery of emerging Asia in 2009 has generated foreign capital inflows into the region, which pushed up stock prices in the second half of 2009.

Bond yields in most emerging Asian economies started to exhibit a downward trend in 2005, particularly in Indonesia and the PRC where declines in bond yields were quite substantial. However, in other countries the timing of the start of the downward trend in bond yields was later than that of the upward trend in equity prices, presumably due to the lagged spillover effects from equity to bond markets. Most foreign capital inflows went to the stock markets, partly because emerging Asian economies had relatively underdeveloped and less open domestic bond markets. However, as stock prices rose, expected returns on equities dropped and bonds became more attractive to investors, who bid up bond prices, thus lowering bond yields. In 2008, bond yields for emerging Asian economies rose, but stabilized in the subsequent year at lower levels. In 2009, capital flows into bond markets resumed.

Policy Implications

Asia faces the challenge of dealing with volatile capital flows and large exchange rate movements. The expansion of global liquidity created by advanced economy central banks to stabilize the financial systems and stimulate domestic demand with record low interest rates—as well as quantitative easing—could push more capital, particularly of short maturity, into fast-growing emerging Asian economies.[9] This would pose serious policy challenges to emerging Asia for macroeconomic management, exchange rate policy, and financial sector supervision.

The necessary policy measures can be classified as structural, macroeconomic and macroprudential.

Structural measures   The first best solution would be to enhance the capacity of domestic financial markets to absorb large capital inflows by accelerating reforms to develop and deepen domestic financial markets and to put in place efficient market infrastructure. The presence of a deep and liquid domestic financial market would make the domestic economy more resilient to large capital inflows and outflows. In Asian emerging economies, the growth of domestic debt markets would also provide alternative channels for intermediating the ample domestic savings and foreign funds for domestic long-term investment and would help alleviate the burden put largely on the banking sector. However, this is a long-term solution.

9. In late 2010 the short-term interest rates in advanced economies ranged from close to zero (in Japan and the United States) to at most 1 percent (in the euro zone). These rates were well below those of emerging Asian economies.

Other structural measures that are effective in the short run would include the liberalization of imports and capital outflows. These measures would mitigate the upward pressure on the currency by reducing the trade balance and/or net capital inflows rather than reducing gross capital inflows per se. The policy of easing restrictions on capital outflows was pursued by a number of East Asian economies, such as Japan, Korea, and Taipei,China during earlier periods of large balance of payments surpluses. It has been adopted by China and India in recent years. It must be kept in mind, however, that a more liberal capital outflow policy could invite more capital inflows.

Macroeconomic measures   Sterilized intervention has been the favorite tool applied by many emerging Asian economies to prevent nominal exchange rate appreciation and economic overheating. Between 2000 and 2007, intervention in the foreign exchange market had been unidirectional, making sterilization an increasingly costly method of preventing overheating of the economy. Doing the same in the post-crisis period could lead to more foreign reserve accumulation, which cannot be sustained indefinitely. Hence, the need to allow greater exchange rate flexibility in times of surges in capital inflows is thus becoming more compelling. Making this an attractive policy option for the region's authorities is an important challenge.

Allowing one's currency to appreciate in response to persistent capital inflows is desirable—to better contain domestic inflationary pressure and incipient asset price bubbles and so improve macroeconomic and financial sector outcomes—because this can limit the accumulation of foreign exchange reserves, enable the central bank to pursue a more independent and prudent monetary policy, and set the ground for facilitating possible external adjustment. However, exchange rate appreciation, if pursued unilaterally, could damage the international price competitiveness of the countries concerned.

Another macroeconomic policy option would be to adopt easy monetary policy—through reducing policy interest rates—to cope with large capital inflows as this would narrow international interest rate differentials and, thus, reduce incentives for capital inflows to the economy. However, this policy option faces a few potential problems. First, easy monetary policy would be undesirable in economies where inflation rates are already high or risk accelerating. Second, easy monetary policy could increase asset prices and further invite capital inflows into the asset markets, thereby creating financial stability risks.

A third option would be to tighten fiscal policy as an instrument for managing large capital inflows, particularly when the economy shows signs of a boom. Evidence from various national experiences suggests that countries that use fiscal tightening tend to perform better than others in managing the adverse consequences of large capital inflows (Schadler 2010). Tightening fiscal policy, or more generally making the fiscal policy stance countercyclical to surges in capital inflows, has often been found to help reduce the risk of overheating the economy and the appreciation pressure on the domestic currency. But the presence of policy lags—for designing, implementing, and impacting—would reduce short-run policy effectiveness. A realistic option for emerging Asia would be to strengthen the automatic stabilizer function of the budget by establishing a strong social sector protection framework as a medium-term solution.

Macroprudential measures Macroprudential policy seeks to contain systemic financial risk by developing appropriate policy responses for the entire financial system. These measures would include countercyclical provisioning, loan to value ratio limits, loan to deposit limits, tighter liquidity requirements, and direct controls on lending to specific sectors. When these measures are targeted at cross-border credit flows—such as international borrowing by banks, nonbank financial firms, corporations, and households—or at foreign exchange markets, they are called capital controls. Examples include market-based regulations designed to reduce the incentives for capital inflows, limits on open foreign exchange positions, and constraints on the type of foreign currency assets allowed to be held or the type of cross-border investors allowed to operate.

Capital controls are an increasingly common tool for limiting capital inflows in emerging market economies. For countries that have substantially liberalized the capital account, market-based controls—such as the unremunerated reserve requirement (URR) Chile and other Latin American countries imposed on capital inflows—have been the predominant option in recent years.[10] Brazil imposed a tax on fixed-income and equity inflows in October 2009 in response to surges in capital inflows and, in the following month, imposed another tax on some trades to prevent circumvention. However, designing and implementing capital inflow controls is not an easy task. Administering capital controls requires highly

10. Thailand adopted this measure in December 2006, but encountered a severe reaction in rapidly falling stock prices, prompting the authorities to exempt stock market investments. Despite this measure, the baht continued to appreciate in 2007. The Thai authorities lifted the URR in March 2008.

competent regulatory authorities because they must constantly look out for unwanted flows—often disguised—entering through other channels. For these economies, returning to the days of draconian capital controls or recreating a system of extensive administrative controls is no longer a viable option.[11]

Evidence on the effectiveness of capital inflow controls is mixed (Kawai and Takagi 2010). Country experiences suggest that the best market-based controls can be expected to achieve is to lengthen the maturity of inflows, while exerting little impact on the overall volume. The effectiveness of capital control measures tends to weaken over time as agents in the markets find ways to circumvent them. At the same time, capital controls can produce adverse effects: they tend to increase domestic financing costs, reduce market discipline, lead to inefficient allocations of financial capital, and distort decisionmaking at the firm level.

Regional Monetary and Financial Cooperation

The consensus in the academic and policy literature is that none of the available tools to deal with large capital inflows at the individual country level is a panacea. However, in the absence of definitive national measures destined to succeed in managing excessive capital flows, one may consider the possibility of collective action at the regional level, which can expand the menu of options available to individual countries. Among the few relevant dimensions of regional cooperation in Asia are financial market surveillance and exchange rate policy coordination.

Regional Financial Market Surveillance and Integration　One of the main factors leading to the Asian financial crisis was the large inflow of short-term capital into economies with inadequately supervised financial systems in the pre-crisis period, which led to excess liquidity, overinvestment, and asset market bubbles. Once the market started to lose confidence in the sustainability of a country's exchange rate, rapid and sudden capital

11. The story may be different for countries such as the PRC and India, which have not substantially opened their capital accounts and maintain restrictions on some types of capital transactions. They have successfully managed the process of gradual capital account liberalization by adopting investor-based controls and prudential-like measures. For these countries, capital account liberalization needs to be well sequenced, proceed within an integrated framework to improve macroeconomic and financial sector management, and be accompanied by the development of institutions that can ensure markets' continued stability. See Kawai and Takagi (2010) for a discussion of the pace and sequencing of capital account liberalization and von Hagen and Siedschlag (2010) for the case of central and eastern Europe.

outflows occurred, exerting large downward pressure on the currencies and putting the brakes suddenly on overextended economic activities. The spread of the Thai baht crisis to other ASEAN countries and Korea also affected financial systems and economies throughout the region.

To prevent capital inflows from affecting financial systems, it is important for the region's policymakers to intensify their monitoring of financial markets and exchange information on a continuous basis. Once a crisis breaks out in one country, regional policy dialogue becomes even more important in mitigating the impact of investor herd behavior and financial contagion. From this perspective, the surveillance and monitoring of regional financial markets is an important area for regional cooperation.[12]

It is high time for the region to introduce institutions that would conduct meaningful financial market surveillance, identify financial sector vulnerabilities, help take concerted actions to contain them, and address other common issues for financial market deepening and integration. This could be best accomplished by establishing a new high-level Asian Financial Stability Dialogue (AFSD) on regional financial sector issues (see box on next page). Such a forum would bring together all responsible authorities—including finance ministries, central banks, and financial supervisors and regulators—to discuss regional financial market vulnerabilities, regional capital flows, common issues for financial sector supervision and regulation, and efforts at regional financial integration.

Once the region faces significant capital inflows, concerted regulatory and supervisory responses will most likely be needed. The reason is that one country's adoption of tighter prudential policies toward capital inflows—such as the capital inflow controls used by Chile—could push foreign capital to other countries. Regional monitoring of capital inflows, policy dialogue on possible responses to and consequences of capital inflows, and information exchange about regional financial sector health through the AFSD would be highly productive. Once such a forum is established and the financial authorities from different countries feel more comfortable working together to deepen collaboration, the AFSD could be encouraged to transform itself into a more systematic body, like an Asian FSB.

Regional Exchange Rate Coordination   If the loss of international price competitiveness is the reason for preventing a country's financial authorities from allowing currency appreciation, the authorities could

12. See Plummer (2010).

Asian Financial Stability Dialogue (AFSD)

To deepen regional financial integration while maintaining regional financial stability, the Asian Development Bank (2008) proposed the creation of an Asian Financial Stability Dialogue (AFSD).

This would be a regional forum that would bring together all responsible authorities—finance ministries, central banks, and financial supervisors and regulators—to address financial market vulnerabilities and strengthen financial supervision and regulation, while promoting financial market development and introducing initiatives for regional financial integration. The global financial crisis underscored the importance of establishing an effective framework for sound financial supervision and regulation to improve market governance at the national level. An important challenge for Asia's emerging economies would be to strike the right balance between pursuing national financial market development and regional financial integration on the one hand and maintaining national and regional financial stability on the other. Regional financial integration would require continued liberalization of domestic financial regulations and cross-border restrictions of financial services and financial flows in many emerging and developing economies. To address these challenges, concerted efforts are needed at the regional level.

The AFSD could help Asian financial authorities coordinate their efforts to promote regional financial stability through information exchange, the mutual recognition of market practices, and the harmonization of minimum supervisory standards. The AFSD could promote regional surveillance of macroeconomic and financial links, including capital flows and asset price movements, so as to spot emerging systemic risks—through early warning mechanisms—and act on them collectively. It could identify systemically important financial firms at the regional level and strengthen monitoring of them. To maximize its effectiveness, it should complement and coordinate with other regional institutions such as the ASEAN + 3 Macroeconomic Research Office (AMRO) that focus mainly on macroeconomic surveillance and policies, as well as monitoring policy implementation. Given that not all Asian economies are members of the FSB or BCBS, the AFSD would need to consolidate Asia's views and positions and make sure that these are heard at the FSB and other global organizations such as the Bank for International Settlements (BIS).

cooperate with other regional counterparts in similar circumstances to take the action simultaneously. Collective currency appreciation against the U.S. dollar—and possibly the euro—is a solution to this dilemma because it would allow the economies experiencing large capital inflows to maintain macroeconomic and financial stability without much affecting the international price competitiveness and, hence, the growth prospects for individual countries within Asia (Kawai 2008). Such collective appreciation would spread the adjustment costs across Asia, thus minimizing and balancing the costs from the perspective of individual economies.

Collective currency appreciation would also reinforce Asia's rising intra-regional economic interdependence, which is furthered by intra-regional exchange rate stability. It would maintain relative currency stability within the region and promote financial and macroeconomic stability, while minimizing the loss of price competitiveness for each economy.

In order for collective currency appreciation to become a viable policy option, there must be an effective mechanism of intensive policy dialogue and cooperation. The existing policy dialogue processes among the region's finance ministers (such as ASEAN+3) and central bank governors (such as EMEAP) can play a critical role in fostering the establishment of such a mechanism.

Conclusion

Lessons drawn from the global financial crisis have led to specific financial reforms at the global level. But there are also unsettled reform agendas. Many of these reforms, undertaken under the G-20 process, are expected to strengthen the financial systems of the United States and Europe, where the crisis originated. Asian economies should not view them as relevant only to these advanced economies but will have to integrate them over time in order to sustain their own economic development and growth and preserve the stability of their financial systems.

Emerging Asian economies face the enormous challenge of developing and deepening their own financial markets, which is part of the unfinished agenda posed by the Asian financial crisis. In economies with rudimentary financial systems, banking sector reform is the first priority, to expand banking businesses and facilitate efficient financial intermediation. Efforts to promote financial inclusion for both households and SMEs are also essential. In economies with sufficiently developed banking sectors, capital market development—including the development of local-currency bond markets and relatively straightforward derivatives—should be promoted in order to achieve more efficient and balanced financial intermediation. Economies with relatively deep financial systems could then be linked more fully with the global and regional financial markets through more open capital accounts and regional cooperation. These efforts could enhance the resilience of Asian economies in the face of volatile capital flows and facilitate the recycling of their large savings to finance long-term investment in the region.

The financial authorities in emerging Asia must step up financial supervision and regulation. First, the authorities need to strengthen microprudential supervision by focusing on the health and stability of individual financial firms. Second, the authorities should conduct an intensive analysis of the financial market and its interaction with the economy, so that they can identify sources of systemic risks and vulnerabilities and take the necessary macroprudential policy actions to address them. Third, they need to reexamine their monetary policy frameworks to ensure that they give adequate weight to asset prices, financial stability, and management of capital flows. Coordination between monetary and supervisory policies at the national and regional levels is essential to contain systemic risks and maintain macroeconomic and financial stability, including possibly introducing a powerful "systemic stability regulator."

Finally, given the rising financial interdependence in Asia, it is important for financial authorities in the region—regulators, central banks, and finance ministries—to work together for regional financial stability. The region should further strengthen the Chiang Mai Initiative Multilateralization and consider establishing a forum to facilitate policy dialogue and joint action among the financial authorities—the AFSD—in order to identify regional financial risks and act on them collectively. Such a forum would also be useful in providing Asian inputs to the FSB for better global financial reforms.

COMMENT BY
HASAN ERSEL

The global financial crisis of 2007–09 produced some puzzling effects. It devastated the financial sector of the developed countries that have advanced financial systems and supposedly sophisticated supervisory capabilities. In contrast, the relatively underdeveloped financial systems of the emerging Asian economies were relatively unaffected by the global financial crisis. In his chapter in this volume, Masahiro Kawai points out the role of the measures taken by these countries in response to the 1997–98 crisis and examines the development of their respective financial systems by considering their efforts at regional cooperation.

The purpose of these comments is to highlight some of the major issues raised by Kawai that may be relevant for developing countries in the other regions of the world.

Some Observations

The recent global crisis brought the following points to the world's attention:

(1) The global crisis was a major blow to the optimistic view that the advanced financial markets can sustain stability and that severe economic crises are a thing of the past for developed economies. In the early 1980s, Hyman Minsky argued that financial systems are "inherently unstable" and advocated the view that they should be carefully regulated and supervised. Minsky's concept of inherent instability did not carry a negative connotation. He was simply drawing attention to the fact that such instability is closely connected to the dynamism of the financial system. Since dynamism is an extremely valuable asset for any financial system the purpose is not to get rid of it; but to develop means to minimize its negative effects while reaping the benefits of its dynamism.[1]

(2) The financial crisis that started in the United States became a financial crisis of the developed world owing to the high degree of integration among advanced financial systems. However it fell short of being a global financial crisis since the financial systems in developing countries, in general, were not seriously affected.[2] Nevertheless, these countries were severely hit through the trade channel. This has two implications: The first

---

1. For a thorough discussion of this view, see Minsky (2008). The relation between instability and the dynamism of a system also drew the attention of engineers. For example, modern fighter planes are constructed to be "structurally unstable" in order to increase their agility.

2. Kawai makes this observation about Asian economies. The available data give the impression that it can be generalized to most developing countries in other regions of the world.

is the visible divergence between the financial systems of the developed and developing economies. The latter have a much narrower spectrum of financial instruments and markets. On the other hand, the financial systems of these countries are connected to the global financial system relatively weakly and through very few markets. As a result of these structural characteristics, the financial systems of the developing countries enjoy partial autonomy from their developed counterparts. Second, the rather strong trade channel effect clearly indicates the increased importance of a dynamic interaction between financial systems and real economies. The financial crisis in the United States and Europe affected their real economies and was transmitted through the trade channel to the developing countries. The interdependence between the financial and real sectors is not confined to the developed countries. Developing countries have achieved a much higher degree of financial sector–real economy integration than they had roughly two decades ago. Thus during the recovery period, the financial systems of "all" countries can be expected to be affected by real sector developments. Therefore Kawai's main message, that developing countries should take urgent measures to strengthen their financial systems, is both justified and important.

(3) The apparent robustness of the financial systems of the developing countries also deserves attention. It is indeed true that the previous experiences of these countries led them to introduce rather dramatic structural reforms to their financial systems and enhance the capabilities of their regulatory and supervisory authorities.[3] On the other hand, for the same reason, these countries paid considerable attention to increasing their foreign exchange reserves and reducing their short-term external debt.[4] These developments undoubtedly helped strengthen their financial systems, but those measures were not innovations; they were simply designed to achieve almost the same regulatory and supervisory standards of the developed countries. However, as the recent experience painfully demonstrated, those standards were not able to prevent a financial crisis in the

3. Asian countries introduced such reforms in the wake of 1997–98 crisis. Some other countries (such as Turkey) followed them after experiencing similar crises.

4. It should be pointed out that Asian economies distinguished themselves from most of the developing countries on these fronts. In Turkey, for example the magnitude of reserve accumulation was not as impressive as Asian economies, and was mostly in terms of borrowed reserves. On the other hand, although Turkey was quite successful in bringing down public sector foreign debt, the reverse trend was observed for the private sector. After 2001 the private sector's foreign debt as well as the share of its short-term portion increased.

developed countries. In other words, this argument, at least, partly fails to answer why such standards work for developing countries but not for developed ones.

At this point, a closer examination of the meaning of the underdeveloped nature of the financial systems of developing countries may help. Underdevelopment in this context refers both to the narrow spectrum of the financial markets and instruments and to the level of competition. The financial systems of the developing countries are less competitive than their counterparts in the developed world. They may therefore achieve higher profitability without resorting to complex financial instruments and/or contracts. However, as Kawai points out, what lies ahead for developing countries is a path that takes them to more sophisticated financial systems, although not necessarily the same ones that today's advanced economies are not happy with. Therefore, developing a satisfactory regulatory and supervisory structure to attain financial stability at the national level should be considered a common goal for both developed and developing countries. Neither group of countries can stay where they are. This point is more relevant for developing countries since, at this point in time, they have less incentive to undertake further costly reforms.

One can deduce from these points that the path to global recovery is not smooth or pain-free and that developing countries cannot hope to remain immune from the same kinds of adverse financial developments experienced by the advanced economies. Therefore devising mechanisms to establish and maintain "global financial stability" is an urgent task for all. However, it is by no means a simple task, since the problem is finding a mechanism to secure an efficient supply of a "global public good" called "global financial stability." Within this framework, Kawai addresses two issues. The first is the need to design a framework to handle the interactions between macroprudential regulation and central banking. The second is the G-20 process, which refers to the international cooperation aspect of the problem. In the rest of these comments I address some aspects of these issues.

Macroprudential Regulation and Central Banking

The recent crisis severely undermined the view that financial stability can be achieved through self-regulation and self-control by individual decisionmakers. In other words, existing regulations are insufficient to protect economies from the devastating consequences of financial instability. First, in some developed countries, violations of existing regulations were commonplace. That fact leads one to question the effectiveness of financial sector supervision in these countries. A more profound issue is the inadequacy of the microprudential regulations. By definition, these regulations are aimed at individual agents and not at the system as a whole, and consequently contribute to supervisors' failure to adequately oversee the actions of individual units. As a result, the methodological inadequacy of the existing supervision approach to detect the accumulation of excessive systemic risk is now better acknowledged.

Most central banks, on the other hand, used to devote themselves to maintaining monetary (price) stability and external stability (exchange rate management). In contrast to the financial supervisors, central banks were concerned with macro issues, albeit defined rather narrowly. For example, most central banks did not consider reacting to asset price movements to be part of their mandate. In a world where monetary stability can be used as a proxy for financial stability and microprudential regulation, and supervision is sufficient for containing systemic risks, such a division of labor may make sense. However, in the recent crisis this mechanism failed to detect the accumulation of systemic risks. Devoting themselves solely to monetary stability was not sufficient for the central banks to monitor financial stability, and microprudential regulation and supervision were inadequate to deal with systemic risk.

Acknowledging the need for macroprudential regulation and supervision inevitably raises two equally important issues. The first is the identification of the set of tools that are needed. The second is designing an efficient institutional structure for this purpose. Macroprudential instruments rely on the adoption of microprudential standards and limits on activities that may increase systemic risk. These instruments need to be adjusted in a countercyclical manner and in line with the change in risk assessment. Inevitably the use of such instruments will influence the effectiveness of the policies pursued by governments and central banks. As Kawai notes, coordination is needed among the government, the central bank, and regulatory bodies. Possible alternatives to institutionalizing coordination have been examined by Kawai and Pomerleano (2010). Whatever form is chosen for the "systemic stability regulator," the central problem of balancing the systemic risk concerns with the policy choices of either the government or the central bank remains. Under these circumstances, governments may consider an independent "systemic stability regulator" more unbearable than an independent central bank.[5] If, on the other hand, governments are allowed to control this authority, then the independence of the central bank will be at stake. The various ways to deal with systemic risk and the divergence of approaches even within the sphere of developed countries reflect the difficulty of finding a broad solution to this problem. Instead, it may be more fruitful to define the tasks of such a systemic stability regulator and let its institutional base vary according to the political, cultural, and other characteristics of each country.

The G-20 Process as a Mechanism to Secure Global Financial Stability

The G-20 does not necessarily seem like a natural forum for dealing with global public goods. It is neither a global authority nor a representative of all countries (unlike the United Nations). It is a self-appointed informal forum that can be described as "G-7 and its guests." It must be admitted, however, that when the G-20 initiative started it received considerable support from international organizations such as the IMF and was mostly welcomed even by the non-G-20 countries. In other words, despite the demonstrated interest of the UN in global financial stability,[6] the G-20 initiative apparently took the lead and still draws the attention of all interested parties.[7]

The G-20, being open to a subset of developing countries, naturally discusses and considers the needs of developed and underdeveloped financial

5. Consider an economy where the banking system is regulated and supervised. Following Bernanke and Gertler (1990) it can be shown that, in general, a regulatory body will reach a lower level of credit supply than banks' profit maximization under risk solution suggests. Assume that the output and therefore employment level is positively correlated with the credit supply. Then the regulatory body's decision will be challenged both by banks and, most likely, by the government. Therefore the conflict between a regulatory body seeking financial stability and the government seeking employment maximization can only be solved when the political authorities appreciate the importance of financial stability. Unfortunately, it usually materializes after the country has experienced the high costs of a financial crisis.

6. This is an interesting point since the G-20 process gained momentum despite the fact that the UN was quick to recognize the severity of the financial crisis and the importance of the UN taking action. The president of the UN General Assembly established a commission of experts in October 2008. Based on the report prepared by the commission, UN member states adopted a rather detailed and substantive statement in June 26, 2010. The report is published in Stiglitz (2010).

7. Although enthusiasm for the G-20 initiative seems to have partially eroded, notably in 2010, this did not trigger a search for another mechanism to replace it.

systems. But it is evident that the G-7 countries have a strong presence within the G-20,[8] and it is unrealistic to expect the G-20 to act contrary to decisions agreed to by the G-7. On the one hand the G-20, besides drawing attention to the problems of the developing world, may also play a significant role when members of the G-7 diverge in their views on global issues. On the other hand, the G-20 has no legal authority to enforce its decisions in any country, including its member countries. This invites the following question: Even if the G-20 is assumed to be a more functional forum than the G-7, is it capable of generating an efficient mechanism to secure global financial stability efficiently?

Since the G-20 does not have the legal right to enforce a set of rules on other countries, and is unwilling to do so, the implied mechanism cannot be conceived as a centralized one.[9] Therefore the problem at hand is to find a decentralized Pareto-efficient mechanism to secure global financial stability. It is not difficult to see that all decentralized mechanisms will not satisfy the efficiency condition. For example, suppose the G-20 agrees on a new set of rules and adopts them, expecting the other countries to follow. If they do, the outcome will be a Stackelberg-Nash equilibrium. As Varian (1994) showed, however, this is not a Pareto-efficient solution. The G-20 can hope to achieve a better result if it commits itself to undertake certain measures conditional on subsequent measures to be taken by the remaining countries. Such a mechanism takes into account both the needs and preferences of all related parties and also makes them aware of the direct and indirect consequences of their own choices. Boadway, Song, and Tremblay (2007) demonstrated that such a commitment mechanism, under certain assumptions, is indeed capable of generating Pareto-efficient outcomes.

8. It should be remembered that the twentieth member of the G-20 is the European Union.

9. The G-20 countries represent around 53 percent of world trade and 83 percent of world GDP (all EU countries included). It may not be misleading to assume that their share in the global financial system could be even more. Although the G-20 as a whole is a major player on a global scale, it doesn't qualify it as a sufficiently powerful agent to impose rules of the game. Following Bowles and Gintis (1992), power can be defined as follows: Consider two players, A and B. "For B to have power over A, it is sufficient that, by imposing or threatening to impose sanctions on A, B is capable of affecting the actions of A in ways to further B's interests, while A lacks this capacity with respect to A." In this case, the G-20 can try to impose rules on other countries by threatening to restrict its economic relations with them unless they abide by them. However, such an act might also negatively affect the well-being of the G-20 members. Therefore, from the G-20's point of view, finding a mechanism that produces reasonably favorable outcomes and is acceptable to other countries is preferable.

These results would suggest that the G-20 process can create an out-come that enables all countries to access the desired level of global finan-cial stability in a decentralized manner. However, such an outcome depends crucially on the institutional setup that governs relations between the G-20 and the non-G-20 countries. At this point one can expect the G-20 to have an advantage over the G-7. Due to its composition, the G-20 can be expected to be more sensitive to the concerns of the develop-ing world. Although this is reassuring, it can hardly be considered sufficient to secure the desired outcome. The G-20, therefore, also needs proper channels to communicate with the non-G-20 countries at the political level. At this juncture, regional cooperation arrangements (on monetary and financial issues, on market surveillance and integration, on exchange rate coordination) may play a significant role in enhancing the effectiveness of such communication. Unfortunately, such regional initiatives are still in their infancy, and for some regions of the world (such as the Middle East) it may take considerably longer for them to play a significant role.

Final Remarks

The 2007–09 global crisis revealed that maintaining financial stability needs well-designed regulatory and supervisory frameworks at the national level. The emphasis on macroprudential regulation, on the other hand, requires a structure that facilitates effective cooperation among govern-ments, central banks, and regulatory bodies. Achieving the desired result will not be easy, especially if due concern is given to the problem of respecting the independence of each country's central bank and regulatory bodies.

A similar mechanism design problem exists in the international sphere. Financial stability is considered a public good. Therefore the most natural way to secure its supply is to seek the cooperation of all countries, which is extremely difficult, if not impossible. This may be a reason to seek alter-native approaches, such as the G-20 process. Whether the G-20 countries can agree on proposals that attract the attention of the rest of the world depends on their joint credibility. However, as indicated above, the effi-ciency of the outcome of the G-20 process depends significantly more on the choice of an operating mechanism. It seems that, at this moment in time, the G-20 has not decided on a mechanism.

Most of the problems of the emerging Asian economies examined by Kawai are also relevant for developing countries in other parts of the world. It should be pointed out, however, that the emerging Asian countries have a considerable advantage over others in developing their domestic financial markets, owing to their significantly higher propensity to save. In addition, the developing countries in the other regions (such as the Middle East) have not reached the level of regional cooperation that emerging Asia enjoys. Progress in this area will not only benefit those countries but also create externalities for all.

References

Adrian, Tobias, and Hyun Song Shin. 2009. "Money, Liquidity, and Monetary Policy." *American Economic Review* 99, no. 2 (May): 600–05.

Arner, Douglas W., and Cyn-Young Park. 2010. "Global Financial Regulatory Reforms: Implications for Developing Asia." ADB Working Paper Series on Regional Economic Integration no. 57 (September). Manila: Asian Development Bank.

Asian Development Bank (ADB). 2008. *Emerging Asian Regionalism: A Partnership for Shared Prosperity*. Manila: Asian Development Bank.

———. 2010. *Asia Bond Monitor* (November). Manila: Asian Development Bank.

Atlantic Council. 2010. *The Danger of Divergence: Transatlantic Cooperation on Financial Reform* (October). Washington: ML Resources, LLC.

Beck, T., A. Demirguc-Kunt, and R. Levine. 2005. "SMEs, Growth, and Poverty: Cross-Country Evidence." *Journal of Economic Growth* 3, no. 9: 199–229.

Beck, Thorsten, and others. 2008. "Finance, Firm Size, and Growth." *Journal of Money, Credit and Banking* 40, no. 7: 1379–405.

Bernanke, B., and M. Gertler. 1990. "Financial Fragility and Economic Performance." *Quarterly Journal of Economics* 105, no. 1: 87–114.

Boadway, R., Z. Song, and J-F. Tremblay. 2007. "Commitment and Matching Contributions to Public Goods." *Journal of Public Economics* 91: 1664–83.

Bowles, S., and H. Gintis. 1992. "Power and Wealth in a Competitive Capitalist Economy." *Philosophy and Public Affairs* 21: 324–53.

Consultative Group to Assist the Poor. 2009. *Financial Access 2009: Measuring Access to Financial Services around the World*. Washington.

Cruz, Prince Christian. 2008. "Why Asia Missed the Global House Price Boom." Investment Analysis (July 10), Global Property Guide (www.globalpropertyguide.com/investment-analysis/Why-Asia-missed-the-global-house-price-boom).

Eichengreen, Barry. 2009. "Out of the Box Thoughts about the International Financial Architecture." IMF Working Paper WP/09/116 (May). Washington: International Monetary Fund.

International Monetary Fund (IMF). 2007. *World Economic Outlook* (April). Washington.

Kawai, Masahiro. 2008. "Toward a Regional Exchange Rate Regime in East Asia." *Pacific Economic Review* 13, no. 1 (February): 83–103.

Kawai, Masahiro, and Shinji Takagi. 2010. "A Survey of the Literature on Managing Capital Inflows." In *Managing Capital Flows: The Search for a Framework*, edited by Masahiro Kawai and Mario B. Lamberte, pp. 46–72. Cheltenham, UK: Edward Elgar.

Kawai, Masahiro, and Michael Pomerleano. 2010. "Regulating Systemic Risk." ADBI Working Paper Series no. 189 (January). Tokyo: Asian Development Bank Institute.

Mayes, David G., Peter J. Morgan, and Hank Lim. 2010. "Deepening the Financial System." In *Rebalancing for Sustainable Growth: Asia's Postcrisis Challenge,* edited by Masahiro Kawai and Jong-Wha Lee. Tokyo: Asian Development Bank Institute.

Minsky, H. 2008. *Stabilizing the Unstable Economy.* New York: McGraw-Hill. First edition published in 1986 by Yale University Press.

Pande, Rohini, and R. Burgess. 2005. "Can Rural Banks Reduce Poverty? Evidence from the Indian Social Banking Experiment." *American Economic Review* 95, no. 3: 780–95.

Plummer, Michael G. 2010. "Regional Monitoring of Capital Flows and Coordination of Financial Regulation: Stakes and Options for Asia." ADBI Working Paper Series no. 201 (February). Tokyo: Asian Development Bank Institute.

Schadler, Susan. 2010. "Managing Large Capital Inflows: Taking Stock of International Experiences." In *Managing Capital Flows: The Search for a Framework,* edited by Masahiro Kawai and Mario B. Lamberte, pp. 105–28. Cheltenham, UK: Edward Elgar.

Stiglitz, J. E. 2010. *The Stiglitz Report—Reforming the Monetary and Financial Systems in the Wake of Financial Crisis.* New York: New Press.

Varian, H. 1994. "Sequential Contributions to Public Goods." *Journal of Public Economics* 53: 165–86.

von Hagen, Jürgen, and Iulia Siedschlag. 2010. "Managing Capital Flows: Experiences from Central and Eastern Europe." In *Managing Capital Flows: The Search for a Framework,* edited by Masahiro Kawai and Mario B. Lamberte, pp. 192–213. Cheltenham, UK: Edward Elgar.

FIVE

The International Monetary System through the Lens of Emerging Asia

DOMENICO LOMBARDI

Our experience in the past has shown that international organizations have tended to approach all problems from the point of view of the advanced countries of the West.

—Sir Shanmukham Chetty, Indian Delegate,
Bretton Woods Conference, July 1944

As the world economy tries to leave behind the worst recession in almost a century, in 2010 emerging Asia has led the global recovery with stronger than anticipated growth, projected at 10.5 percent for the People's Republic of China (hereafter PRC) and 9.7 percent for India.[1] Building on the resilience of their aggregate demand, the soundness of their policy fundamentals, and their swift response to the crisis, emerging Asian nations have been able to weather the global crisis that sent other countries to the brink of economic depression.

This is in stark contrast to the financial crisis that affected the region in the late 1990s, which resulted in a sharp contraction in economic activity and, in some cases, social and political turmoil. In that crisis, the IMF intervened with programs that were subsequently found to be limited in size,

I would like to acknowledge helpful comments and suggestions from Kemal Derviş, Mario Lamberte, and Maria F. Viola, although they are not responsible for the contents of the chapter. I am grateful to Karim Foda and Sarah Puritz for excellent research assistance.

1. IMF (2010b). Overall, emerging and developing Asia is expected to grow at 9.4 percent in 2010.

inappropriate in their conditionality, and inadequately designed to confront the challenges at hand.

In the recent crisis, and in contrast to the 1990s, the IMF has emerged forcefully, with unprecedented institutional vigor. Early on, it established a new facility—the Flexible Credit Line (FCL)—with uncapped access to its resources for countries with a sound track record, upgraded its lending framework, and pledged to better serve its members. Moreover, it has become the central international organization supporting the G-20 leader summits. It has provided critical analysis and recommendations that have served as the basis for concerted official actions crucial for containing the extraordinary potential devastation of the recent crisis. Although several countries have taken advantage of the institution's greater responsiveness, the only Asian nations that have turned to the IMF for help are Pakistan and Sri Lanka.[2] Singapore and the Republic of Korea (hereafter Korea), however, sought and obtained the support of the U.S. Federal Reserve through bilateral currency arrangements. Under the latter, each country was guaranteed access to US$30 billion directly from the issuer of the main international reserve currency to support their respective financial systems at a time when global capital markets had dried up.[3]

More recently, Korea, as the 2010 G-20 chair, proposed a new global swap regime as a way to encourage countries to reduce their reliance on exports, ultimately reducing the need for accumulating very large precautionary reserves.[4] Days after the Korean proposal, East Asian nations officially launched the Chiang Mai Initiative Multilateralization (CMIM)—a $120 billion regional currency swap agreement that covers Korea, the PRC, Japan, and the ten-member Association of Southeast Asian Nations (ASEAN).[5] The CMIM builds on the previous CMI bilateral swap network to facilitate simultaneous currency swap transactions by adopting a

2. In this chapter, *Asia* refers to the region's eastern and southern countries, unless otherwise noted.

3. See the press release of the U.S. Federal Reserve of October 29, 2008. In Singapore, the monetary authorities did not draw on the facility, which expired on February 1, 2010 (Monetary Authority of Singapore Press Release, January 28, 2010). In Korea, the central bank distributed the swap dollars to Korean banks through competitive tender in the form of temporary dollar liquidity support over 84–85 days. The Bank of Korea used a total of $16.3 billion, which it began returning to the Federal Reserve as of March 19, 2009, and had fully repaid on December 18, 2009 (see http://eng.bok.or.kr/eng/engMain.action).

4. See "South Korea Pushes for Global Swaps Regime," *Financial Times,* March 1, 2010.

5. See the Joint Press Release "Chiang Mai Initiative Multilateralization (CMIM) Comes Into Effect," available at www.boj.or.jp/en/type/release/adhoc10/un1003e.htm.

common decisionmaking mechanism under a single contract and establishing an independent regional surveillance unit.[6] In other words, the CMIM represents an embryonic Asian Monetary Fund.

These recent developments underscore the difficulties that persist in the relationship between Asia and the IMF, despite various reforms that are either under consideration or have already been enacted. In this chapter, after a brief review of the IMF's role in the Asian crisis of 1997–1998, I explore the recent policy and institutional changes at the IMF by dissecting their impact on emerging Asia. I argue that Asia is more interested in pursuing reforms of the structural features of the international monetary system (IMS). As a result, institutional changes at the IMF disconnected from the latter objective are likely to be of limited interest to the region. I conclude that only by linking IMF reforms to structural changes in the IMS will the IMF gain strong support from emerging Asian countries as the central institution of a reformed and truly global monetary system.

Lessons from the IMF's Role in the 1997–98 Asian Crisis

In the recent history of the IMF, the 1997–98 Asian crisis stands as a landmark. It made clear that the domestic and international policy implications arising from the magnitude and scope of short-term capital flows had not, before then, been fully understood. As a result of the increasing integration of emerging economies with global capital markets, the Asian crisis was preceded by large capital flows into the countries later hit by the turmoil, and triggered by sudden shifts in market sentiment that led to massive capital flow reversals.[7]

The swift outflow of capital led to capital account corrections that were followed by contractions in aggregate demand and depreciation of the exchange rate, which, by interacting with domestic balance sheet

6. On the establishment of a regional surveillance unit in Singapore, see the Joint Ministerial Statement of the 13th ASEAN+3 Finance Ministers' Meeting, Tashkent, Uzbekistan, May 2, 2010 (www.aseansec.org/documents/JMS_13th_AFMM+3.pdf). On the CMI, see Kawai (2007) and Kuroda and Kawai (2002).

7. There is now a vast body of literature on the Asian crisis and the role of the IMF. See, for instance, Kawai and Rana (2009); Ito (2007); IEO (2003); Radelet and Sachs (1998); Sachs (1998); and Stiglitz (1998). This literature has investigated broader design issues of the IMF programs with the Asian countries hit by the crisis, including Fund recommendations for fiscal and monetary policies. While an exhaustive treatment of the Asian crisis is beyond the scope of this chapter, the aim of the following paragraphs is to briefly recall the main events of the crisis and the role that the IMF played.

vulnerabilities, in turn induced further contractionary effects.[8] The potential of suddenly withdrawn international capital flows to induce fluctuations far wider than those typically observed in a current account crisis is, however, not the only lesson arising from the Asian crisis. The other lesson is the scope for financial contagion: a capital account crisis can rapidly be transmitted to other, often neighboring, economies via market spreads and capital flows.[9] This is exactly what happened to some countries in the region, such as Thailand, in the early summer of 1997.

Following the floating of the Thai baht in early July of 1997, the IMF announced a US$4 billion program in late August that, combined with bilateral lines of credit and loans from other multilateral organizations, amounted to US$17.2 billion. But as the overall package was falling short of the forward commitments owed by the Thai central bank (standing at US$23.4 billion), not to mention the outstanding foreign short-term debt of the private sector, market participants reacted unfavorably by further depleting the central bank's official reserves, which then prompted another depreciation of the baht soon after the program was announced.

In the weeks that followed, the crisis spread to other Asian countries, such as Korea and Indonesia, whose currencies, already under pressure, began to slide. Until early October 1997, the IMF still considered Indonesian fundamentals to be "sound." However, shortly after the approval of the IMF program with Indonesia, confidence in its domestic financial system began to wane when the closure of sixteen banks was announced. Market participants started to wonder what criteria had underpinned such a decision, while uncertainty clouded the terms of deposit guarantees and cast doubt on the broader political resolve of the then-president of Indonesia to thoroughly implement the agreed-upon program.

These factors, combined with further uncertainty about the effective size of the total external financing available, sent the country into a political, social, and economic tailspin. Overall, total foreign assistance agreed upon amounted to US$40 billion, of which one fourth would come from the IMF alone. However, unlike in the case of Thailand, the so-called "second line of defense" portion of funding, consisting of more than half of the overall package, would only kick in at the end of the three-year standby arrangement with the IMF, leaving market participants to wonder whether it would ever become available at all.

---

8. On this, see, among others, Cavallo and Frankel (2008).
9. On financial contagion, see, for instance, Kaminsky, Reinhart, and Vegh (2003).

In reaction to an economywide crisis and in an attempt to compensate for a perceived lack of ownership by the highest echelons of the Indonesian leadership, a follow-up program with the IMF was agreed upon in January 1998. But it included so many policy measures unrelated to the root causes of the crisis that it suddenly became the archetype of what a well-designed IMF program should not be. Like the previous program, it still lacked a comprehensive strategy to tackle the critical areas of bank and corporate debt restructuring.

In November 1997, Korea became the latest Asian country to be hit by the crisis. Foreign investors stopped rolling over loans to the country's private sector, and the Bank of Korea depleted its reserves to enable the banking sector to repay its foreign loans. The next step was for Korea to request IMF assistance, which it obtained in the form of the newly created Supplemental Reserve Facility. Korea would be allowed Fund assistance equal to twenty times its own quota at the Fund, or US$21 billion, in addition to some US$36 billion pledged by other multilateral organizations and official creditors. As in the case of Indonesia, there was uncertainty whether, and under what terms, the second line of defense would materialize.

Like the IMF's program with Thailand, the one announced with Korea in early December failed to impress market participants. The Korean won continued to slide, until the G-7 resorted to "moral suasion," by asking foreign commercial banks to roll over their loans to the country. Only at this point did the situation finally begin to stabilize. In the words of the IMF's own Independent Evaluation Office, the "[IMF] program failed because it was underfinanced, given the absence of a coordinated rollover agreement and the immediate non availability of the second line of defense."[10]

As noted by Takatoshi Ito, while Thailand, Indonesia, and Korea differed in the soundness of their macroeconomic fundamentals, they all shared a high ratio of short-term debt to official reserves, with Korea's being the highest at 2.1, leaving their respective economies vulnerable to herd behavior by foreign investors.[11] In hindsight, the fact that all three countries recovered by 1999 highlights the important role that international liquidity shortages played, reflecting the potentially devastating effects of sudden reversals in speculative flows, and their scope

10. IEO (2003, 20).
11. See Ito (2007).

for contagion, when interacting with the economic and financial vulnerabilities of each country.

In drawing the lessons from the Asian crisis, for the purposes of this
chapter it is important to emphasize the need for timely, predictable, and
adequate external financing that is consistent with the nature of a capital account crisis, rather than a current account crisis. In Asia in the late
1990s, external financing usually did not meet these criteria: uncertainty
over the size, the terms, and the timing of the disbursements jeopardized
the prospect of stabilizing the expectations of market participants. Ultimately, capital outflows continued, which led to (further) contractions
in aggregate demands and (further) exchange rate depreciation, which
then resulted, by interacting with balance-sheet vulnerabilities, in even
more severe contractions in output, all of which spread to neighboring
economies.[12]

In the aftermath of the crisis, various efforts were made to strengthen
the regulatory framework and improve policy transparency and data
dissemination. Building on the premise that well-regulated financial systems are essential for macroeconomic and financial stability in a world
of increased capital flows, the Financial Sector Assessment Program
(FSAP), a joint IMF and World Bank initiative introduced in May 1999,
was set up to promote the soundness of domestic systems in member
countries.

This initiative was complemented by related efforts, through the
Reports on the Observance of Standards and Codes (ROSCs), to assess
compliance with key international standards in areas such as accounting,
auditing, anti–money laundering, countering the financing of terrorism,
banking supervision, corporate governance, data dissemination, fiscal
transparency, insolvency and creditor rights, insurance supervision, monetary and financial policy transparency, payments systems, and securities
regulation.

These efforts finally culminated in the IMF's introduction of a new
facility—the Contingent Credit Line (CCL)—designed to provide a precautionary line of defense for members with sound policies but who are
vulnerable to contagion effects from capital account crises in other countries. This facility, however, failed to elicit active interest on the part of

---

12. In this regard, the IMF's Independent Evaluation Office (IEO 2003, 11) stated that
contagion in the Asian crisis was an "important factor."

the membership owing to restrictions on the amount of unconditional access and the limited duration of the borrowing, and thus was discontinued in late 2003.

In part because of the resistance of Western countries, there was an insufficient effort, however, to put the lessons of the Asian crisis into the broader context of the reforms needed in the IMS following the extraordinary wave of economic and financial globalization of recent decades. As it turned out, the aforementioned efforts failed to attract any significant interest from emerging Asia, which instead started to accumulate large-scale reserves in defiance of the very purpose for which the IMF was established.

Struggling to Adapt: Economic and Financial Globalization in the Face of an Asymmetric International Monetary System

Despite the increasing adoption of flexible exchange rates since the demise of the Bretton Woods fixed exchange rate system in the early 1970s, the appetite for international reserves has grown steadily. As shown in figure 5-1, the demand for reserves increased fourfold in the first decade of the 2000s. Emerging Asia, in particular, accounts for the bulk of the sustained demand, although emerging economies outside of Asia have also contributed in the most recent years. Overall, the share of world total reserves of emerging Asian countries increased from 27 percent in 1995 to 48 percent in 2009 (see figure 5-2).

Notwithstanding some changes that have occurred in the three decades between 1980 and 2010, the current IMS has maintained key asymmetric features that have affected the increasing globalization of economic and financial activities driven by the integration of emerging economies. Specifically, they have produced a pattern of reserve accumulation by several emerging and developing economies (figure 5-1) that cannot simply be traced to traditional mercantilistic motives. The IMF estimated that in 2009 global reserve accumulation driven by self-insurance accounted for between US$4 and 4.5 trillion—that is, some two-thirds of the world stock of international reserves and over half of the increase witnessed over the decade begun in 2000.[13]

13. Mateos y Lago, Duttagupta, and Goyal (2009). Their estimates draw on Obstfeld, Shambaugh, and Taylor (2010).

FIGURE 5-1. Stock of International Reserves, 1999–2009

Trillions of U.S. dollars

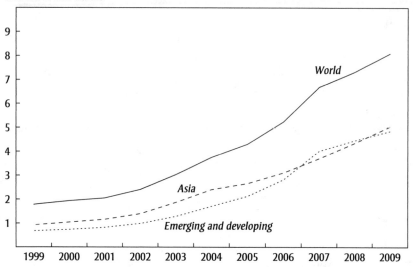

Trillions of U.S. dollars

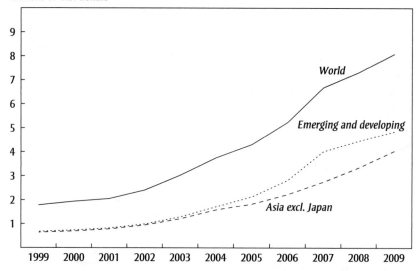

Source: IMF, Currency Composition of Official Exchange Reserves (COFER) (www.imf.org/external/np/sta/cofer/eng/index.htm); CEIC Data Company (www.ceicdata.com/); IMF, International Financial Statistics (IFS) (www.imf.org/external/pubs/cat/longres.cfm?sk=397.0).

Note: Asia includes the PRC; Hong Kong, China; India; Indonesia; Japan; Korea; Malaysia; the Philippines; Singapore; Taipei,China; Thailand; and Viet Nam.

FIGURE 5-2. Shares of World Reserves, Various Years

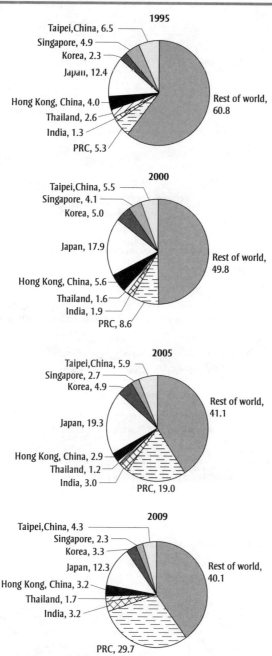

Source: CEIC Data Company (www.ceicdata.com/); IMF, International Financial Statistics (IFS) (www.imf.org/external/pubs/cat/longres.cfm?sk=397.0).

The economic growth recorded in the past fifty years in emerging and developing countries has been coupled with an overall increase in volatility as a result of their integration into the global economy. On average, output volatility in these countries has, in fact, been higher than in OECD countries.[14] While developing and emerging economies have experienced higher volatility due to more frequent terms-of-trade shocks, they are also made more vulnerable by their trading with similarly volatile economies.

In this setting, international capital flows, which should facilitate the smoothing of real shocks on output, have instead acted as a source of further destabilization owing to their highly procyclical nature.[15] Compounding matters is the growing financial openness experienced by many developing and emerging economies and their vulnerability to contagion from the effects of financial crises experienced first in other economies. Not surprisingly, developing and emerging economies have therefore endured a number of currency and financial crises, like the one experienced by several Asian countries in the late 1990s.

The sustained financial globalization witnessed over the past few decades is in direct contrast to the remarkably little evolution observed in the IMS, which has, if anything, contributed to further reducing the policy space for emerging and developing economies, even as they have become more and more integrated in, and vulnerable to, the global economy.

Global Deflationary Bias

The first structural asymmetry of the IMS relates to the well-documented feature whereby any adjustment in external accounts hinges on deficit countries rather than those in surplus. This feature was first noted by Lord Keynes in his preparatory work for the Bretton Woods Conference in 1944. He pointed out that this fundamental asymmetry in the global monetary system would generate a global deflationary bias in the absence of any corrective mechanism.

Under the current system, it is usually not feasible for balance-of-payments surpluses and deficits to be resolved without negatively affecting global economic activity. When confronted with insufficient financing,

---

14. See the comparative analysis presented in Perry (2009), which includes Asian countries.

15. Prasad and others (2009); Kose, Prasad, and Terrones (2003).

deficit countries must sooner or later make an adjustment to balance their external accounts; surplus countries, however, do not face a similar pressure, and do not have to engage in expansionary policies.[16]

Awareness of this asymmetry implicitly affected the founding discussions of the current IMS at the Bretton Woods Conference, resulting in the important, albeit ambiguous, wording in Article I of the IMF's Articles of Agreement, namely that the Fund's purpose is "to promote international monetary cooperation through a permanent institution which provides the machinery for consultation and collaboration on international monetary problems."

This provision was operationalized by making the IMF the overseer of countries' efforts to liberalize their current account transactions and to uphold a rule-based system of exchange rates. That is, the Bretton Woods economic order aimed to spur international trade and growth by ensuring that all countries would make their currencies convertible for the purpose of current account transactions and that the exchange rate system overall would be stable. In a way, the global deflationary bias was being softened by setting the long-run foundations for an open global economy and by providing the Fund with the related regulatory powers.[17] In this setting, the IMF would provide temporary balance-of-payment financing to ease adjustment, though the basic asymmetry of the system would remain, as the burden of adjustment would ultimately fall on the deficit country.

After the Bretton Woods fixed parities system was abandoned in the early 1970s, the IMF's Interim Committee met in Jamaica in 1976 to begin

16. Keynes (1930; 1943). In Keynes's vision of international monetary cooperation, a fundamental premise was that creditor as well as debtor nations should assume responsibility for balance-of-payments adjustments. This symmetric aspect of the IMS was to be elaborated more clearly in his later plan for an international clearing union.

17. Article IV provides the legal foundation for members' obligations to the Fund with regard to the so-called code of conduct. Specifically, Section I stipulates the cooperative behavior required of a member country in formulating its own economic policies so as to contribute to an "orderly economic growth with reasonable price stability." Section III establishes the role of the IMF as the "overseer" of the international monetary system and outlines the obligations that each member must fulfill and for which the Fund must verify compliance. Article VIII stipulates another set of obligations associated with IMF membership; namely, it prevents any member from imposing "restrictions on the making of payments and transfers for current international transactions" without the approval of the Fund. It also prevents a member from engaging "in any discriminatory currency arrangements or multiple currency practices . . . except as authorized under this Agreement or approved by the Fund." Moreover, it states in detail the minimum information requirements for each IMF member.

amending the institution's Articles of Agreement. The result was the Second Amendment of 1978, which set up the framework for the Fund's modern surveillance function. In essence, the new framework reflected the desire of member countries, led by the United States, to create a flexible regime that would foster adjustment through regular consultations, but would also allow individual countries to determine the conditions for attaining domestic macroeconomic objectives. This was a great change from the original Bretton Woods regime, whereby the anchor provided by the pegged exchange rate—overseen by the IMF—dictated the required internal adjustment.

In the absence of clear international rules, the new system placed great weight on consultations and national-level responsibility. At the heart of the revised Article IV, there was a shift in authority back to member countries and away from the IMF. The IMF still bore the task of helping its members avoid unilateral setting of exchange rate policies by individual nations, but the IMF was left with few, if any, instruments with which to fulfill this task.[18]

Fund efforts to build a genuine multilateral consultation system suffered another blow with the initiative of some key members—France, Germany, Japan, the United Kingdom, and the United States—to set up their own multilateral surveillance forum over monetary and exchange rate policies in 1982. While they agreed that the exercise would be conducted in cooperation with the IMF, it became clear at the start that the G-5 (which would become the G-7 with the inclusion of Italy and Canada) would play a lead role.

The lack of an authentic multilateral forum to discuss and formulate policy responses to global developments has thus left developing and emerging economies more vulnerable in an increasingly interdependent world. In the context of the global consultations on IMF reform organized by civil society in 2007 and 2008, participants remarked on the increasing spillover effect across economies and the growing need for multilateral surveillance.[19] They complained, however, that advanced countries do not take into adequate consideration how their policy spillovers affect the rest of the global economy.

---

18. See Lombardi and Woods (2007).
19. The consultations were organized by the Centre for International Governance Innovation, New Rules for Global Finance, and the University of Oxford. See Lombardi (2008).

International Currency Bias

An additional structural source of instability in the IMS is the central position that the U.S. dollar enjoys as a global reserve asset. By 2010, U.S. dollar–denominated assets made up about 60 percent of world reserves, though the share of the U.S. dollar has declined over time as a result of the rise in euro-denominated assets, as figure 5-3 shows. The reliance on the domestic currency of a single country as the principal international reserve asset makes it difficult for U.S. policymakers to reconcile, in the long run, their domestic macroeconomic goals with the (increasing) need for a net supply of dollar-denominated international assets, leaving the IMS vulnerable to unilateral adjustments in the economic policies of the issuer country.

The implication of the de facto fiduciary dollar standard has been, in practice, that the United States has run current account deficits and other countries have accumulated net dollar assets; yet this same deficit in the U.S. current account tends to weaken confidence in the dollar as an international reserve asset, since it requires corrections at some point to restore its credibility; all the while amplifying the system's deflationary bias.[20] It is true that U.S. dollars can and have also been supplied through the capital account, with the United States accumulating foreign currency–denominated assets by investing abroad, and the rest of the world acquiring dollar assets. There is demand for "safe" U.S. treasury bonds. But the accumulation of these U.S. liabilities by foreign central banks or other financial institutions requires the United States to run a budget deficit.[21] Caught between the conflicting needs of achieving domestic objectives or maintaining the international public good of monetary stability, U.S. authorities will likely opt for the former, if they have to.

But as long as confidence in the dollar remains stable, U.S. policymakers enjoy the unique privilege of running monetary policies relatively independently from the determinants of exchange rates with other currencies, and thus they are able to finance large amounts of imports through the issuance of low-interest liquid liabilities—a modern form of international seigniorage made possible by the dollar's preeminent position in the global

---

20. This is a revised version of the so-called "Triffin Dilemma." See Triffin (1961; 1968). In theory, it would also be possible for the United States to export long-term capital matched by short-term placements of capital-importing countries in dollar assets.

21. See, among others, Akyüz (2010).

FIGURE 5-3. Currency Composition of Reserves, 1999–2009

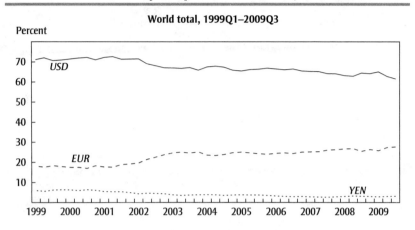

World total, 1999Q1–2009Q3

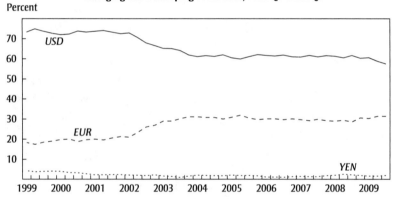

Emerging and developing economies, 1999Q1–2009Q3

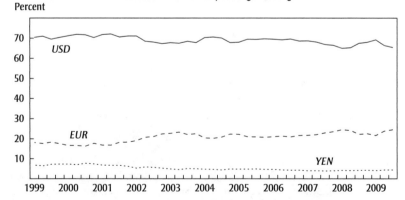

Advanced economies, 1999Q1–2009Q3

Source: IMF, Currency Composition of Official Exchange Reserves (COFER) (www.imf.org/external/np/sta/cofer/eng/index.htm).

reserve system. In contrast to Keynes's global deflationary bias, the issuer of the principal international reserve currency might even contribute to an inflationary bias, as long as the foreign demand for dollar-denominated assets generates downward pressure on U.S. interest rates.[22]

The status of the dollar as the main global reserve asset was formally codified in the Bretton Woods fixed exchange rate system by setting the U.S. currency as the anchor for the IMS, with all other currencies required to fix their value in relation to the dollar. After the demise of the Bretton Woods system in 1973, U.S. policymakers benefited from increasingly greater macroeconomic policy space as the previous, albeit imperfectly binding, constraint that countries could convert dollars into gold disappeared.[23] In turn, the IMS evolved from a "gold-exchange standard" to a "fiduciary dollar standard."[24]

At the height of the 2007–09 global financial crisis, despite the fact that the United States was at the center of the financial turmoil, the dollar enjoyed remarkable stability thanks to the sustained international demand for safe assets, mainly in the form of U.S. Treasury bills, with the U.S. central bank even acting as a provider of international liquidity to selected emerging economies.[25] In contrast, economies that do not issue international reserve assets cannot supply a monetary base without facing a decline in the external value of their respective currencies, which severely constrains the scope of their policy interventions.

In this regard, the IMS has been remarkably resistant to change. The only relevant development was the creation, under the auspices of the IMF, of the special drawing rights (SDRs) in 1969 to support the Bretton Woods fixed exchange rate system. SDRs supplemented the limited international supply of the two key reserve assets, namely gold and the U.S. dollar, which were still insufficient in the face of ongoing world trade expansion and financial development.[26]

22. See Ocampo (2010).

23. For an analysis of how the gold constraint did not fully operate on U.S. economic policies, see Eichengreen (2006).

24. See Ocampo (2010) for an excellent treatment of this issue.

25. As a result, interest rates on U.S. Treasury bills even declined throughout the crisis, as noted in various issues of the IMF's Global Financial Stability Reports.

26. The value of an SDR is currently based on a basket of four key international currencies: the dollar, the euro, the yen, and the pound sterling. SDRs are costless assets. However, if a member's SDR holdings rise above its allocation, the member earns interest on the excess; conversely, if a member holds fewer SDRs than allocated, it pays interest on the shortfall. In other words, SDRs provide the option of attaining a loan without maturity, whose cost is indexed to money market interest rates.

The SDR is not a currency per se; nor is it a claim on the IMF. It represents only a potential claim on the freely usable currencies of IMF members. Allocations of SDRs are determined on the basis of a long-term global need to supplement existing reserve assets, and have been made only twice since they were established. The first allocation, for a total amount of SDR 9.3 billion, took place from 1970 to 1972 and was distributed in yearly installments. The second, for SDR 12.1 billion, took place from 1979 to 1981, again in yearly installments.

In contrast with the obligation set forth in Article VIII about "making the special drawing right the principal reserve asset in the international monetary system," SDRs have played a marginal role as international reserves, which is symptomatic of the decline in the IMF's perceived importance. It is significant, in light of the need for reserve assets in the past few decades, that no additional SDRs were issued before 2009 (see next section). Even the stock of the two previous allocations represented a very small fraction of total international reserves.[27]

By its very nature, the SDR implies a mainly passive role for the IMF. Once a decision on an allocation of SDRs has been made by member countries representing at least 85 percent of the institution's voting power, the IMF has no discretionary control over how the allocation is used. As the system currently stands, exchanges of SDRs for national currencies may take place in two ways: as voluntary bilateral transactions or as designations by the IMF of member countries with an external surplus that may accept SDRs in exchange for their currencies. So even if the IMF plays a brokering role by matching demand and supply of SDRs, the transactions remain essentially bilateral.

Institutional Bias

A third asymmetric element of the IMS is associated with the governance of the institution charged with the regulatory task of overseeing it. The current distribution of voting power within the IMF, as has been well documented, is heavily biased toward Western countries and points to a serious legitimacy gap.[28] The G-7 countries, for instance, together account for almost half of overall voting power and thus constitute the most powerful

27. As of June 2008, SDRs accounted for less than 0.5 percent of global (non-gold) reserves. See Truman (2010).

28. See Bryant (2010) and Mirakhor and Zaidi (2009), among others. These aspects have also been the focus of the 2009 global consultations on IMF reform. See Lombardi (2009).

TABLE 5-1. Aggregate Power of Informal Coalitions on the IMF Executive Board

Informal coalitions	Voting power (country based)	Voting power (constituency based)
G-7[a]	44.39	46.05
EURIMF[b]	32.02	33.34
G-11[c]	—	27.01
Asia-Pacific group[d]	18.95	18.95

Source: Author's elaborations from www.imf.org. Voting power data as of March 22, 2010.

a. The country-based voting power is the sum of the votes of the United States, Japan, Germany, France, the United Kingdom, Italy, and Canada. The constituency-based voting power includes, in addition to the voting shares of the United States, Japan, Germany, France, and the United Kingdom, those of the constituencies led by Italy and Canada.

b. The country-based voting power is the sum of the voting power of Austria, Belgium, Bulgaria, Cyprus, the Czech Republic, Denmark, Estonia, Finland, France, Germany, Greece, Hungary, Ireland, Italy, Latvia, Lithuania, Luxembourg, Malta, the Netherlands, Poland, Portugal, Romania, Slovakia, Slovenia, Spain, Sweden, and the United Kingdom. The constituency-based voting power is the sum of the voting power of the chairs led by Belgium, Denmark, France, Germany, Italy, the Netherlands, Spain, and the United Kingdom.

c. The constituency-based voting power is the sum of the voting power of the chairs led by Argentina, Brazil, the PRC, Egypt, India, Iran, Rwanda, Sierra Leone, Saudi Arabia, and Thailand. If the Central American constituency, currently led by Spain, were to be included, the aggregate voting power would increase to 31.45 percent. Country-based voting power is blank because the G-11 is a chair-based coalition. See Woods and Lombardi (2006).

d. The country-based voting power is the sum of the voting power of India, Bangladesh, Bhutan, Sri Lanka, Japan, the PRC, Brunei Darussalam, Cambodia, the Fiji Islands, Indonesia, the Lao People's Democratic Republic, Malaysia, Myanmar, Nepal, the Philippines, Singapore, Thailand, Tonga, Viet Nam, Australia, Kiribati, Korea, the Marshall Islands, the Federal States of Micronesia, Mongolia, New Zealand, Palau, Papua New Guinea, Samoa, Seychelles, Solomon Islands, and Vanuatu. The constituency-based voting power is the sum of the voting power of the chairs led by the PRC, Korea, India, Japan, and Thailand.

bloc around which to aggregate additional votes, as shown in table 5-1. The aggregation of the votes of EU member states and non-European G-7 states largely exceeds a (simple) majority of votes, which is sufficient to pass most decisions, including the election of the managing director of the Fund.

The asymmetric distribution of voting power is magnified by a skewed pattern of representation that privileges advanced economies, mostly European. As shown in table 5-2, European countries are represented by eight or nine chairs, depending on the intra-constituency rotational patterns, while most Asian countries are clustered into two constituencies, led by India and Thailand, respectively. There are, in addition, two single-country Asian chairs, namely the PRC and Japan. In 2010 the aggregate voting power of all four chairs stands at 15.53 percent, which increases to 16.86 percent when Korea's votes are included.

Yet the chair of the constituency to which Korea belongs rotates with Australia. This makes it unlikely that the former would steer the chair's

TABLE 5-2. IMF Executive Board Chairs

Country	Voting power	Legal status	Internal governance arrangements
United States	16.74	appointed	
Japan	6.01	appointed	Each executive director is appointed by the respective
Germany	5.87	appointed	country authorities and serves at their pleasure.
France	4.85	appointed	
United Kingdom	4.85	appointed	
PRC	3.65	elected	
Saudi Arabia	3.16	elected	Single-country constituencies
Russia	2.69	elected	
Belgium	5.13	elected	Multi-country constituency chaired by Belgium
The Netherlands	4.77	elected	Multi-country constituency chaired by the Netherlands
Spain	4.44	elected	Multi-country constituency with chair rotating among Mexico, Spain, and Venezuela
Italy	4.10	elected	Multi-country constituency chaired by Italy
Canada	3.63	elected	Multi-country constituency chaired by Canada
Thailand	3.52	elected	Multi-country constituency with chair rotating among Indonesia, Malaysia, Singapore, and Thailand
Korea	3.44	elected	Multi-country constituency with chair rotating between Australia and Korea
Denmark	3.43	elected	Multi-country constituency with chair rotating among Denmark, Finland, Iceland, Sweden
Egypt	3.19	elected	Multi-country constituency chaired by Egypt
Sierra Leone	3.01	elected	Multi-country constituency with chair rotating among all members
Switzerland	2.78	elected	Multi-country constituency chaired by Switzerland
Brazil	2.42	elected	Multi-country constituency chaired by Brazil
Iran	2.42	elected	Multi-country constituency chaired by Iran
India	2.35	elected	Multi-country constituency chaired by India
Argentina	1.95	elected	Multi-country constituency with chair rotating among Argentina, Chile, and Peru
Rwanda	1.34	elected	Multi-country constituency with chair rotating among all members

position any way other than that supported by Australia, the largest shareholder within the constituency. Korea's membership in the Australian constituency therefore poses a trade-off. On the one hand, it enables it to leverage the weight of a relatively large shareholder like Australia, which recently agreed to rotate the chair of the constituency with the Asian country, providing the latter with unprecedented visibility and prestige on the

IMF Board. On the other hand, it may entail some dilution of the voting power that Asia can leverage whenever it intends to promote a policy agenda that Australia and New Zealand, another key country of the constituency, do not wish to support.

Recent research has underscored the importance of informal arrangements in IMF governance, and thus of relevant lobbying and agenda-setting outside the sphere of the formal governance channels.[29] In this setting, cross-coalitions tend to be a pervasive feature of the IMF Board's informal politics, with every chair being a member of one or more informal groupings. The aim is to leverage preferential access to Fund senior management and staff to affect the institutional agenda at an early stage, before it is formalized in specific items brought before the Executive Board.

Asian chairs have their own informal grouping—the Asia-Pacific Group—which is used by the Chinese, Indian, Japanese, Korean, and Thai representatives for exchanging views and discussing issues of common interest, with the aim of shaping a common position. A recent comparative analysis of informal coalitions on the IMF Board, however, has found that the leverage of this group has had a limited effect on Board dynamics compared to that of the G-7 or the EU, because of both its relative diversity and its limited voting power.[30] As shown in table 5-1, this group is the least powerful on the IMF Board, although it has been quite successful in forging a common view on the need to claim a greater role for the region in the governance of the IMF through reforms of the quota system and current representation on the Executive Board.

All in all, the skewed distribution of voting power, magnified by patterns of governance within constituencies and the operation of informal coalitions, makes for substantial asymmetry. A small number of members hold the majority of votes and promote decisions that affect the membership at large. This same small group may also unilaterally exclude itself from compliance, again because of its majority control over the decision-making of the institution. Accordingly, the relatively minor share of voting power of emerging Asian members jeopardizes incentives for their meaningful engagement in the institution's deliberations.

IMF governance cannot be interpreted separately from its policies or the implementation of its regulatory powers. Since many emerging Asian

29. Woods and Lombardi (2006).
30. Woods and Lombardi (2006).

countries have carried inadequate weight in Fund decisionmaking, their positions, even on matters in which they may have the most incisive and immediate experience or knowledge, are less likely to be incorporated in the IMF's own policies and programs.[31] This asymmetry is most noticeable as it pertains to Fund surveillance. As part of the global consultations on IMF reform initiated by managing director Dominique Strauss-Kahn in the spring of 2009, participants concurred that the institution's ability to predict the recent international crisis was hindered by the asymmetric role of the United States in IMF governance. But had the IMF been able to foresee the unfolding of the U.S. financial crisis, it still would not have had any leverage over its own largest shareholder. The United States tended to want the IMF to focus on the Chinese exchange rate—an important part of the U.S. international economic agenda, but still merely one aspect of the global imbalance problem.[32]

The approval of the 2007 Surveillance Decision with the alleged abstention of two Eastern and Central Asian chairs is another case in point. The decision was intended to offer greater guidance on the conduct of exchange rate policy by making clear the notion of exchange rate manipulation, when and how it is desirable to intervene in foreign exchange markets, and the need to avoid exchange rate policies that result in external instability. It also included some appraisal indicators to help the IMF determine when it needs to initiate discussions with members about their economic policies, requiring the Fund to label currencies that deviate significantly from equilibrium as "fundamentally misaligned." Emerging market chairs, most notably from Asia, however, felt targeted by the decision and resented that its content and timing were motivated by the need to sanction their policies.[33]

31. See, for instance, the analysis developed in Woods (2009).

32. Along similar lines, Miranda Xafa, a former member of the IMF Executive Board, notes that the fact that the financial crisis originated in advanced economies, which in practice tend to be outside of the purview of the Fund's crisis prevention efforts, contributed to complacency. She concludes that more even-handed surveillance would have enhanced the Fund's effectiveness (Xafa 2010).

33. Other instances regarding the link between IMF governance and policies were documented in the context of the 2009 global consultations on IMF reform. Concerns were raised about influential member countries using their power in some cases to influence Fund policy in their favor. For example, it was pointed out that there have been cases of programs with policy measures unnecessary for resolving a country crisis, but indicative of contentious areas in bilateral commercial relations with major creditor countries. The conditionality of the IMF program with Korea on liberalizing imports of car components, a contentious item in commercial relations between Korea and the United States for several years, is a case in

Another instance in which the IMF's governance has affected the asymmetries of the IMS is that, against the need for increased reserves, the issuance of "synthetic" assets such as SDRs requires approval of 85 percent of the voting power of the IMF membership. Besides the potential veto that such a large supermajority affords to a few countries or groupings, the governance arrangements underpinning the creation of SDRs have reduced the IMF's ability to be responsive to the liquidity needs experienced by some segments of its membership. At the same time, it embeds a tension in the institutional mandate to pursue systemic stability, as it leaves decisions on regulating global liquidity in the hands of those countries issuing the hard currencies used as international reserve assets. To the extent that the distribution of quotas is skewed toward some segments of the membership, general allocations of SDRs would only reinforce that fundamental asymmetry, given that they are usually allocated on the basis of a member's quota.

Innovations of the IMS

Building on the framework developed in the previous section, this section reviews recent and ongoing reforms of the IMS by assessing their broader implications for emerging Asia.

Global Deflationary Bias

In September 2009, leaders at the G-20 summit in Pittsburgh agreed to the so-called "Framework for Strong, Sustainable, and Balanced Growth," proposed by the United States. Through this framework, they pledged to devise a method for setting objectives, to develop policies to support such objectives, and to assess outcomes through mutual evaluation. The IMF's involvement has been sought in providing analysis on various national or regional policy frameworks and how they fit together. The end goal is

---

point. Others have included capital account liberalization and the privatization of major services or banks. Similarly, participants noted that major shareholders have tried to use Fund-supported programs as a vehicle to force borrowing countries to adopt policies that would generate adequate balance-of-payments surpluses to service their debt obligations, as in the case of the programs with Indonesia. It was clear to observers inside and outside the Fund alike that the program would generate a sizable shock and exacerbate the effects of the financial crisis on the country's real economy, and yet the primary objective of the assistance program was to generate as great a balance-of-payments surplus as possible, in as little time as possible, to guarantee that outstanding creditors would be repaid. See Lombardi (2009).

"strong, sustainable, and balanced growth" in which the improvement of living standards in emerging market and developing countries is supposed to be a critical element. To accomplish this, the G-20 has also devised a standard template for national policy frameworks that will allow countries to indicate key forward-looking elements of their policy plans and to outline the expected impact of policies both on their domestic economy and, more broadly, on their national forecasts for key economic variables for the subsequent three to five years.

Based on country submissions received between January and March 2010, the IMF has been tasked with uncovering inconsistencies in national assumptions, analyzing the mutual compatibility of various country frameworks and policies, and calculating the aggregate impact of the national frameworks and policies on the global economy. The bulk of this work has fed into an initial report by the Fund for the G-20 deputies and for their finance ministers and central bank governors. It has developed two alternative scenarios—one upside and one downside—to explore the benefits of further G-20 policy action toward their shared objectives of strong, sustainable, and balanced growth.[34] Following the completion of the initial phase of the mutual assessment process at the June 2010 summit in Toronto, the G-20 has focused on the implementation aspects of the agreed-upon policies as well as on follow-ups.[35]

This is the first relevant multilateral surveillance exercise on a global scale in recent history, and it introduces two main innovations. First, it is the first time in recent history that the United States has agreed, even proposed, to submit itself to a full peer-review process. Even in the context of the Jamaica Amendment, when the current IMF surveillance framework was discussed and approved in 1978, the United States only reluctantly accepted its basic premise.[36] Second, it implies a shift from the recent past,

---

34. In a follow-up assessment shared with the G-20 leaders at the Toronto summit, the IMF has quantified the benefits from mutually consistent and collaborative policy actions in terms of global GDP growth higher relative to the G-20 baseline by 2.5 percent over the medium term, worldwide employment gains in the neighborhood of 30 million additional jobs, and 33 million people lifted out of poverty (IMF 2010a).

35. The role of the IMF in this process is spelled out in IMF (2009).

36. Earlier, under the Bretton Woods system, every member country that had not made its currency fully convertible had to consult with the IMF. Consultations went on even after countries had moved toward full convertibility, in response to the desire of the United States for an "activist" IMF that would monitor European economies—owing to counterbalancing European demands—on a strictly "voluntary" basis and while monitoring the United States as well (the first such consultation was held with the United Kingdom in 1961). See Lombardi and Woods (2007).

when multilateral surveillance on the global economy was in practice dealt with in the more restricted forum of the G-7 nations. In contrast, the G-20 convenes all the systemically important countries, including the largest emerging Asian economies—the PRC, India, and Indonesia, along with Korea and Japan—providing an immediate, alternative platform through which Asia can engage, in the face of an institution like the IMF still perceived to be dominated by Europe and North America. In fact, the choice of the G-20 as the primary forum for international policymaking was meant to promptly accommodate rising powers, mainly from Asia, in the multilateral system.[37]

There are, however, two main challenges for G-20-led multilateral surveillance. First, the exercise appears, so far, mainly geared toward making national policymakers aware of the international spillovers of their policies and providing a context in which they can exercise mutual pressure, as the Toronto and Seoul summits exemplify.[38] Whether and to what extent this will feed into substantially revised national frameworks, along the lines, for instance, recommended in the upside scenario envisaged by the IMF, is highly uncertain because it presupposes a shared vision of the costs and benefits from coordination. This may require some countries to grow less in order to preserve the overall stability of the global economy and/or to accept higher risks by revisiting their precautionary reserve accumulation policy. Or it may require some other countries not to withdraw their stimulus early on in order to preserve their contribution to the global economic recovery, even if this may result in temporary higher fiscal deficits than are politically feasible. The G-20 countries have committed to a peer-review process for their economic policies and to a broadly defined policy objective. This is not the same as committing to numerical policy targets—consistent with quantitatively defined objectives set for the overall group—for which they can be held accountable in a multilateral forum. Even if the Toronto summit produced some broad numerical goals with regard to reducing fiscal deficits, they largely reflect commitments already taken by the respective national authorities.[39]

37. Mo and Kim (2009).

38. The respective communiqués are available at www.g20.utoronto.ca/2010/g20_declaration_en.pdf and www.g20.utoronto.ca/2010/g20seoul.html.

39. In fact, at the G-20 Finance Ministers meeting in Gyeongju, Korea, on October 23, 2010, the secretary of the U.S. Treasury proposed to target a predefined ratio of current account balance over GDP in the process of adjusting external imbalances but his proposal did not elicit support from other systemic economies. See "Trade Imbalance Targets Elude G20," *Financial Times*, October 23, 2010.

The effectiveness of this multilateral exercise will also hinge on the extent to which emerging Asian countries are willing to fully articulate their vision of how international economic coordination should work in practice. This is no small task, especially for a group of countries with a historically weak sense of regional identity. If Asia does not rise to the occasion and express some collective initiative with regard to the G-20 agenda, there is a real risk that the G-20 will become a mouthpiece for Europe and North America, which is in direct opposition to the reason it was deemed the premier forum for global economic policymaking in the first place.

International Currency Bias

As the crisis unfolded and developing countries' economies increasingly needed to bolster their reserve asset position, the G-20 supported a general allocation of SDRs equivalent to $250 billion, and the IMF quickly implemented the leaders' proposal, effective August 28, 2009.[40] The potential credit that SDR holdings provided was meant as liquidity support with unconditional financing, aimed at limiting the need for adjustment and giving greater space to countercyclical policies in countries with no hard currency.

For countries that might be tempted to accumulate greater reserve assets in response to the systemic uncertainty stemming from the crisis, the more general aim was to ease worry by managing their currency exchange rates so as to generate large trade surpluses. Yet, because the allocation of SDRs follows the distribution of voting power across the membership, those emerging market economies whose quotas are underrepresented also received fewer SDRs. All in all, the SDRs allocated to emerging Asia totaled $28 billion—that is, almost 1 percent of their total 2008 reserve stock or slightly less than 5 percent of the aggregate variation in the 2008–2009 stocks. For individual countries, however, the allocation of SDRs as compared to the variation of reserve stocks ranges from a low of 2 percent for the PRC to a high of 84 percent for Malaysia, as reported in table 5-3.[41]

---

40. In addition, the Fourth Amendment to the IMF's Articles of Agreement, which allows a special one-time allocation of SDRs, went into effect on August 10, 2009, as a separate measure. This special allocation, which was made to IMF members on September 9, 2009, was in the amount of SDR 21.5 billion (about $33 billion).

41. Low-income countries received about $20 billion. To put this figure in perspective, it by far exceeds the World Bank's International Development Association (IDA) commitments and support to low-income countries, which totaled US$14 billion in the fiscal year that ended in June 2009.

TABLE 5-3. **2009 SDR Allocations for Emerging Asian Countries**
$US billions

Country	Foreign exchange reserves			SDR allocations		
	2008	2009	Annual change	Nominal amounts	Percent of 2008 stock	Percent of annual change
PRC	1,946.03	2,399.20	453.17	10.65	0.55	2.35
India	246.60	258.58	11.98	5.20	2.11	43.42
Indonesia	49.34	60.57	11.23	2.75	5.57	24.46
Korea	200.48	265.20	64.72	3.68	1.83	5.68
Malaysia	90.61	92.87	2.26	1.90	2.10	84.27
Philippines	33.05	36.60	3.55	1.14	3.44	32.03
Singapore	173.65	186.01	12.36	1.15	0.66	9.29
Thailand	108.32	133.60	25.28	1.40	1.29	5.53
Viet Nam	23.88	NA	NA	0.42	1.76	NA

Source: Author's elaborations from www.imf.org. Reserves data are from IMF IFS.

Note: SDR allocations for 2009, which include both general and special allocations, have been converted into U.S. dollars at the September 2009 average exchange rate, available at: www.imf.org/external/np/tre/sdr/proposal/2009/0709.htm.

In light of recent developments, a UN Commission of Experts has called for expanding the role of the SDR through regular or cyclically adjusted issuance of SDRs, as a way of managing international economic risks posed for countries that do not issue hard currencies (see United Nations 2009).

Because SDRs are an artificial unit of account with limited scope for use within the existing parameters, the head of the Chinese central bank recently proposed a significant overhaul to increase the role of the SDR.[42] Specifically, he has recommended: transforming the SDR from a "synthetic" basket currency into one backed by actual assets; designing a settlement system between the SDR and national money to make the SDR easily "convertible" into national currencies; and strengthening the link between the SDR and the IMF, its issuing institution. It bears mention that the Chinese proposal, in this regard, is based on the underlying premise of a truly supranational IMF that oversees the IMS. For this reason, the proposal also envisages a political bargain between structural reforms of the IMS and the restoration of the IMF's centrality in it.

42. Zhou (2009).

In the interim, the IMF has expressed some interest in proposals for strengthening the SDR,[43] and the IMF managing director has suggested that the yuan could be included in the basket of currencies that makes up the SDR as soon as its external value becomes market based.[44] The 2011 French presidency of the G-20 aims to strengthen the role of the SDR, and the IMF's executive board is already assessing relevant options (see IMF 2011).

Institutional Bias

Since a country's share of quotas is the key to decisionmaking power and provides the metrics for access to Fund financing and for the allocation of SDRs, calls for IMF reform have focused mostly on realigning the distribution of voting power to better represent the rising economic weight of many emerging market economies.

In March 2008, a package of quota and voice reforms was agreed on by the IMF's Executive Board and was endorsed by the Board of Governors one month later. The reform builds on an initial step taken by the IMF's membership in September 2006 to grant ad hoc quota increases to four countries—the PRC, Korea, Mexico, and Turkey. The 2008 reform package foresees ad hoc quota increases for fifty-four countries that were underrepresented under the new quota formula, a tripling of basic votes and provisions aimed to ensure that the share of basic votes remains proportionate to total voting power. Finally, it envisages the allocation of additional resources for the two largest African constituencies through an additional alternate executive director.[45]

The 2008 reform package now awaits approval by three-fifths of the membership—that is, 112 member countries representing at least 85 percent of total voting power—before it can go into effect. As of the end of 2010, a total of 101 members, equivalent to about 83 percent of total vot-

---

43. The managing director of the IMF has stated that "SDR allocations could be made more responsive to global developments and flexible to country circumstances." See Strauss-Kahn (2009).

44. See "IMF Chief Says Would Consider Yuan for SDR Basket," Reuters, June 28, 2010.

45. Basic votes reflect the principle of equality among states and are meant to provide the smallest members of the institution with a stronger voice in deliberations. While basic votes stood at 11 percent in proportion to the total voting power of the institution in its early days, their relative weight has subsequently declined through successive general quota increases to the current 2 percent.

TABLE 5-4. Quotas of Selected Asian Countries

Country	Actual quota shares	Post–second round quota shares	Calculated quota shares (based on data through 2005)
PRC	3.72	4.00	6.39
India	1.91	2.44	2.00
Indonesia	0.96	0.87	0.90
Korea	1.35	1.41	2.25
Malaysia	0.68	0.74	0.86
Philippines	0.40	0.43	0.47
Singapore	0.40	0.59	1.03
Thailand	0.50	0.60	0.84
Viet Nam	0.15	0.19	0.23
Subtotal	10.07	11.28	14.95
Japan	6.12	6.56	8.03
Total	16.19	17.84	22.98

Source: www.imf.org

ing power, had accepted. Although the proposed reform package helps in realigning quota and voting shares, actual quota shares for many members remain considerably out of line with their calculated quota shares. As reported in table 5-4, the 2008 reform package entails slightly more than a 1 percent shift of voting power to emerging Asia. Based on calculated quotas, however, emerging Asia should have received an increase of almost 5 percent.

This supports the view of those who have argued that governance reforms have not yet gone far enough in winning the confidence of emerging market economies. Reacting to these circumstances, in April 2009, the International Monetary and Financial Committee called for a prompt start to the Fourteenth General Review of Quotas so as to complete it by January 2011—some two years ahead of the original schedule. In September 2009, at the G-20 summit in Pittsburgh, leaders endorsed a greater shift in voting power in favor of "dynamic" economies.[46] At the G-20

46. The relevant excerpt from the G-20 communiqué states that "the distribution of quotas should reflect the relative weights of its members in the world economy, which have changed substantially in view of the strong growth in dynamic emerging market and developing countries. To this end, we are committed to a shift in quota share to dynamic emerging market and developing countries of at least five percent from over-represented to under-represented countries using the current IMF quota formula as the basis to work from." The communiqué is available at www.pittsburghsummit.gov/mediacenter/129639.htm.

meeting in Gyeongju, in October 2010, the finance ministers agreed on a package of reforms that went beyond reasonable expectations by endorsing a shift of about 6 percent of voting power to dynamic and underrepresented economies.[47] According to this agreement, already approved by the institution's executive board and board of governors,[48] the PRC will become the IMF's third shareholder, with Brazil and India among the top ten members on the basis of their revised quotas. Moreover, the quota review, to enter into effect by the IMF's annual meetings in 2012, will be linked to a recomposition of the board itself, with Western Europeans giving up two seats at any given time.[49]

Another area where the IMF has introduced far-reaching reforms is its lending framework, with the doubling of access limits, simplification of conditionality, and the establishment of a new facility for crisis prevention, the FCL, which provides qualified countries with large, upfront, and potentially uncapped access to Fund resources with no (ex post) conditions. The FCL can be approved for countries meeting pre-set qualification criteria.[50]

Late in 2010 the IMF's executive board enhanced its crisis prevention toolkit by increasing the duration of the FCL and establishing a new Precautionary Credit Line (PCL) for members with "sound policies who nevertheless may not meet FCL's high qualification requirements."[51] The PCL

47. The communiqué is available at www.g20.utoronto.ca/2010/g20finance101023.html.

48. See the IMF's press release 10/477of December 16, 2010, available at www.imf.org/external/np/sec/pr/2010/pr10477.htm.

49. More details are available at www.imf.org/external/np/sec/pr/2010/pr10418.htm.

50. These criteria are "that the member (a) has very strong economic fundamentals and institutional policy frameworks; (b) is implementing—and has a sustained track record of implementing—very strong policies, and (c) remains committed to maintaining such policies in the future. The relevant criteria for the purposes of assessing qualification for an FCL arrangement include: (i) a sustainable external position; (ii) a capital account position dominated by private flows; (iii) a track record of steady sovereign access to international capital markets at favorable terms; (iv) a reserve position that is relatively comfortable when the FCL is requested on a precautionary basis; (v) sound public finances, including a sustainable public debt position; (vi) low and stable inflation, in the context of a sound monetary and exchange rate policy framework; (vii) the absence of bank solvency problems that pose an immediate threat of a systemic banking crisis; (viii) effective financial sector supervision; and (ix) data transparency and integrity." See www.imf.org/external/np/pdr/fac/2009/032409.htm.

51. See the IMF's press release 10/321 of August 30, 2010, available at www.imf.org/external/np/sec/pr/2010/pr10321.htm.

allows members to access large resources, on a precautionary basis, with streamlined ex post conditionality aimed at reducing the economic vulnerabilities identified in the qualification process.

Building on its revamped lending toolkit, the IMF is working on a proposal for a framework (Global Stabilization Mechanism; GSM) aimed at preserving confidence in the global financial system and at limiting contagion in the face of a systemic shock. Should a systemic event occur, the GSM would be set in motion and would proactively channel financial assistance to help countries cope with large-scale liquidity shortages through FCLs for multiple qualifying countries of systemic importance.[52]

At the height of the 2007–09 financial crisis, Mexico, Poland, and Colombia all requested, obtained, and later renewed, IMF assistance under the FCL terms, but apparently no Asian country has yet shown interest in the facility. On the whole, Asian countries had strong economic fundamentals and did not really need IMF support. As noted earlier, however, some Asian countries did enter into swap agreements with the U.S. Federal Reserve, while at the same time strengthening the regional financing framework through the recently announced multilateralization of the Chiang Mai Initiative. Despite wider consultations on IMF reforms, which culminated in the increasing role played by the G-20, of which emerging Asia is an important part, it is still unclear whether the IMF has broadly reshaped its relationship with emerging market economies enough to win their confidence.[53]

Given that emerging Asia is still underrepresented in the various layers of IMF decisionmaking, these countries have understandably been reluctant to submit their economic policies to the scrutiny of an institution in which they feel they have little ownership. Recent reforms do not tackle in a substantial way the current biases of the IMS. For instance, even if the ongoing quota discussions will result in a sizable ad hoc increase in quotas to dynamic economies, the 85 percent supermajority needed to approve SDR allocations will still give the largest shareholder a clear veto power. Moreover, as emerging market economies need large international liquidity buffers to counter potential sudden shifts in international capital flows, then they may have an incentive to directly approach the issuer of the main

---

52. See IMF (2010c), (2010d) and (2010e).
53. See Woods (2010).

reserve assets, or the U.S. Federal Reserve, rather than the IMF, which in turn has to draw from the monetary authorities of hard currency issuers.[54]

Concluding Remarks

The analysis developed in this chapter has elaborated on the asymmetry between the sustained globalization of economic and financial activities driven by the integration in the world economy of emerging economies, many of which are in Asia, and the resilience shown by the IMS to adapt accordingly. The lack of an authentic multilateral forum and the greater weight placed on consultations and national-level responsibility in the conduct of each member's economic policies have prevented emerging market economies from meaningfully engaging advanced countries on the increased uncertainty they face. At a time when they have become increasingly more integrated in, and vulnerable to, the global economy, this has encouraged self-relying policies that, taken in the aggregate, defy the very notion of a global monetary system and challenge the central role of the IMF. The resilience of the IMS is exemplified in the embedded instability of a national currency, namely the dollar, taking on international currency status. As exemplified by the policy debate in emerging countries on the consequences for their economies from the expansionary stance of the U.S. Federal Reserve (referred to as "QE2"), this makes the IMS more exposed to the domestic policymaking of the world's largest economy, despite provisions in the Fund's Articles that the SDR would become the premier world reserve asset. Such issues have been raised publicly and privately by the Fund's managing director in an attempt to focus senior policymakers on the need to reform structural aspects of the IMS.[55]

The current asymmetric features of the IMS have been reinforced by the institutional framework underpinning the IMF, which has acted, in some instances, to amplify rather than reduce the built-in instability of the IMS. In fact, its regulatory role needs to be continuously underpinned by

54. IMF credit is only formally denominated in SDR since it consists mostly of foreign exchange in hard currencies. As an alternative to the current scheme, Polak (2005) has proposed SDR-funded IMF financing. His proposal is supported by Ocampo (2010), among others.

55. See, for instance, Strauss-Kahn (2009), as well as the high-level conferences that the IMF has organized with Korea, the G-20 chair, in February and July 2010. Details are available on the IMF's website: www.imf.org.

decisions of its governance bodies, where a handful of countries hold a majority of votes. Even when a supermajority of votes is required, as is the case with SDR allocations, a few select countries or groups still hold potential veto power; this rule thus limits the IMF's ability to address liquidity needs among increasingly important segments of its membership. It also implies a tension in the Fund's mandate to ensure systemic stability, since it puts decisions on regulating global liquidity in the hands of the very countries issuing the hard currencies adopted as international reserve assets. As a result, until 2009, SDRs had rarely been issued, despite an increasing appetite for reserve assets shown by several emerging economies, especially in Asia.

The shift brought about in the recent crisis with the increased role of the G-20 (which includes large emerging market economies), its potential as a high-level political forum for global economic policymaking, and the apparent availability of advanced economies to strengthen the Fund's governance may reduce some of these asymmetries. A substantial realignment of the voting power within the IMF membership in the next few years will provide the means to emerging Asia to meaningfully engage with the global membership of the Fund and to promote long-range reforms of the IMS that respond to the needs of increasingly important segments of the Fund's global membership.

As long as countries with large stocks of reserves, like emerging Asian economies, perceive a gap between their relative international economic status and the position they hold within the IMF's membership, they have an incentive to break away from the IMF and to set up regional or plurilateral pooling facilities. Should they ever need substantial dollar-denominated official funding to counter the effects of a systemic crisis, they can then negotiate (precautionary) lines of credit with the U.S. monetary authorities.

With its elevation to the leaders level, the G-20 has vigorously emerged from the recent international financial crisis by carving for itself a role as the premier forum for international economic cooperation. Differently from the G-7, its inclusion of emerging market economies, especially from Asia, provides for a more legitimate forum where the heads of state and government from various regions of the world can, for the first time in history, discuss far-ranging reforms of the IMS. By providing unprecedented political capital to the IMF, they are in the unique position to give impetus to an ambitious agenda for reform that builds on the stream of initiatives already enacted, or proposed, by the IMF's managing director and to broaden that agenda to a significant overhaul of the international monetary system.

COMMENT BY
JIM O'NEILL

Domenico Lombardi lays out in great clarity and detail what has been obvious to many observers, including this one, for years. If I have any gripe with the chapter, it is with its title! It is not only through an Asian lens that the IMF and the international monetary system (IMS) are remarkably distorted. It is plainly obvious to anyone who looks at them through the lens of the modern diversified world. Indeed, this is partly what motivated me back in 2001 to first think of the "BRIC" (Brazil, Russia, India, and China) concept, which led to my publishing the paper "Building Better Global Economic BRICs" in 2001.[1]

In tables 5-1 and 5-2, Lombardi shows how the voting power of the IMF is distributed. The position of Belgium is perhaps the best example of the ludicrous state of affairs. Belgium still has a weight of 5.13 percent in IMF voting rights while the People's Republic of China (PRC) stands at 3.65 percent. How can this be right? During the decade 2000–09, the increase in the U.S. dollar value of the PRC's GDP was around $3.5 trillion, about 75 percent that of the United States. The PRC's GDP increased by more than seven times that of Japan, the country with still the second highest share of votes. Of the top ten contributors to global GDP growth, four were from the euro area, but suffice it to say that Belgium was not among them. They were France, Germany, Italy, and Spain. Collectively they contributed a similar amount to GDP expansion as the PRC. Their combined voting weights in the IMF remain at 19.3 percent, more than three times that of the PRC (see table 5-5). Ludicrous. You don't have to be born in Asia to think that, although if you were, and if you end up being an economic policymaker, you can understand why Asians might not be too enamored of IMF advice, or with the world's monetary system, in which the Fund is supposed to have a central role. The combined weight of these four European countries is actually bigger than that of the four BRIC countries put together. There is urgent need for more radical change.

1. O'Neill (2001).

TABLE 5-5. Countries' IMF Voting Power in Comparison with Their Share of World GDP

Percent

Countries or country groups	Votes in IMF	Share of world GDP
United States	16.74	26
Euro 4[a]	15.29	18
PRC	3.65	9
BRICs[b]	9.60	17
European Union	32.02	30

Source: IMF; GS Global Economics, Commodities, Strategy Research.
a. Euro 4: France, Germany, Italy, and Spain.
b. BRICs: Brazil, Russia, India, and China.

If you compare the voting rights to the current size of GDP, Europe's combined position doesn't seem too out of line if looked at in the aggregate (see figure 5-4). When you compare it to the BRICs, it does look excessive, but, ironically, not quite as inappropriate as the low share of the United States. In fact, this comparison suggests that other emerging nations perhaps have too big a share for their size, including those in Africa and Latin America, although given that they typically vote as part of multi-country groups, this is debatable. The overall oddity gets even bigger when you look at the decade ahead. According to Goldman Sachs projections for 2010–2019, no single euro area country will be among the top ten contributors to global growth, not one. France will be the closest, in eleventh place. The PRC is likely to see its dollar value of GDP increase by more than $7 trillion. This will be equivalent to double that of the United States, or close. By 2018, we expect that the BRIC countries' GDP will actually match that of the United States, with the PRC alone about two thirds. In this regard, the conclusions of the G-20 meeting in Gyeongju in October of 2010 highlight a potentially important set of governance reforms whose implementation will be helpful in addressing current gaps.

A major question will be: By 2020, will the IMF still exist if it has not changed radically? If the relative size of economies is a relevant guide, then the PRC will need to see its share of votes in the IMF at least treble. The other BRIC countries, Brazil, India, and Russia, will need to see their influence on the Fund grow significantly by more than what is implied in the decision of the IMF executive board following the Gyeongju meeting in October 2010.

FIGURE 5-4. Change in Size of GDP from 2000 to 2009, by Country

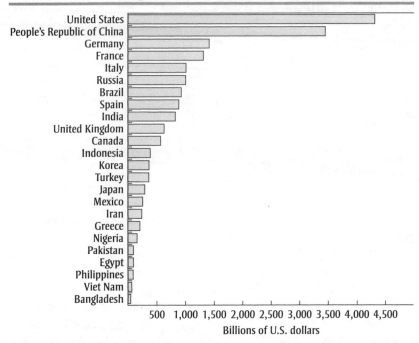

Billions of U.S. dollars

Source: IMF, *World Economic Outlook,* various years; GS Global Economics, Commodities, Strategy Research.
Note: 2000 GDP was adjusted for the updated 2003 rebase of the series.

Reading Lombardi's chapter raises another issue that has dogged me for many months, in fact ever since March 2009, when People's Bank of China Governor Zhou suggested a bigger role for the SDR in the world's monetary system. His suggestions are very consistent with the flavor of Lombardi's observations, if not the specific recommendations. On the many occasions when I have thought about Zhou's proposals, I have repeatedly wondered what could give the SDR a more interesting role in life? The answer I always reach is that, if its basket were to be adjusted, its constituents should include the yuan and some of the other BRIC currencies. Indeed, in a recent Goldman Sachs paper Michael Buchanan and I suggested that this is inevitable in the next decade.[2] He and I frequently debate how this can happen without their currencies being truly convert-

2. Buchanan and O'Neill (2010).

ible and free for use by others around the world. This is effectively a requirement by the IMF. However, Lombardi's chapter makes me wonder whether the PRC and the other BRIC countries might dispute this rule as we progress through the decade and they get bigger. Indeed, one wonders whether they could develop a "BRIC currency" as an offset to a freely floating dollar. There are already some tentative signs of the four countries exploring ways of using each other's currency for bilateral trade; perhaps this idea will take root unless the IMF evolves in a much more radical fashion than it is doing today.

One of the other revealing factors made evident by Lombardi is the remarkable level of foreign exchange reserves controlled by Asian countries. Again within Asia, the PRC's position stands out, although the size of reserves of many other Asian countries is often eye catching. Seen from Western eyes, and probably often those of the IMF, these levels of reserves can be translated into evidence that Asian exchange rates are deliberately kept from appreciating to support export-based models of development and growth. While there may be some partial justification for this thinking, I am not entirely convinced that this is a primary motive. We all know the considerable limitations of exchange rate models, but the model preferred by Goldman Sachs, GSDEER,[3] actually suggests that the yuan is not particularly undervalued, with the valuation mismatch having been resolved in the past five years. What does seem feasible, from Lombardi's excellent discussion of these historical developments, is that, in the 1997 Asian crisis, in response to the subsequent advice handed out by the IMF and their shock at the speed with which their economies collapsed, many Asian countries decided "never again." In this regard, and as suggested by Lombardi, it is interesting that no Asian countries have recently gone to the IMF for "help"; and other policy prescriptions, such as those adopted by Korea, are seen as more desirable. Why take advice from someone who is primarily a representative of others' interests?

So what should change? I would not want to give the false impression that the IMF and its main historical backers are asleep. In fact, just as the global credit crisis was arguably good for the PRC, by forcing it to change its model from that of an unsustainable low-value exporter to a more domestically driven economy, the IMF has benefited from the crisis. The emergence of the G-20 and the spirit in which the G-20 addressed its challenges during 2009 have both allowed, and actually

3. See O'Neill and others (2005).

demanded, a change in behavior and thinking at the IMF. The decision to encourage the IMF to study the economic outlook for G-20 members in the context of their global compatibility, and to report back, is, for example, a welcome development. Similarly, the request for the IMF to opine with greater clarity and purpose on truly global matters, including misaligned exchange rates, are all steps in the right direction. The move by the United States, in August 2010, to question the number of seats at the IMF board opens up a unique opportunity for the Fund to seize the moment.

As is clearly shown by Lombardi, on a number of different fronts, the IMF has not been representative of the modern global economy and its balance. As he points out, this appears to be especially true with respect to Asia, and, within it, the PRC. As I write this, the PRC has announced that it will allow more flexibility in its foreign exchange policies, including implicitly some strengthening of the yuan. Seen in the context of a number of policy developments and the performance of the Chinese economy since late 2008, the PRC is doing a number of things that the West and the IMF should be impressed by. As the next decade progresses, if the PRC and other Asian economies, notably India, are to regard the IMF as being at the center of the world's monetary system, it will be increasingly important for the IMF to become less G-7-centric, and especially less Euro-centric.

References

Akyüz, Yilmaz. 2010. "Why the IMF and the International Monetary System Need More than Cosmetic Reform." Geneva: The South Center.

Bryant, Ralph. 2010. "Governance Shares for the International Monetary Fund: Principles, Guidelines, Current Status." Draft. Washington: Brookings.

Buchanan, Michael, and Jim O'Neill. 2010. "Global Reserve Currencies and the SDR," Global Economics Paper 196. May 26. New York: Goldman Sachs.

Cavallo, Eduardo A., and Jeffrey A. Frankel. 2008. "Does Openness to Trade Make Countries More Vulnerable to Sudden Stops, or Less? Using Gravity to Establish Causality." *Journal of International Money and Finance* 27, no. 8 (December): 1430–52.

Derviş, Kemal. 2009. "Precautionary Resources and Long-Term Development Finance: The Financial Role of the Bretton Woods Institutions after the Crisis." Richard H. Sabot Lecture Series. Washington: Center for Global Development.

Eichengreen, Barry. 2006. *Global Imbalances and the Lessons of Bretton Woods*. MIT Press.

Eichengreen, Barry, Ricardo Hausmann, and Ugo Panizza. 2007. "Currency Mismatches, Debt Intolerance, and the Original Sin: Why They Are Not the Same and

Why It Matters." In *Capital Controls and Capital Flows in Emerging Economies: Policies, Practices and Consequences,* edited by Sebastian Edwards, pp. 121–70. Cambridge, Mass.: National Bureau of Economic Research.

Independent Evaluation Office (IEO). 2003. "The IMF and Recent Capital Account Crises: Indonesia, Korea, Brazil." An Evaluation by the Independent Evaluation Office (IEO) of the IMF. Washington: International Monetary Fund.

———. 2006. "An Evaluation of the IMF's Multilateral Surveillance." Evaluation by the Independent Evaluation Office (IEO) of the IMF. Washington: International Monetary Fund.

International Monetary Fund (IMF). 2009. "The G-20 Mutual Assessment Process and the Role of the Fund." Washington.

———. 2010a. "The G-20 Mutual Assessment Process—Alternative Policy Scenarios." Washington.

———. 2010b. *World Economic Outlook. October 2010.* Washington.

———. 2010c. "The Fund's Mandate: The Future Financing Role: Revised Reform Proposals." March 25. Washington.

———. 2010d. "The Fund's Mandate: The Future Financing Role: Revised Reform Proposals." June 29. Washington.

———. 2010e. "The Fund's Mandate: The Future Financing Role: Revised Reform Proposals." August 25. Washington.

———. 2011. "Enhancing International Monetary Stability—A Role for the SDR?" January 7. Washington.

Ito, Takatoshi. 2007. "Asian Currency Crisis and the International Monetary Fund, 10 Years Later: Overview." *Asian Economic Policy Review* 2: 16–49.

Kaminsky, Graciela L., Carmen Reinhart, and Carlos A. Vegh. 2003. "The Unholy Trinity of Financial Contagion." *Journal of Economic Perspectives* 17, no. 4 (Fall): 51–74.

Kawai, Masahiro. 2007. "East Asia Economic Regionalism: Update." In *The International Monetary System, the IMF, and the G-20: A Great Transformation in the Making?* edited by Richard Samans, Marc Uzan, and Augusto Lopez-Carlos. Basingstoke, U.K.: Palgrave Macmillan.

Kawai, Masahiro, and Pradumna B. Rana. 2009. "The Asian Financial Crisis Revisited: Lessons, Responses, and New Challenges." In *Lessons from the Asian Financial Crisis,* edited by Richard Carney, pp. 155–97. New York: Routledge.

Keynes, John Maynard. 1930. *Treatise on Money.* New York: Harcourt, Brace.

———. 1941. "Keynes to Montagu Norman, Governor of the Bank of England, 19 December." In *Collected Writings,* vol. 25, pp. 98–99.

Kose, M. Ayhan, Eswar Prasad, and Marco Terrones. 2003. "Financial Integration and Macroeconomic Volatility." IMF Working Paper 03/50. Washington: International Monetary Fund.

Kuroda, Haruhiko, and Masahiro Kawai. 2002. "Strengthening Regional Financial Cooperation in Asia." *Pacific Economic Papers* 332: 1–35.

Lombardi, Domenico. 2008. "Bringing Balance to the IMF Reform Debate." *World Economics* 9, no. 4: 13–26.

———. 2009. "Report to the IMF Managing Director on the Civil Society (Fourth Pillar) Consultations with the IMF on Reform of IMF Governance." Washington: International Monetary Fund.

Lombardi, Domenico, and Ngaire Woods. 2007. "The Political Economy of IMF Surveillance." CIGI Working Paper 17. Waterloo, Canada: Centre for International
Governance Innovation (February).

———. 2008. "The Politics of Influence: An Analysis of IMF Surveillance." *Review of
International Political Economy* 15, no. 5: 711–39.

Mateos y Lago, Isabelle, Rupa Duttagupta, and Rishi Goyal. 2009. "The Debate on
the International Monetary System." IMF Staff Position Note. Washington: International Monetary Fund (November).

Mirakhor, Abbas, and Iqbal Zaidi. 2009. "Rethinking the Governance of the International Monetary Fund." In *Finance, Development, and the IMF,* edited by James
Boughton and Domenico Lombardi. Oxford University Press.

Mo, Jongryn, and Chiwook Kim. 2009. "Power and Responsibility: Can East Asian
Leadership Rise to the Challenge?" Working Paper 09-01. Seoul: Hills Governance
Center at Yonsei.

Obstfeld, Maurice, Jay C. Shambaugh, and Alan M. Taylor. 2010. "Financial Stability, the Trilemma, and International Reserves." *American Economic Journal:
Macroeconomics* 2, no. 2: 57–94.

Ocampo, José Antonio. 2010. "Reforming the Global Reserve System." In *Time for a
Visible Hand: Lessons from the 2008 World Financial Crisis,* edited by Stephany
Griffith-Jones, José Antonio Ocampo, and Joseph E. Stiglitz. Oxford University
Press.

O'Neill, Jim. 2001. "Building Better Global Economic BRICs." Global Economics
Paper 66. November 30. New York: Goldman Sachs.

O'Neill, Jim, Alberto Ades, Hina Choksy, Jens Nordvig, and Thomas Stolper.
2005. "Merging GSDEER and GSDEEMER: A Global Approach to Equilibrium
Exchange Rate Modelling." Global Economics Paper 124. New York: Goldman
Sachs.

Perry, Guillermo. 2009. *Beyond Lending—How Multilateral Banks Can Help Developing Countries Manage Volatility.* Washington: Center for Global Development.

Polak, Jacques J. 2005. *Economic Theory and Financial Policy: Selected Essays of
Jacques J. Polak 1994–2004,* edited by James Boughton. Armonk, N.Y.: M. E.
Sharpe.

Prasad, Eswar, Ayhan Kose, Kenneth Rogoff, and Shang-Jin Wei. 2009. "Financial
Globalization: A Reappraisal." *IMF Staff Papers* 56: 8–62.

Radelet, Steven, and Jeffrey Sachs. 1998. "The East Asian Financial Crises: Diagnosis,
Remedies, Prospects." *Brookings Papers on Economic Activity* 1: 1–90.

Sachs, Jeffrey. 1998. "The IMF and the Asian Flu." *American Prospect* 37
(March–April): 16–21.

Stiglitz, Joseph E. 1998. "The Asian Crisis and the Future of the International Architecture." *World Economic Affairs* (September).

Strauss-Kahn, Dominique. 2009. "Beyond the Crisis: Sustainable Growth and a Stable
International Monetary System." Sixth Annual Bundesbank Lecture, Berlin, September 4.

Triffin, Robert. 1961. *Gold and the Dollar.* Yale University Press.

———. 1968. *Our International Monetary System: Yesterday, Today and Tomorrow.*
New York: Random House.

Truman, Edwin. 2010. "The IMF and Regulatory Challenges." *International Specta-
tor* 45, no. 1 (March).

United Nations. 2009. "Recommendations by the Commission of Experts of the President of the UN General Assembly on Reforms of the International Monetary and Financial System." New York: United Nations.

Woods, Ngaire. 2009. "Governance Matters: The IMF and Sub-Saharan Africa." In *Finance, Development, and the IMF,* edited by James Boughton and Domenico Lombardi. Oxford University Press.

———. 2010. "Global Governance after the Financial Crisis: A New Multilateralism or the Last Gasp of the Great Powers?" *Global Policy* 1, no. 1: 51–63.

Woods, Ngaire, and Domenico Lombardi. 2006. "Uneven Patterns of Governance: How Developing Countries Are Represented in the IMF." *Review of International Political Economy* 13, no. 3: 480–515.

Xafa, Miranda. 2010. "Role of the IMF in the Global Financial Crisis." *Cato Journal* 30, no. 3 (Fall): 475–89.

Zhou, Xiaochuan. 2009. "Reform the International Monetary System." Speech presented at the People's Bank of China, March (www.pbc.gov.cn/english/detail.asp?col=6500&id=178).

Contributors

Dony Alex
ICRIER, New Delhi

Kemal Derviş
Brookings Institution

Hasan Ersel
Sabanci University

Karim Foda
Brookings Institution

Yiping Huang
Peking University

Masahiro Kawai
Asian Development Bank Institute

Rajiv Kumar
FICCI, New Delhi

Domenico Lombardi
University of Oxford and Brookings Institution

José Antonio Ocampo
Columbia University

Jim O'Neill
Goldman Sachs

Index

Account balances: and exchange rates, 52–53; and global imbalances, 6, 57, 77–80, 85–88, 97; "outer space" account surplus, 44–45, 50, 55; and "rebalancing" debate, 43–51, 54; and savings rates, 46–47, 60–61. *See also* China, account surplus in; United States, account deficit in

Akyüz, Yilmaz, 58, 62

Alex, Dony, 8–11, 69, 96–97, 98, 100

ASEAN+3 nations, vii–viii, 13, 93, 125

ASEAN+4 nations, 10, 92, 96, 97

ASEAN sub-region, 10, 88, 90, 138, 151

ASEAN Trade in Goods Agreement (ATIGA), 92

Asia. *See* Emerging Asia

Asian Bond Fund (ABF), 13, 125–26

Asian Bond Markets Initiative (ABMI), 13, 125

Asian Development Bank (ADB), 10, 92, 93, 94, 139

Asian financial crisis of 1997–98: causes of, 116; and economic growth, 19; and G-20, 185–86; and IMF, 152–57, 185–86; and macroeconomic imbalances, 9, 73–74

Asian Financial Stability Dialogue (AFSD), 14, 138–39, 141

Asian Investment Bank (AIB), 10–11, 92, 94, 96, 97

Asian Monetary Fund, 153

Asian Tigers, economic growth in, 3, 19

Asia-Pacific Group, 169

Balances. *See* Account balances

Banking systems: central, 106, 144–45, 147–48; reform of, 118–22, 140, 144–45; shadow, 106, 111–12, 113; soundness indicators, 116–17, 118

Bank of Korea, 155

Bankruptcy regimes, 115

Barro, R. J., 33

Basel II framework, 118–21

Basel Committee on Bank Supervision (BCBS), 107, 108, 115, 121, 139

Basel III standards, 12, 108

Belgium, IMF voting rights of, 182

Bernanke, Ben, 9, 71

Biases. *See* Currency biases; Deflationary biases; Institutional biases

Boadway, R., 147

Bond market development, 13, 124–26, 134

Bosworth, Barry, 29, 30

"Bottom-up" approach to regulation and supervision, 12, 112

Bretton Woods Conference and regime, 15, 160–61, 162, 165

Asian Development Bank Institute

The Asian Development Bank Institute is a subsidiary of ADB that functions as its think tank and focuses on knowledge creation and information dissemination for development in the Asia and Pacific region. Based in Tokyo, it helps ADB's developing member economies build knowledge, capacity, and skills to reduce poverty and support other areas that contribute to long-term growth and competitiveness in the region. This is done through policy-oriented research, seminars and workshops designed to disseminate thinking about best practices, and a range of other capacity building and training initiatives.

Brookings Institution

The Brookings Institution is a private nonprofit organization devoted to research, education, and publication on important issues of domestic and foreign policy. Its principal purpose is to bring the highest quality independent research and analysis to bear on current and emerging policy problems. The Institution was founded on December 8, 1927, to merge the activities of the Institute for Government Research, founded in 1916, the Institute of Economics, founded in 1922, and the Robert Brookings Graduate School of Economics and Government, founded in 1924. Interpretations or conclusions in Brookings publications should be understood to be solely those of the authors.